P9-DUA-367

DATE DUE

UE 13/99		

DEMCO 38-296

CHINESE PROPAGANDA POSTERS

FROM REVOLUTION TO MODERNIZATION

我们要处处为人民着想，为国家兴旺着想。在新的一年里，要抓紧揭批"四人邦"这个纲，加强人的思想革命化，加速实现四个现代化，创出高速度。

我国二十三年实现四个现代化，关键是前八年。这八年的发展速度，要超过过去的二十八年。

战斗的号召 光辉的榜样

CHINESE PROPAGANDA POSTERS

FROM REVOLUTION TO MODERNIZATION

Stefan Landsberger

An East Gate Book

M.E. Sharpe

Riverside Community College
Library
4800 Magnolia Avenue
Riverside, CA 92506

JQ 1512 .Z13 P85 1995

Landsberger, Stefan.

Chinese propaganda posters

ACKNOWLEDGMENTS

This study of the visual propaganda in China during the 1980s is the result of some twenty years of poster collecting, research and analysis. During this period I have been helped by a great many people, to all of whom I feel deeply grateful. For their respective roles — all of vital importance to the realization of this project — the following must be mentioned.

I am greatly indebted to Tony Saich (The Ford Foundation, Beijing) and Tim Cheek (The Colorado College, Colorado Springs), who gave invaluable support in guiding me through the process of writing, by judiciously meting out praise and blame.

In China, many people went out of their way to help me acquire posters. Ingrid d'Hooghe, Jan van der Made, Peter Peverelli, Tony Saich, and many others, made it possible to bring together the wealth of material presented here. Others who have contributed, often unwittingly, and who should be mentioned are Claudia Landsberger, Kate Hartford, Marien van der Heijden, Michel Hockx, Christina Jansen, Burchard Mansvelt Beck, Frank Pieke, and Kurt Radtke.

Thanks to Paul Wijdeveld, commissioning editor with The Pepin Press, this book has been published. His and the publisher's suggestions helped to turn the initial version of this study into a book of interest to a scholarly and a more general audience alike.

Mention should also be made of the team of Jennifer Stoots, Juliette Carchedi and Wouter Thorn Leeson, whose outstanding work resulted in a publication of the highest standard.

Without LinDai Boogerman's continuous support and assistance, this book never would have seen the light. Her ability to boost my confidence made me finish the poster project and it is to her that this book is dedicated.

Copyright © 1995 Pepin Van Roojen
Copyright text © 1995 Stefan R. Landsberger

All rights reserved. No part of this book may be reproduced in any form and by any means without permission in writing from the copyright holder.

First published in 1995 by The Pepin Press ᴮ/ᵥ,
POB 10349, 1001 EH Amsterdam, the netherlands

This edition published by M.E. Sharpe, Inc.,
80 Business Park Drive, Armonk, NY 10504

Library of Congress Cataloging-in-publication data:

Landsberger, Stefan.
    Chinese Propaganda Posters : from revolution to modernization /
Stefan Landsberger.
        p.   cm.
    "An East Gate Book."
    Includes bibliographical references and index.
    ISBN 1-56324-688-0 (alk. paper)
    1. Propaganda, Chinese. 2. Posters—China—History—20th century.
I. Title
JQ1512.Z13P85   1995
306'0951'09048—dc20   95-9042
                                                  CIP

Printed and bound in Singapore

FRONT COVER ILLUSTRATION: 'Little guests in the Moon Palace' *(Yuegong xiao keren)*, early 1970's.

BACK COVER ILLUSTRATION: 'Chinese braves for the first time trail the Changjiang' *(Zhonghua yongshi shou piao Changjiang)*, 1987.

FRONTISPIECE: 'A call to struggle, glorious example' *(Zhandoude haozhao, guangyaode bangyang)*, 1978.

PAGE 4: 'Chairman Hua, the people of all nationalities warmly love you!' *(Hua zhuxi, gezu renmin re'ai nin!)*, 1978.

CONTENTS

8

沿着有中国特色的社会主义道路奋勇前进！

INTRODUCTION

9

PREVIOUS PAGE: 'Advance bravely along the road of socialism with Chinese characteristics' *(Yanzhe you Zhongguo tesede shehui zhuyi daolu fenyong qianjin)*, 1989.

RIGHT: 'Only socialism can save China, only socialism can develop China' *(Zhi you shehui zhuyi cai neng qiu Zhongguo, zhi you shehui zhuyi cai neng fazhan Zhongguo)*, 1989.

In December 1978, the Third Plenum of the Eleventh Central Committee of the Chinese Communist Party (CCP) adopted a comprehensive framework for the modernization of agriculture, industry, national defence and science and technology. At that time, there were no indications that these policies would effectively spawn a second revolution, which would irrevocably change both China and Chinese society. Known as the Four Modernizations, the program was originally based on plans formulated by Zhou Enlai in 1964, in cooperation with Deng Xiaoping. Despite an initial lack of acceptance, the plans were once again proposed, albeit unsuccessfully, by Deng in 1975. After his second return from political disgrace in 1977, Deng proposed them yet again to no avail. Although economic modernization was one of the main policy planks formulated by Hua Guofeng in 1978, only later in that year the program was actually adopted as policy. Its official aim consisted of the

all-round modernization of agriculture, industry, national defence and science and technology by the end of the century so that our economy can take its place in the front ranks of the world, [...and become...] a modern, powerful socialist country.

In the 1980s, these goals were more concisely formulated as

quadrupling the gross industrial and agricultural output value, [...and] building the country into a modern socialist country with a high degree of civilization and democracy by the year 2000.

Economic reform required social order and political predictability. The stress on 'spiritual development' (the exaltation of will power and the human, subjective dimensions of history that had characterized the mobilization campaigns during the rule of Mao Zedong) was de-emphasized in favour of all-out 'material development'. The idea that the Four Modernizations were to once again make China 'rich and strong' *(fuqiang)* was more important to many Chinese; the People's Republic of China, as a socialist state, would then take its rightful place among the ranks of the advanced (mostly Western) countries. Indeed, by the end of the 1970s, the CCP saw the rehabilitation of the economy as an ideal way to shore up its damaged image, apparently without foreseeing the erosive effects that this rehabilitation would ultimately have on society and the party's legitimacy to rule the country.

As the successes of the modernization policies began to directly benefit ever-increasing numbers of the people, if only in the form of significantly-improved living conditions, it became apparent to the population that they were permitted to enjoy 'the freedom to have fun' for the first time since the founding of the People's Republic of China in 1949. The new policy was made all the more enticing by the fact that an Open Door policy formed an

学习雷锋好榜样
发扬艰苦奋斗的精神

LEFT: 'Study Lei Feng's fine example — Develop the spirit for bitter struggle' *(Xuexi Lei Feng hao bangyang — fayang jianku fendoude jingshen)*, no date.

OVERLEAF: 'The Commune's Fishpond', 1973.

important part of the Four Modernizations. People were given the opportunity to become acquainted with non-Chinese, or Overseas Chinese, visitors. Various elements of other cultures and life-styles soon entered China in their wake. The availability of radio and television provided yet another Open Door to the Chinese people. The latter medium in particular came to be seen as the ultimate symbol of the success of modernization, and its presence in the homes of the people was an indication of personal economic prosperity.

As a result of these changes, and also as a consequence of decreased political intrusion by the CCP into an increasingly heterogeneous society, the strident primacy of politics that had previously characterized Chinese society was reduced to a seemingly inconsequential accompaniment to the development of the increasingly lively, free-wheeling and entrepreneurial society of the 1980s. For the first time in the history of the People's Republic of China, the well-organized system for propaganda, agitational and political education, modelled on the traditional and centuries-old Confucian mechanisms of social control, had to compete with the 'informal penetration' of national sovereignty by electronic media, through mail flows, popular literature and other media likely to escape official scrutiny. This continuous stream of non-political

and non-pedagogic messages from abroad interfered with what until then had been the 'Voice of China': all media under tight central control, so that the CCP kept a grip on the thought and behaviour of the Chinese people.

This study is devoted to one aspect of the communications practices of the People's Republic of China, namely, the visual or figurative propaganda that was produced between 1978 and 1987, and within the specific ideological framework of the Four Modernizations. The focus will be on the analysis of a body of some 1,000 posters of 'low-end use' visual propaganda, consisting of gouaches, oil paintings, water colours, brush and ink drawings, and wood block prints that were printed in large quantities and sold through the national network of *Xinhua* (New China) bookshops. This visual propaganda usually played a supportive role in campaigns waged through other mass-media, and was part and parcel of a mechanism of rectification that had been developed by the CCP during its stay in the Yan'an area in the 1940s. Originally intended solely for cadres and Party-members, the population at large was increasingly exposed to this mechanism of rectification, which reached a climax during the Cultural Revolution.

Not included in the study is the more ephemeral visual propaganda specifically designed for use on the huge billboards located along the streets and avenues of China's urban areas. These billboards also contained political and ideological exhortations to behave and think in a specific way, or to work toward a specific goal. They appeared in the form of quotations from the writings of Mao Zedong, slogans formulated by the Party in line with the current policy, or large visual representations of a

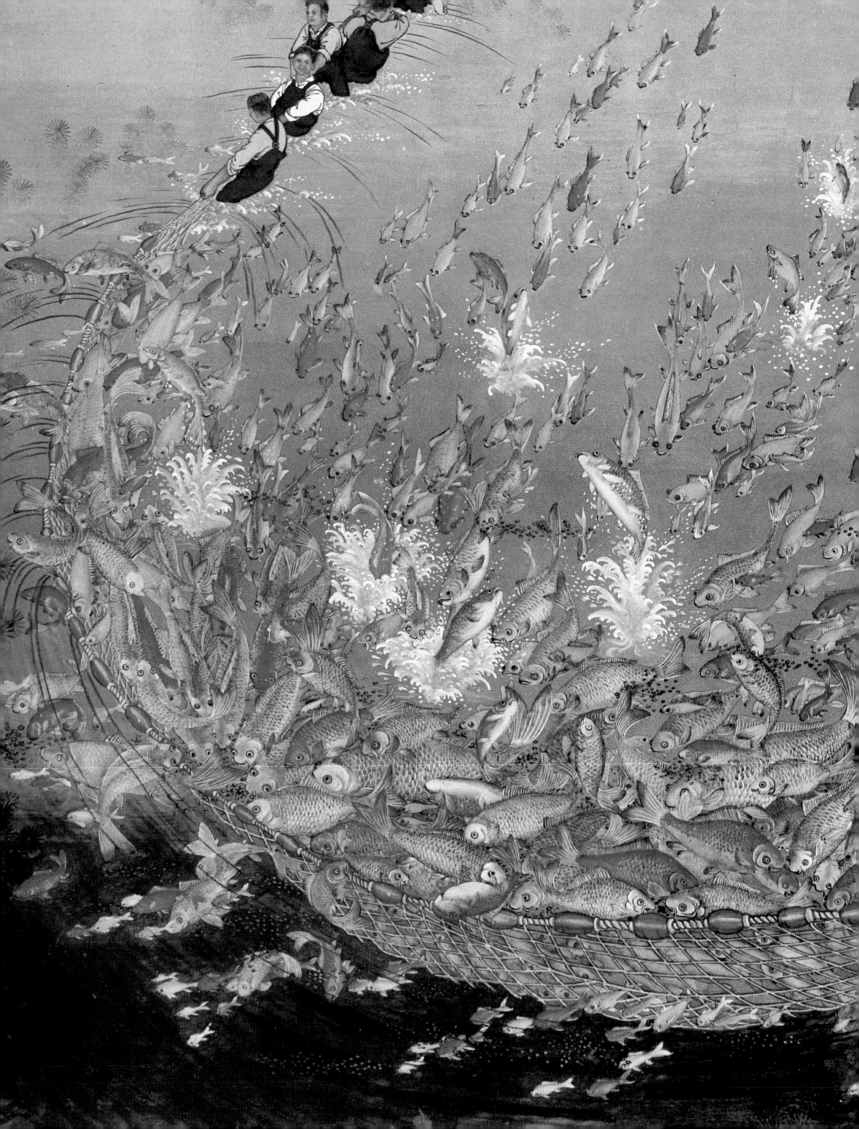

'National women's volleyball team' *(Zhongguo nüpai)*, from the series *Zhonghua hao ernü*, 1990.

future Communist Utopia. However, the images on these billboards were not produced on a national scale.

Personal impressions gathered while travelling in the People's Republic of China in the 1980s and 1990s, were that the local propaganda departments had considerable leeway in the production of these billboards. Nonetheless, the general contents were to remain within the political and ideological limits of the national campaigns for which the exhortations were used. In the Four Modernizations decade the billboards grew in number but came to be reserved primarily for a more persuasive and pervasive type of propaganda: they carried advertisements of Chinese and foreign companies for consumer goods and products. Following the bloody crackdown on pro-democracy demonstrators in June 1989, however, intensified political and economic retrenchment brought the political billboards back to the streets.

The posters in the study typically measure 53 cm x 77 cm (21" x 30"); large-size posters typically measure 105 cm x 77 cm (44" x 30"). These measurements may include a white margin around the image. Most posters supply the names of the artist, the publisher, printer and distributor, as well as information pertaining to the number of print runs and their respective quantities (varying from a few thousand to two or three million), date of publication, an index number (in more recent examples, an ISBN number), and the price.

Due to a lack of publishers' catalogues on the production of visual propaganda, it is hard to say how representative these particular posters are. They shed light on the changing conceptions of the leadership regarding the modernization and reform process itself, and the effects

which they believed the process would have on Chinese society. This raises questions concerning the symbolism of the Four Modernizations and how it was manifested through the use of propaganda posters. Did this symbolism gradually change, in line with shifts in policy or perception, or in line with the changes in relative power of the various ruling factions? Did this symbolism have the same meaning for both the leadership and the population, thus suggesting a common culture through which their interaction was mediated? Have various target groups been approached with different symbols or can one single Four Modernizations symbolism be ascertained?

Widespread as the initial appeal of the prints may have been, it has been impossible to gauge their success in propagandizing their 'unnoticed' political contents. Until the mid-1980s, a large variety of these low-priced propaganda posters intended for a mass audience could be obtained at the *Xinhua* bookshops. In the second half of that decade, politically inspired printed matter almost completely disappeared, only to be reintroduced with a vengeance after the Tian'anmen incident of June 1989. Even then, however, propaganda posters had lost most of their previous staying power. A number of posters appeared which extolled the qualities of perseverance, obedience and loyalty to the Party as espoused by Lei Feng, Zhou Enlai, the national women's volleyball team, and other 'Excellent sons and daughters of China'. After the appearance of these posters, such visual propaganda seems to have disappeared.

Alternatives to propaganda posters, however, became available in the mid-1980s. These were more in line with the popular demand for aesthetically pleasing decorations, preferably without any explicit or implicit political contents, and the masses did not hesitate to switch to these new materials. The leadership turned to other media, particularly the electronic media of radio and television, to propagate behavioural norms. These media were no longer employed as tools of class struggle, but as tools for modernization, symbolically and functionally contributing to the economic and ideological dimensions of reform. Proof of the diminished use of the posters, and the decreased reliance on them by the leadership, can be found in quite unexpected sources. For example, the 'Yearbooks of Chinese Publishing', published in Beijing by Shangwu Yinshuguan, invariably contained a chapter devoted to accomplishments in the production of propaganda posters and New Year prints in the preceding year. After 1984, however, this section vanished from the yearbooks.

The decline in the use of the propaganda poster as a medium for communicating political messages, and its reduced appeal to the population, raise a number of interesting questions concerning the effectiveness of the poster.

First, had the method of propagating behaviour through propaganda prints become obsolete in a society which strived for modernization? Secondly, were the propagated behaviours themselves no longer relevant to the actual attitudes and abilities demanded by the rapidly changing social and economic reality? In relation to this question, one must ask whether or not the contents of the posters were in line with the changing aesthetic appreciation of the population. A fourth question that must be addressed is whether the propaganda poster as a means of communication was applicable to a society that was abandoning more 'primitive' communication techniques, necessitated by the lack of infrastructure and a high level of illiteracy, for the use of electronic media.

In the first chapter of this book, the more theoretical aspects of the propagation of behaviour, both in pre-modern and 20th century China, will be explored. This includes an analysis of the merging of salient aspects of Confucianism and Marxism-Leninism, which led to the formulation of Mao Zedong Thought. Also, the consequence this merger had on the propaganda produced between 1949 and 1978 will be discussed. The second chapter will focus on developments made during the Four Modernizations period. After outlining the newly-formulated policies of this period, their effects on the development of poster art will be closely scrutinized. The third chapter of the book is devoted to analyses of the contents of propaganda posters of the 1980s. These analyses will not only concentrate on questions related to the target groups of such propaganda, but will also deal with the specific stimuli which were formulated for these groups, and with the symbolism and imagery with which these stimuli were presented.

TRADITIONAL AND MODERN PROPAGATION OF BEHAVIOUR IN CHINA

PREVIOUS PAGE: 'Young pines
struggle to develop the magnificence of mountains and streams'
*(Qingsong jingzhang shanhe
zhuang)*, 1977.

BELOW: 'Buddha hands', from the
Ten Bamboo Studio Painting
Manual, after J. Tschichold, *Der
Holzschneider und Bilddrucker
Hu Cheng-yen*, 1943.

PRECURSORS OF VISUAL PROPAGANDA IN TRADITIONAL CHINA

CONFUCIAN ROLE-MODELLING

Throughout the centuries, models of desired behaviour have functioned as forceful mechanisms to inculcate behavioral traits among the Chinese people. In pre-modern China, the state engaged in an early form of propaganda which was based on the idea of the 'malleability of man'. This concept was strongly influenced by the teachings of the philosopher Confucius (551-?479 BC), who was firmly convinced that persuasion and education would be more effective than the use of force or punishments in achieving a state of social harmony. He combined this conviction with a belief in the efficacy of role-modelling. The Confucian exegetist and philosopher Mencius (372-289? BC) also believed that human beings automatically would be inclined to modify their own behaviour when confronted with examples of impeccable moral qualities.

The belief in the socially beneficial effects of role-modelling was based on the perception that mental and intellectual activities were clustered, namely, that processes of knowing and believing were accompanied by promptings to act. Schematically, the mechanism of clustering works as follows: 'knowing' involves an understanding of the distinctions between things in the natural world and their correspondence to distinctions in the human world which are marked by language and the recognition of moral principles, some of which can have a normative dimension. 'Believing' is clustered with knowing through

a process of evaluation, namely, by assessing what is recognized and what actions correspond with that knowledge. 'Promptings to act' take place in a manner which is relevant to knowing or believing. 'Thought' is understood to first activate and consequently direct behaviour. As such, it is considered to be more important than action itself. If people know what is right or wrong, or what is good or bad (in terms of behaviour, thought, etcetera), or are taught the distinction between each, they will be prompted to behave in a way consistent with that knowledge.

By using previous virtuous rulers as role models for

impeccable behaviour, Confucius tried to teach his various patrons how to rule in an exemplary way: through observance of the correct rules of behaviour *(li)*, entailing both rights and responsibilities, and through constant self-criticism and self-improvement. This was based on the idea, dating back to at least the Shang dynasty, that the right to rule was founded on merit, namely, moral authority. Correct behaviour consisted of observing the Five Cardinal Relations, the hierarchically structured relationships between ruler and ruled, father and son, elder brother and younger brother, husband and wife, and between friends (the *wulun)* and interpreting one's role in life accordingly. The supreme importance attached to the principle of filial piety *(xiao)*, as part of the Five Cardinal Relations, reinforced the necessity to follow the example set by a senior. This could be a father or a father-figure, like the ruler. Any king groomed to be a virtuous person *(junzi)* earned the right to rule by committing deeds that deserved the support of the ruled. By simply functioning as a moral example, or role model, he could lead his subjects; they would behave in accordance with the roles prescribed by the relationships they were in. Then, an utopian state of 'Grand Harmony' *(Datong)* would be reached, in which all relationships would flourish.

Confucianism was made the ideology of the State during the first century of the rule of the Han dynasty (206 BC - 220 AD). One of the main reasons for its adoption was that Confucianism emphasizes the duty of officials to serve their rulers with dispassionate loyalty. By defining the ideal interpersonal relationship as an hierarchical one, it ensured the subordination of all people to authority figures. Model emulation became a standard feature of all subsequent dynasties. Its efficacy was based on the premise that correct ideas stem from proper, or correct, behaviour, and that orthopraxy ideally would lead to orthodoxy (believing what was considered proper to believe). The models did not necessarily engage in saintly behaviour; negative models could also serve the purposes of 'perfectibility' and 'educability', although not in terms of attraction or conscious imitation. Their common characteristic was that they functioned as the concrete embodiment of abstract moral principles.

Education played a major role in the dynamics of belief control. A thorough and universal education in the Confucian virtues, and the behavioural codes derived from them, was seen as one of the most important aids to the development of specific desirable tendencies in the population. Being steeped in Confucian knowledge would automatically lead to the acceptance of the Confucian code as the absolute criterion of thought and conduct. As the legitimacy of the state was firmly rooted in this code, education became a desirable function of government.

Examples of models presented in texts used in formal education include, among others, the 'Classic of Filial Piety' *(Xiaojing)*, providing 24 models of filial behaviour; relevant sections of the dynastic histories; written versions of popular legends *(mengqiu)*; and popular morality books *(shan shu)*. Exemplary female behaviour was described in a significantly smaller number of sources including the 'Classic of Exemplary Women' *(Lie nü zhuan)* and 'Instructions for Women' (Ban Zhao's *Nü Jie)*. Visual models could be found in the gallery of

BELOW LEFT: 'Queen Victoria',
after *Dianshizhai Huabao*, 1884
or later.
BELOW RIGHT: 'Tibetan tribute
bearers', after Bauer, *China und
die Fremden*, 1980.

images and portraits in the ritual centre of the Confucian temple, and in the erection of memorial arches *(dafang)* for virtuous widows, a practice started during the Qing dynasty. Those taking part in formal education, which was supported by the state, were usually members of the gentry. Having passed the State examinations, based on a thorough knowledge of the Confucian classics, one not only joined the educated elite, but also the ruling class. As a 'grammatocracy', this class exercised power according to time-honoured Confucian prescriptions. The socialization process, then, was intimately linked with literacy. The 'community compact' system *(xiangyue)*, developed under the Ming dynasty and re-instituted at the beginning of the Qing, went even further than earlier belief control. It could be seen as an extension of the formal state education. The *xiangyue* lectures brought the official interpretation of Confucianism to the vast and mostly ignorant rural population. It consisted of a public reading of the 'Six Maxims' *(Liu Yu)* written by the Shunzhi Emperor, and was later replaced by the 'Imperial Sacred Edict' *(Sheng Yu)* written by the Kangxi Emperor. The latter's maxims were, in turn, superseded by the Amplified Instructions, laid down by the Yongzhen Emperor. The essence of the Confucian ethic was expounded in the reading; moreover, it paid great attention to preventing behaviour not in line with the expounded ideals (such as adherence to 'false doctrines' *(quxue)* or an unwillingness to supply the state with produce). The maxims ideally were to be expounded twice a month by local Imperial graduates, or other dignitaries, and the activity could be accompanied by awe-inspiring rituals which usually ended with the recording of the good and evil

BELOW: 'Anti-Christian protest prints' (c. 1860), after Ellen Johnston Laing; *The Winking Owl: Art in the People's Republic of China*, 1988.

deeds of the population. This latter practice created both positive and negative local models that could be easily recognized by the population. In order to drive the intended message of the readings home, from the late-Ming period onward various officials published private versions of 'explanations', some of which contained illustrations to show to the peasantry.

A further enmeshing of the largely illiterate population in the Confucian tradition took place by means of legends, drama, folk stories and folk songs. These were created for the ordinary people by scholar-bureaucrats, namely, those schooled in Confucianism who had failed to enter government service. Entertainment, by visually and orally transmitting historical 'facts' and cultural values, 'provided a cultural indoctrination of immense strength'. A number of early publications contained illustrations of desired behaviour. Although they were originally destined for lit-

erate audiences, and therefore probably did not reach the population at large, they can be considered part of the early visual tradition of role-modelling.

PRECURSORS OF THE CHINESE PROPAGANDA POSTER

The pre-existing visual tradition, originally geared to the demands of literate audiences, was based on a number of influences, both domestic and foreign. Early examples include publications such as the 'Ten Bamboo Studio Painting Manual' and the 'Mustard Seed Garden Painting Manual' from late-Ming/early-Qing times. A series of woodcut texts, first published during the Southern Song dynasty (1127-1279), but better known in its Qing edition, portrayed and described a variety of contemporary labour and commercial activities. 'Pictures of Tilling and

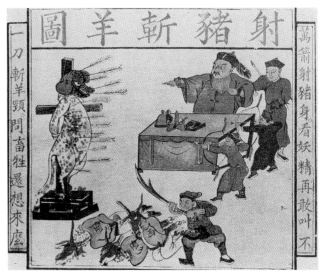

RIGHT AND FAR RIGHT: 'Yu Chi and Qin Qiong', pair of door-gods, after Wang Shucun, *Ancient Chinese Woodblock New Year Prints*, 1985.

Weaving', for example, which showed the step-by-step process of cultivating rice, and the production of linen and silk, documented for the first time the labours of the peasantry instead of activities of the elite.

In later years, the emergence of popular illustrated journals was instrumental in the creation of a mass culture. The journals popularized the visual tradition among the increasingly powerful group of non-elite merchants who had sprung up in the urban centres. One of the most influential of these journals was the Dianshizhai Pictorial *(Dianshizhai huabao)*, a magazine published in Shanghai between 1884 and 1895 by one of the first lithographic printing shops in China, and devoted to current affairs and sensational events. Its illustrations showed, for example, Queen Victoria and Tibetan tribute bearers (see page 20).

Another means of visual communication that should be considered as a precursor of the propaganda print was the protest print. The earliest forms, designed during the 16th century, mainly expressed anti-Western and anti-Christian sentiments. Although created by dissatisfied members of the elite, they were intended to induce a hostile attitude among the population at large. These visual protests, which increased in number during the second half of the 19th century, either took the form of Western prints which were re-cut to invert their original contents, or they were inspired by the style of traditional Chinese black-and-white book illustrations (see page 21). No matter what visual or artistic form these protests took, their meaning was clear to everyone, including the illiterate. This cross-class appeal was made possible by the use of traditional images, in a standardized, accepted and

popular visual idiom. The most important influence on the visual propaganda produced by the CCP, however, was the New Year picture. Employing various elements of folk art and symbolism, these pictures catered to the tastes and beliefs in the countryside, expressing wishes for happiness and good luck. According to Wang Shucun, the most well-known expert on the New Year prints of the People's Republic of China

During the New Year festival, more than 20 varieties of New Year prints would be stuck on the front gates, doors onto the courtyard, walls of a room, besides a room's windows, or on the water vat, rice cabinet, granary, or livestock fold. Colourful and floral prints would be everywhere in the house to express the hopes and joy of the festival.

These prints did not necessarily spell out officially sanctioned behaviour. On the contrary, they utilized symbols that were traditionally seen as auspicious, including those promoting long life, a government career, and wealth.

This undoubtedly contributed to their popularity among large sections of the population. Often, they featured mythological personages like the Kitchen God, the Door God and the God of Longevity, by turning them into magical charms to drive away bad luck. They were, however, created in an environment that had centuries of experience dictating thought and action. Their creators, moreover, were often artists who had been educated in the basics of Confucianism. New Year prints, then, were necessarily permeated by behavioural indications, thus consolidating the Confucian values of the educated, urban elite among the illiterate peasant population. When Daniel Kulp went to Phenix Village in Guangdong Province at the end of the 1910s for sociological research and fieldwork, he concluded that the art forms he encountered

...are so conventional and fixed that they supply no new or divergent forces to conflict with other forms of village behaviour. They set limits beyond which the person does not go, and so constitute one type of social control. Thus, they play a role in the village schematization of conduct and conduce to stabilization of personality.

The origins of these New Year prints were clearly utilitarian-magical. They evolved from the practice of painting images of gods *(menshen)* on doors so as to ward off ghosts and wild beasts. This form of religious art is comparable to Russian *ikons*, printed icons and amulets produced by Buddhist and Taoist monasteries from the fifth century AD, and the so-called 'paper pictures' *(zhihua)* common during the Song dynasty (although the latter have only survived as references in old texts).

During the Ming and Qing, the subject matter of New Year prints broadened and became more secularized. The new types included genre prints, usually showing the households of the rich and the opulent interiors of their houses, while simultaneously reflecting the working of Confucian principles within the household. Content also included literary themes, theatrical subjects, landscape prints, and pictures devoted to various aspects of political life in the second half of the 19th and early 20th centuries. During the 18th century, considered to be the golden age of New Year picture *(nianhua)* production by Chinese scholars, the popularity of New Year picture art reached its highest point, and the prints began to circulate throughout the whole country.

Although Western prints were known from the 16th century onward, and many Western artistic devices were absorbed into the Chinese popular print, their techniques were never imitated on a wholesale basis. Originality, ingenuity and individual experimentation in any of the arts were qualities that were not admired in pre-modern China, nor would they lead to an artist's success. An average artist usually spent the greater part of his life copying the works of his master, in an attempt to surpass the quality of the original. Art education was devoted to traditional ink and watercolour painting, aerial perspective and linear design. In the wake of the Reform Movement of 1898, which set out to modernize society, art students were increasingly exposed to Western techniques such as oil painting, two-point perspective and the treatment of light and shade in painting *(chiaroscuro)*. These techniques were seen as successfully combatting the tradition of imitation. Western influences led to widespread artistic experimentation with a plethora of artistic movements and styles from abroad. Artists applied these imported techniques without any real understanding of the political, social and artistic developments that had brought such techniques into use in the West.

The presence of numerous foreign companies and their advertising agencies in the foreign settlements along the Eastern seaboard, promoted the use and appreciation of Western art techniques by the population at large. These companies were instrumental in bringing large amounts of visual materials to the people, in the form of illustrated calendars, posters, handbills, scrolls, etcetera. These were often designed by Chinese artists to cater to Chinese tastes, and were produced on some of the most sophisticated imported printing facilities and distributed free of charge. They penetrated China and entered the poorest and the wealthiest homes, particularly in the countryside. There, they would compete with New Year pictures for the attention of the household.

COMMUNIST VISUAL PROPAGANDA

ROLE-MODELLING IN CHINESE MARXISM

Mao Zedong and the other leaders of the CCP had all been subjected to a socialization process that included the various traditional practices to maintain social order. Although they rejected the more typically Confucian aspects of these practices, such as filial piety and the overriding concern with the maintenance of social harmony, they still believed in the perfectibility of the people. Moreover, they were convinced that by participating in revolutionary activities new social relationships would emerge among the people which would cultivate a 'New Man', as expressed by Marx and Lenin.

Neither Marx nor Engels clearly spelled out how the proletariat would be made to embrace the new ideology they were formulating, but elements of their writings did influence propaganda practices in the Soviet Union in three major ways. First, on the basis of the Marxist doctrine of materialism, and similar to Confucianism, it was held that ideas are determined by the social environment, in which the economic system is ultimately decisive. At the same time, the role of psychological factors as an

LEFT: 'Having a surplus year after year' *(Niannian youyu)*, date unknown.
BELOW: 'Celebrating an abundant harvest' (1904).
Both after Wang Shucun, *Ancient Chinese Woodblock New Year Prints*, 1985.

influence on the development of society was played down. Secondly, the Marxist theory of dialectics saw struggle, or contradiction, as an essential and ultimately creative force in nature and society. This made struggle, either against internal or external enemies or against nature, a predominant theme in communist propaganda. Thirdly, the appeal to reason, which stemmed from Marx's belief that he had formulated a science, was to become one of the cornerstones of the Soviet propaganda message.

Although never drafting any specific plans for mass indoctrination through propaganda, Lenin rejected Marx's materialist notion that workers would spontaneously develop the class consciousness necessary to bring about revolution. Instead, he stressed the need for a type of propaganda which would take the form of political education. This would help the proletariat to gain an understanding of its interests, an impossibility without aid from outside, and give them the correct interpretation of their immediate and long-range goals. On the basis of the idea that propaganda and organization are opposite sides of the same coin, Lenin considered it absolutely necessary to have a vanguard to lead and educate the proletariat. The Communist Party, in being such a vanguard, should use the most advanced elements in its ranks to show the correctness and applicability of the Party's abstract ideology and policy blueprints. Lenin, moreover, saw propaganda, albeit in an educational form, as a necessary precondition for the achievement of every goal. He was convinced that 'a certain element of pedagogy was and always will be' part of the Party's work.

In Mao Zedong Thought, the CCP leadership's adaptation of Marxist-Leninist elements and Soviet experiences to the uniquely Chinese conditions, the use of models is advocated as a means to bring about social or attitudinal change: with the advanced acting as models for the intermediate, and the intermediate as models for the backward, all of society would develop through emulation. Mao Zedong Thought, termed 'Confucian Leninism' by Lucian Pye, combines the controlling elements of both Confucianism and Leninism, and makes everyone constantly aware of what constitutes behaviour in accordance with the definition of one's role, and what conduct is deemed unacceptable. In one of Liu Shaoqi's important contributions to Mao Zedong Thought, the connection between Confucianism and Leninism is made even more explicit. Liu applied the time-honoured Confucian term 'self-cultivation' to the process of remoulding one's self and raising one's revolutionary level. His grafting of the concept of the 'New Man',

inherited from the Soviet Union, onto Chinese circumstances was an attempt to create a replacement for the Confucian ideal of the sage, or *junzi*. To become a 'New Man', or a good Communist, the cultivation of the self would follow the model of the words, deeds, work and qualities of the founders of Marxism and Leninism. Likewise, on the basis of filial piety, authority figures, in their role as benevolent fathers, should be revered and unconditionally accepted as models. Ironically, this was seen as eradicating the influences of the old society, and protecting the Party and its members from being corrupted by its newly-acquired power.

In both Confucian and Maoist theory, confrontation with a model that is held up for emulation will stir a desire in a person to imitate desired behavior. This results in an internal contradiction between the individual's existing, internalized values and the ones to which he now compares himself. The struggle between the two value systems leads to a new equilibrium, in which the new values are internalized. The process does not stop there because, when confronted with a new model, the equilibrium gives way to a new internal contradiction. In this way, an eternal cycle of confrontation, internalization and renewed confrontation is created, leading to ever-higher levels of human perfection or social development. As such, the emulation of models follows the Marxian dialectical process and fits neatly into the 'struggle-unity-struggle' scheme which was developed in Mao's epistemology. To quote Mao's own words:

'Little Yu Gong's on the fields of Dazhai' *(Dazhai tianshang xiao Yu Gong)*, 1977.

it is only through repeated education by positive and negative examples and through comparisons and contrasts that revolutionary parties and revolutionary people can temper themselves, become mature and make sure of victory.

Along these same lines, he later increasingly valued the use of models in the mass campaigns that were designed to overcome difficulties created by lagging industrialization and mechanization. Particularly from the Great Leap Forward onward, the models presented by the CCP had to demonstrate that, by relying on will power, and by giving supremacy to the human, subjective dimensions of history, the people would be able to quickly transform the concrete obstacles they encountered in the physical world. This was the result of an exaggerated belief in the power of ideology on human consciousness, a belief that reached its climax in the 'Little Red Book' cult of the Cultural Revolution.

THE USE OF MODELS BY THE CHINESE COMMUNIST PARTY

In general, the CCP's use of models is based on a pervasive belief in the power of form over substance, with the idea that a population can be controlled by merely providing examples of orthopraxy, or sanctioned behaviour. The use of models in the visual arts, as well as in literature, reflects the leadership's analysis of the current political or economic situation at any given time, as well as its ideas about the behaviour that is needed to bring about envisaged changes. Consequently, these models, and the ideas they represent, are made into learning objects which are translated and developed by the propaganda apparatus into appropriate stimuli and images.

A model should be someone who is recognizable and in whom everyone can see elements of his or her own life or experience, made larger than life. It is assumed that the public will react positively when they are told which behaviour is desired. Presenting a model is often seen as solving a behavioural problem, but there is no clear attempt to evaluate beforehand the effects of the behaviour that is so strongly promoted. Ideally, a model functions as a positive moral example by presenting behaviour, values and attitudes which the leadership wants the masses to emulate. The subject can be a person, a commune *(Dazhai)*, an oil field *(Daqing)* or a factory. A model can set an example of his or her technical or innovative abilities in order to help others integrate that ability with certain value-laden feelings, or exhort them to act in accordance with some durable norm or recently-promulgated official regulation. As a 'conveyor belt', a model should pass on officially-sanctioned information to the masses.

In his treatise 'Some Questions Concerning Methods of Leadership', formulated in 1943, Mao institutionalized models as a channel for the two-way communication between leadership and masses. As Mao himself put it, such communication should take place in the following way:

Take the ideas of the masses (scattered and unsystematic ideas) and concentrate them (through study turn them into concentrated and systematic ideas), then go to the masses and propagate and explain these ideas until the masses

'Study a brave spirit, follow a
brave course', (Xue yingxiong
jingshen, zuo yingxiong daolu),
early 1970s.

embrace them as their own, hold fast to them and translate them into action, and test the correctness of these ideas in such action. Then once again concentrate ideas from the masses and once again go to the masses so that the ideas are persevered in and carried through. And so on, over and over again in an endless spiral, with the ideas becoming more correct, more vital and richer each time.

In this view, models are the concentrated and systematic version of the scattered and unsystematic ideas of the masses, and convey the ideas of the leadership concerning the contents of certain behavioural roles. This 'conveyor belt' function is based on three principles. First, models are able to illustrate abstract universal values because, by seeing the particular, the universal will be understood. Secondly, a model is more effective when he or she not only is able to pinpoint public attention to a single aspect of a problem, but is also able to suggest a solution. Thirdly, a model demonstrates how this solution can be concretely executed. As in Confucian times, the most important reward for a model should be the respect of those who emulate him, as an acknowledgement of the sacrifices made, for example by being allowed to take part in the decision-making process of government. The desire to become a model should serve as a stimulus for others.

THE COMMUNIST PROPAGANDA SYSTEM

Ever since the establishment of the CCP in 1920, the formulation of propaganda policy has been the responsibility of its Central Committee. Initially, propagandizing the Party's revolutionary theory and its revolutionary decisions was closely linked with education and, in particular, with combatting illiteracy. Such efforts were to take effect through the printed media and through slogans in which the masses could recognize their own reality. Only during its stay in the revolutionary stronghold Yan'an from 1936 through 1945, did the CCP systematize its propaganda attempts into a comprehensive framework that gave printed material more transformational, agitational and administrative dimensions. This took place through the formulation of a rectification doctrine to bring about the following objectives: the consolidation of CCP leadership over society; the ascendancy of a particular group within that leadership; bureaucratic control in a goal-oriented organization where the goals frequently change; vigorous implementation of new Party policies; improved cadre work style; the elimination of behaviour judged deviant by the Party leadership; and the internalization of values and outlooks promoted by the regime — i.e., genuine attitudinal change. The targets of rectification ranged from members of the CCP Politburo to the lowest officials outside the Party. The doctrine thus confirmed Party legitimacy and was at the root of cadre training and discipline. Aside from merely correcting deviant behaviour and thoughts, rectification also attempted to develop proletarian consciousness, by involving constant education and training in order to raise each person's knowledge of, and commitment to, proletarian values.

The group dynamics developing within the 'small group' *(xiaozu)*, consisting of ten to fifteen persons and set up at every level for the purpose of political activities, facilitated CCP control and played a crucial role in the passing on of propaganda, as envisaged in the rectification doctrine. These groups were initially organized in Yan'an, and later in all residential and work units, particularly in urban areas, and resorted under study committees at all territorial and organizational levels, with the Central Committee and Propaganda Department at the top. Activities included the 'study' and discussion of Party and Government documents, and (self-)criticism. Although it cannot be proven with certainty, it is quite likely that the deeper meaning and intention of visual and literary propaganda was discussed in these groups as well. The mechanism of (self-)criticism makes the 'small group' the most powerful element of the propaganda system. The behaviour or faults of each group member are systematically examined by the others, and this creates enormous group pressure for behavioural and attitudinal conformity.

Once people have been coerced or persuaded into changing their behaviour, they seek information on which to base their new outlook. If this is to correspond to leadership demands, the leadership must be able to control information so that only that which affirms desired opinions reaches those undergoing change. The CCP's monopoly on the means of mass communications greatly facilitated such informational control, by allowing the constant repetition of approved ideas, barring all heterodox interpretations of events, and censoring facts that may have challenged the official line. Propaganda posters played an important role in this comprehensive, controlled media system that was designed to support attitudinal change and rectification by providing easily- understood visual information that spelled out the desired behaviour.

THE PROPAGANDA DEPARTMENT

Before the founding of the People's Republic of China in 1949, the CCP attempted to control the ideological agenda via public communication, entertainment media, and by using traditional means of communicating its objectives (for example through New Year prints), or by adopting

methods that had been developed in the Soviet Union (for example propaganda plays and wall newspapers). After 1949, the State, acting through the unchallengeable authority of the CCP and in the name of the people, would decide what people should know and do; thought and characteristic modes of everyday life would be made thoroughly predictable. The presentation of models, whether in the printed or broadcast media, in art or in literature, was instrumental in this process. In the name of protecting the people against their own ideological lapses, and in order to supply unequivocal behavioural guidelines, the CCP's autocratic, paternalistic management of culture (namely, constant evaluation and correction of artists and intellectuals), was justified.

Until the start of the Cultural Revolution in 1966, the Central Committee issued all major propaganda policies through the Propaganda Department which functioned under its auspices. The Propaganda Department, in turn, disseminated these policies through the Propaganda Departments of the Party Committees at each administrative level, through the mass media, through the government's Ministry of Culture, and through the mass organizations (the Youth League, Women's Federation, Federation of Trade Unions, etcetera). As such, it played a crucial role in the political process of the CCP: it transformed the propaganda policies that were centrally dictated by CCP-leaders, into policies 'of the people and by the people' by activating its apparatus.

The jurisdiction of the Propaganda Department, as a policy-making and coordinating organization, originally was extremely broad and encompassed 'culture' in all its aspects. Not only was it responsible for day-to-day administration and propaganda, but its sub-departments also oversaw all activities taking place in various sectors: science and technology; literature and art; newspapers and journals; press and publication; education; public health and sports; cultural education; Marxist-Leninist research; editing and translation; policy research; international liaison; and a political department. As a result of the wide-ranging responsibilities of the Department, newspapers and journals, teaching materials, literary works, the cinema, and other means of communication, including neighbourhood posters, billboards and blackboards, came to be employed as propaganda devices. It became central to the implementation of socialism under the CCP that these media provide shining, single-minded and idealistic visions within the official ideological rhetoric. All these devices mutually reinforced the centrally-formulated or more localized propaganda messages. These tools were to sustain and cement the short-term mobilization which rectification was designed to promote.

After 1966, the Propaganda Department ceased to exist; its functions and activities were taken over by the Cultural Revolution Small Group headed by Jiang Qing, until her arrest in the second half of 1976. After this, the Cultural Revolution was officially called to a close. Most Party and government organizations, and their political and ideological practices that had been either disbanded or terminated in 1966, were revived and in some cases reorganized. The formulation of propaganda policies was resumed by the Central Committee, and the Propaganda Department once more took on the function of a conduit for those policies, although the size of the Department

LEFT: Woodcut by Li Hua 'Roar,
China' (Nuhuo ba! Zhongguo;
1935), after Zhu and Chen,
Zhongguo xihua wushi nian.
RIGHT: Woodcut by Li Hua, clear-
ly inspired by Käthe Kollwitz,
'Figures' (c. 1936) after Laing, The
Winking Owl.

significantly decreased. In the 1980s, the Department's activities started to focus more strictly on the supervision of all forms of ideological communication aimed at both Party members and the public. This implied that its previous control of the mass media, the educational system, and the mass organizations, was renewed and strengthened.

THE COMMUNIST PROPAGANDA POSTER UNTIL THE FOUR MODERNIZATIONS ERA

ART BEFORE AND AFTER THE MAY FOURTH MOVEMENT

After the founding of the Republic in 1912, China was torn between a desire to modernize and to regain its rightful place among civilized nations, and the desire to salvage as much tradition as possible. In the arts, this led to the search for a new 'national form'. The intellectual Hu Shi called for complete Westernization, whereas the writer-scholar Lu Xun advocated a more critical attitude.

These calls reached a climax on the 4th of May, 1919, when student demonstrations organized to protest the Versailles Peace Conference (at which the Allies signed away China's rights to territory formerly held by Germany), escalated into a national movement, demanding progressive changes in all fields. This May Fourth Movement, which lasted roughly until 1921, succeeded in bringing about important cultural, educational and political reforms. In the words of Chow Tse-tung, the May Fourth Movement, although termed by some a 'Chinese Renaissance', can be better

defined as a complicated phenomenon including the 'new thought tide', the literary revolution, the student movement, the merchants' and workers' strikes, and the boycott against Japan, as well as other social and political activities of the new intellectuals, all inspired [...] by the spirit of Western learning and the desire to re-evaluate tradition in the light of science and democracy in order to build a new China.

The refusal of China's territorial demands led to dissatisfaction with the West, and a desire to follow the example set by the successful October 1917 Revolution in the Soviet Union, where an autocratic imperial government had been replaced by popular rule. This prepared the ground for growing popular support of socialist ideas. At the same time, Soviet inspiration also influenced developments in the world of literature and the arts.

The post-May Fourth reorientation of the art world came in two divergent forms which each were to strive for supremacy in the decades to come. On the one hand, Western influences continued to have a profound impact. The images of the late Art Nouveau period, an Asian-inspired design movement, on Chinese art and design in the 1920s needed little adaptation to Chinese tastes. The style of Art Deco, originating in 1925, likewise called for little change to gain acceptance. As the Shanghai style, in which Art Deco, Cubist and traditional Chinese patterns and motifs were blended, it was to prove appealing to a cosmopolitan audience. Another foreign style that gained widespread popularity in the 1930s was Futurism.

On the other hand, a group of politically progressive designers and artists, inspired by the ideas of Lu Xun,

'Develop dynamiting in the militia', block print designed by Yan Han, early 1940's.

rejected the direct importation of foreign images and called for the development of a style that would do more justice to the national aesthetic and artistic identity. Lu Xun was aware of the fact that literature and art in the past had catered exclusively to the tastes of the educated elite, and he sought forms that would support his belief that, by paying special attention to the inequities of modern life and to the needs of the growing new audience in the urban middle class, artistic expression had a social responsibility.

Lu was deeply influenced by the works of Western woodcut-artists: Käthe Kollwitz (Germany, 1867-1945), Frans Masereel (Belgium, 1889-1971), and the Soviet printmakers, Vladimir Favorsky (1886-1964), Alexei Kravchenko (1889-1940), and Pavel Pavlinov (b. 1881). In their engravings, which portrayed the dark side of life in the tradition of 19th century European realism, he saw parallels with the fate of China's own lower classes, and an opportunity to expose the social and economic evils of his time. In order to promote these examples of socially conscious art, he published nine volumes of prints from his own collection between 1929 and 1936, and sponsored three exhibitions of prints in the international settlement in Shanghai between 1930 and 1933, as well as a travelling exhibition in 1936. The exhibited works focused on scenes of peasant life, workers in factories and scenes from urban working class districts. The peasants, however, when confronted with these Western-style prints, did not particularly like them. According to this audience, the prints lacked colour and significant content.

In order to popularize graphics as an art form, and par-

ticularly as one that would have an agitational effect in China, Lu aimed at a combination of Western styles and wood block techniques, in particular realism, with traditional styles such as Han dynasty bas-reliefs, Ming and Qing book illustrations and New Year pictures. The medium of woodcut prints was to end the primacy of Western influences. It was not until the late 1920s and the early 1930s, however, that the New Woodcut Movement took off, mainly through the large-scale founding of woodcut clubs and societies. From the start, the Nationalist authorities suspected these clubs and societies to be under communist influence. Most of the Chinese wood block artists active in the early 1930s, however, often did little more than directly copy Western examples in style and subject matter. Although the artists sympathized with the plight of the worker and peasant, the general tone of their works was more one of pessimism than of a belief in the agitational effects of their art. The two woodcuts by Li Hua on pages 30 and 31 show the gloominess, on the one hand ('Roar, China', 1935) and the inspiration by Kollwitz, ('Figures', ca. 1936) on the other hand.

'Supporting an Army of the People and for the People' (*Yonghu zanmen laobaixing zijide jundui*), a block print designed by Gu Yuan, early 1940s.

THE BIRTH OF AN AGITATIONAL STYLE

Historical circumstances in the late 1930s greatly influenced the birth of a new, agitational style in the visual arts. After the outbreak of the Anti-Japanese War in 1937, China was divided into roughly three political spheres. The Northeast and the coastal areas (including major population centres such as Beijing, Shanghai and Canton) were basically under Japanese control; the Nationalist Government held parts of the inland provinces (including Sichuan, where the war-time capital Chongqing was established), while the Communist-held base areas included the CCP-headquarters in Yan'an, in Shaanxi Province.

In the Japanese-controlled areas, visual arts were mainly employed to propagandize the Japanese aim of creating an East-Asian Cooperation Sphere, to justify the Japanese military presence in China and gain popular support for it, and to warn the population against cooperating with either the Nationalists or the Communists. To this end, calendars, newspapers, magazines, handbills and posters that made use of indigenous forms of popular current art were produced. Among these were the traditional Buddhist 'Judges of Hell' pictures.

In the areas under Nationalist domination, the Western-inspired style of wood engraving and other urban forms of popular art were employed to portray the war atrocities committed by the Japanese, and to bolster popular support for resistance against the invaders. The medium of photo-montage also gained popularity among those artists who criticized the Nationalist regime and its inability to address political and economic ills. The clipping and pasting together of images from pictures guaranteed some form of anonymity for the artists.

Art in the base-areas was largely under the control of the CCP. Large numbers of artists, who were more motivated by idealism and antipathy to the feeble Guomindang-resistance against the Japanese, rather than staunch communists, travelled to the base areas. There, they usually followed short courses at the Lu Xun Academy of Literature and Art *(Luyi)*, established in Yan'an in 1938 to teach drawing, propaganda painting, caricature, print-making and art history. Posters, serial stories and cartoons were used to maintain the anti-Japanese sentiments among the peasant population, to mobilize popular resistance against the invaders, and to educate the masses. To counter the lack of peasant interest in the Western-inspired woodcuts and the Japanese use of traditional elements of popular culture, a search was undertaken for a new style that was to parallel the forms of art popular among the people. In 1940, during the New Year's Propaganda Movement, the decision to use traditional Chinese New Year prints was made.

This was important in two respects. First, the peasantry responded positively to the old visual idiom and symbolism used in the colourful, popular New Year prints. They liked realistic New Year pictures, as long as the portrayal

'Well-clothed and well-fed'
(Fengyi zushi) after Zhu and
Chen, *Zhongguo xihua wushi
nian.*

was a little more beautiful than reality. This was evident from the numerous prints that were successfully employed in combatting illiteracy in the Northwestern rural areas. Secondly, this encouraged the use of the age-old techniques of water-printing, which corresponded more with the unsophisticated means of mass reproduction available in the base areas. The images were to be based entirely on traditional Chinese popular arts and were to replace the use of the expressionist style, so instrumental in the creation of an agitational visual idiom in the 1930s. Simple forms and lines and flat colours were used to depict more realistic figures against a white background, with a sparing use of the depressing black so typical of the expressionist woodcuts.

In Yan'an, the use of art as a catalyst of cultural change among the peasantry was put into practice. Propaganda art was specifically created to reinforce propaganda campaigns that were primarily waged through other media. They could take the form of 'hortatory propaganda pictures' *(xuanchuanhua)*, for which soldiers, workers and militiamen posed, and which were painted on city walls, village houses or on huge pieces of white cloth. One form of propaganda picture that probably was derived from Soviet practice, and that was used from 1943 onward, was the 'leader's portrait'. It featured local, national and international figures, military and political leaders (Mao Zedong, amongst others), and labour and hygiene models. These pictures were sold, but they could also be awarded as prizes. In this way, they were incorporated into rituals which enhanced their value and conferred status on their recipients.

THE YAN'AN CONFERENCE ON LITERATURE AND ART

The widespread use by the CCP of visual propaganda that employed traditional modes of expression, such as New Year prints, was decided on during the Yan'an Conference on Literature and Art, a meeting of artists and intellectuals in the revolutionary base area of Yan'an in 1942. On this occasion, the theoretical dimensions of, and limitations on, art in the socialist society under CCP-rule were defined. In essence, the Yan'an Talks elaborated upon decisions that had been reached at the Gutian Conference of 1929. At this previous conference, where advocates of 'political warfare' (Mao and others) and representatives of the 'purely military viewpoint' (commanders of the Red Army) had clashed, guidelines were set which basically shifted the organization of propaganda work from the army to the CCP.

First of all, it was decided that propaganda should be aimed at a range of distinct social groups with different cultural backgrounds, occupations and levels of education. Thus, not only the mass base of the CCP would be addressed, but also potentially hostile social groups could be won over or neutralized. Secondly, all target groups were to be addressed in terms of their own psychology and experience. General political issues were to be linked with everyday life. To successfully bring this about, the pre-existing values and forms of China's 'old culture' were linked to the new political ideals and, where necessary, were manipulated to further the aims of the revolution. Thirdly, it was decided that all propaganda was to have 'time quality' *(shijianxing)* and 'local quality' *(difangxing)*. With regards to the latter element,

'Hygiene Model', c. 1942, after
Laing, *The Winking Owl*.

propaganda that failed to take local differences into account was, at best, irrelevant and unintelligible.

At the Yan'an Talks, Mao presented both the opening and closing speeches, spelling out the most important guidelines to be followed once the CCP had gained control over the whole nation. Mao's remarks were to guide all artistic expression until the present day, although in varying intensity. After a relative lull in the 1950s, the Talks regained their former prominence during the Cultural Revolution. Likewise, although lip service was paid to the Talks during the early 1980s, they once more became cultural dogma after the conservatives gained their 1989 victory over the reformers. In his introduction, Mao clearly stated that the arts were to play an important role in the political socialization of the population:

Literature and art [must] become a component part of the whole revolutionary machinery, so they can act as a powerful weapon in uniting and educating the people while attacking and annihilating the enemy, and help the people achieve solidarity in their struggle against the enemy.

In outlining how this was to be brought about, Mao first objected to the wholesale, uncritical importation of foreign images, as well as their use in Chinese art (with the exception of the Soviet examples). Moreover, he rejected the notion of 'art for art's sake' as bourgeois, and he rejected the notions of art above class, fellow-travelling and politically-independent art. Instead, he advocated the use of the 'rich, lively language of the masses'. There was no room for art forms that were popular among the more cosmopolitan urbanites, or the 'bourgeoisie' in the cities;

after all, in employing the idiom of 'the masses', art had to serve peasants, workers and soldiers.

The overall purpose of serving the broad masses of the people was to satisfy their demands *(puji,* popularization) while at the same time raising their cultural standards *(tigao).* Mao made it clear, however, that popularization, a conscious application of the artistic modes of expression current among the population, should be the main objective of the arts. More importantly, arts and artists had to serve politics by following the demands made by the CCP, which, after all, represented the masses. Mao summed up his expectations of revolutionary literature and art as follows:

What we demand is a unity of politics and art, a unity of content and form, a unity of revolutionary political content and the most perfect artistic form possible.

This unity was to be brought about by combining the 'old forms', or the already existing sense of style among the common people, with new contents: a political meaning.

The decision to use 'old forms' was an integral part of the mandate construction in which the CCP was involved (namely, fulfilling the conditions for the accession to politico-moral authority implied in the Mandate of Heaven). By substituting rather than abolishing old visual elements, by manipulating symbols used in traditional popular culture and traditional values that underlie these symbols, the CCP set out to move the social totality from its existing state to a future of socialism or communism. Secondly, as the arts were primarily needed to show the

people how to act and what to say, and not merely who their enemies were, it was important that the prints conveyed the positive aspects of peasant life in areas under communist control. They were not to depict scenes of the guerrilla warfare waged by the communists, nor were they to urge popular support for the People's Liberation Army (PLA). A well-known example of militarily inspired prints was 'Develop dynamiting in the militia' (see page 32). Instead, the arts had to supply images of rural scenes, structured around optimistic themes, such as the fruits of socialist cooperation and the prosperity and security of the base areas (see pages 34 and 35, 'Well-clothed and well-fed', and 'Hygiene Model'.)

PROPAGANDA ART DURING THE CIVIL WAR (1946-1949)

After the Japanese capitulation in 1945, under the guidance of the CCP, the visual arts again underwent a reorientation. After their success in transforming the thoughts and sympathies of large sections of a predominantly rural audience, the arts were now to be directed toward an audience of urbanites who were still largely unfamiliar with, and possibly hostile toward, communism. The themes of the woodcuts that had previously been so popular in the countryside were not suited to depicting construction and industrial scenes, and the CCP hoped to learn a propaganda method that would have more appeal to the sophisticated tastes of Chinese city-dwellers. Ideally, it would take the form of a fusion between the technical and visual advances of the pre-war Shanghai style and the ideological correctness of the

Yan'an style. Following Mao's favourable remarks in Yan'an about the Soviet experience and its use as a guideline for both popularization and raising standards, Soviet propaganda methods and their implementation were studied. There, a two-decade experience in visualizing the post-revolutionary phase of construction had been gained. As a result, Chinese literature and art would follow the guidelines set by the theory of Socialist Realism, the dominant aesthetic style in the Soviet Union since the 1930s. This was facilitated by the fact that, from 1949 until 1957, Chinese writers and painters studied in the Soviet Union. The reaction of both the public and the artists to Western-style realism was favourable because, according to a 1959 retrospective,

it enabled Chinese artists to grasp the world of reality and to cure the indifference to nature which caused the decay of Chinese traditional art, [while at the same time] it was the most popular form of art, which was also easiest to grasp.

During the Civil War period in China, the first instances of this new hybrid Chinese style, touted as a mass revolutionary design style, were visible already. At the same time, the decline of the woodcuts became apparent.

PROPAGANDA ART IN THE 1950s

In the early 1950s, the popularizing function of the arts was again stressed over their ability to raise cultural awareness. A large proportion of the population, which was to be influenced by the new ideology and the goals of socialist construction, had to be reached. The Korean

FAR LEFT: 'Our revolutionary bell is still resounding: workers and peasants, unite to fight new battles and win new victories! Set the Red Cavalry against the White! Sign up now for the Red Cavalry!' (c. 1919).
LEFT: 'The Motherland summons you!' (c. 1941).
Both after Nina Baburina, *The Soviet Political Poster, 1917-1980*.

RIGHT: 'Graphs of the First Five Year Plan (1953-1957) for the Development of the National Economy of the People's Republic of China' *(Zhonghua renmin gongheguo fazhan guomin jingjide di'yige wunian jihua (1953-1957) tujie)*.

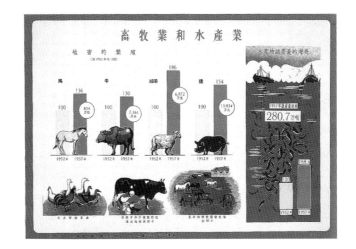

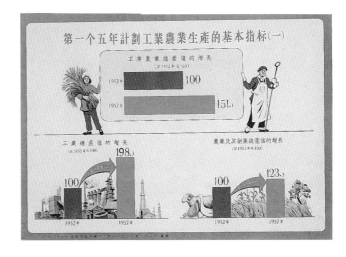

conflict, which started in 1950, called for the elimination of all foreign, especially Western, artistic influences; this sounded the death-knell for the Shanghai style. The production of New Year prints, considered to be prime examples and expressions of 'people's art', surged. In some, traditional visual elements were used to convey new messages, while others depicted completely new subjects, retaining only the bright colours and emphasis on detail which were reminiscent of the original New Year pictures.

With the visual arts geared to the process of popularization, the need for the development of a new, national revolutionary style was even more acutely felt. During the period between 1951 and 1953, Zhou Yang (1907-1990), the most powerful official in the artistic hierarchy in the first three decades of the People's Republic of China, advocated the basic introduction of Soviet-styled Socialist Realism. He called for its blending with traditional elements and specific Chinese artistic techniques. The resulting hybrid would be the most correct and important guidance for the arts. Socialist Realism, with its combination of the reality of today and the ideals of a better future, was deemed appropriate, as the leaders felt it would most appeal to the masses. But, it also portrayed idealized social and political models, namely, ordinary men and women engaged in the creation of this better future. They depicted the bright side of the lives of the 'real heroes', representatives of the 'new people' striving for a 'new world', as demanded by Mao in the Yan'an Talks. Socialist Realism was sometimes used for New Year prints, more frequently for oil paintings, and also found its way into works done in a more traditional style.

The pictures of this period reflected the atmosphere of enthusiasm that existed among the population, despite the numerous political campaigns organized to increase or consolidate popular support for various aspects of Communist rule, and the enormous effort that was required to create this new socialist world in a country torn and devastated by decades of war and internal strife. The Hundred Flowers Campaign of 1956 and 1957 initiated a short period in which constructive criticisms of the CCP leadership could be voiced. The political relaxation was matched by a relaxation in art policy, resulting in a revival of traditional forms and less stress on the need to paint in the Socialist Realist style. When the amount and intensity of criticism exceeded the leadership's wildest expectations, the Hundred Flowers Campaign was restructured into an Anti-Rightist Campaign, in which the more outspoken critics were prosecuted with a vengeance.

'Ask for a new battle assignment'
(Zai qing zhan), 1975.

During the subsequent Great Leap Forward Campaign, with its calls for 'more, faster, better, [and] cheaper' production, Mao called for Soviet Socialist Realism to be replaced with a 'fusion of revolutionary realism and revolutionary romanticism' in the arts. As the poet, scholar and politician Guo Moruo put it,

revolutionary realism takes realism as its keynote, and blends it with romanticism, whereas revolutionary romanticism takes romanticism as its keynote, but blends it with realism.

On this basis, the visual arts were intended

to convey the most romantic and glamorous views of the motherland; social, economic and political triumphs; the strength, courage, and resourcefulness of the people; and the wisdom of their leaders.

Clearly, the non-Soviet element of romanticism was introduced to make the arts more visionary, in order to imbue the population with the necessary spirit of self-sacrifice, hope and enthusiasm to overcome concrete obstacles by pure will power. At the same time, this eliminated the inappropriate gloominess often found in 'pure' Soviet Socialist Realism. To accurately reflect the spirit of the times, an alternative medium had to be found in which the lofty ideals of the Great Leap could be portrayed with idealistic and heroic images. A new and dynamic illustrative style was developed, which emblazoned the yearly production goals on brilliantly-coloured banners and symbolic monuments. This brought motivational graphics to a higher conceptual level. The propaganda art pro-

duced during the movement achieved an incredible degree of idealization, which was only repeated during the Cultural Revolution.

'Graphs of the First Five Year Plan (1953-1957) for the Development of the National Economy of the People's Republic of China' (see page 37) contain early examples of this 'Illustrator Realism'. To reflect the urgency of the times, art was to be produced in larger quantities and at a faster pace. Posters and magazines were employed to communicate the Great Leap objectives to the population and to inspire and motivate society. The success of posters in mobilizing the work force to a fever pitch convinced the propaganda workers of the poster's usefulness. The increased demand for art created opportunities for amateur painters to arise from among the peasants and workers, and led to a reappraisal of folk themes in the arts; this was reflected by the renewed attention paid to traditional papercuts, and their use on posters and in magazines. Professional artists were supposed to find inspiration by personally gaining labour experience.

PROPAGANDA ART DURING THE PERIOD OF CONSOLIDATION

The disastrous economic results of the Great Leap, exacerbated by three consecutive years of crop failures, forced Mao to step back to 'the second echelon'. Under the rule of Liu Shaoqi and Deng Xiaoping, developments in the fields of politics and economics returned to the predictability of the first half of the 1950s. Mao's political decline led to attempts to replace the guidelines of his Yan'an Talks. To this end, Zhou Yang called for shifting

'It's always spring in the commune' *(Gongshe chun changzai)*,
early 1970s.

attention in Socialist Realist art and literature from politics
and heroic characters to a more balanced treatment of
the so-called 'middle characters' (namely, those who
could neither be classified as heroes, nor as villains).
More room was to be left for personal doubt and individual shortcomings, making the subjects more recognizable
and true to life. As a result, the idealistic and heroic
images were replaced by more romantic visualizations of
the good life that the people led under socialism. Quite a
few 'pretty-girl pictures', art that featured female beauties
in an aesthetically pleasant way, without any political
message, were produced.

The period can be generally characterized as one in
which the raising of standards gained the most attention.
The decrease of stress on the positive proletarian heroes
led to a distinct increase in the professionalization of the
artists; instead of 'learning from the masses', they now
rejoined official art academies. This development was
supported by a new interest in the decorative quality of
art, its roots in traditional (folk) art, and for the poetic
quality of art (namely, whether art expressed the artist's
mood, ideas and feelings). Works of art, moreover, were
judged on the basis of their success in combining techniques originally not employed in their specific medium,
and by their personal style and originality. Traditional
artists who ventured outside their discipline and who
experimented with new techniques and subjects were
lauded. Western techniques of watercolour and oil painting, and their integration with Chinese traditional-style
painting, were singled out for praise.

A sea-change was imminent. In 1962, in a clear bid to
regain his former political prominence and power, Mao

advocated a Socialist Education Movement (SEM) to 'inoc-
ulate' the peasantry against the temptations of feudalism
and the sprouts of capitalism he saw re-emerging in the
countryside. In order to accomplish this, he increasingly
pinned blame on the CCP leadership. The party organization, in the meantime, tried everything to block Mao.
Accusing the CCP of the same 'revisionism' and preference
for technocratic over ideological solutions as seen in the
Soviet Union, he turned toward the only organization he
considered trustworthy: the PLA. The PLA had been active
in the arts during the Japanese and the Civil Wars. In
peacetime, the army largely followed the trends of the
civilian arts world.

Under the leadership of Marshal Lin Biao, who became
Minister of Defence in 1959, the PLA was increasingly
employed to bolster the personality cult of Mao. Lin considered this to be the means by which to ingratiate himself with Mao, a precondition for his own leadership
ambitions. Starting with the compilation of the
'Quotations from Chairman Mao' *(Mao zhuxi yulu)*,
which was for use by the armed forces, Lin turned the
PLA into an organization that functioned along the ideological and political lines Mao desired. The PLA also supplied the behavioural models that corresponded to Mao's
ideas about ideological correctness; the most well-known
of these were the exemplary soldiers Lei Feng and
Ouyang Hai. Lin laid down instructions that art should
unite and educate the people, inspire the struggle of revolutionary people and eliminate the bourgeoisie. Art had
to be revolutionized and guided by Mao Zedong
Thought: its contents had to be militant and reflect real
life. In the summer of 1964, during the Third National

LEFT, FROM TOP TO BOTTOM:
'Heart-to-heart talk' *(Zhixin hua)*,
early 1970s.
'Reporting to Chairman Mao'
(Xiang Mao zhuxi huibao), early
1970s.
'Comrades-in-arms' *(Zhanyou)*,
1977.
'The new struggle starts from
here' *(Xinde zhandou cong zheli
kaishi)*, early 1970s.

Exhibition of PLA Art, most of the paintings echoed Lin's instructions by featuring red paint, army heroes (Lei, Ouyang, and others), Mao and his thoughts. Clearly, proletarian ideology, communist morale and spirit, revolutionary heroism, etcetera, were the messages which took precedence over style and technique in this new hyper-realistic political art.

PROPAGANDA ART DURING THE CULTURAL REVOLUTION (1966-1976)

Visual arts during the Cultural Revolution were largely influenced by the dictates of Jiang Qing. Together with Lin Biao, she and other radicals directed the movement through the Cultural Revolution Small Group. This direction was first limited only to the arts, but gradually spread to all aspects of (political) life. The conceptual dogmas provided by the model operas supported by Jiang Qing became de rigueur in the visual arts. On the basis of her 'three prominences' (stress positive characters, the heroic in them, and stress the most central of the main characters), the subjects were portrayed realistically; and, by employing the techniques of mise en scène, the subjects were always in the centre of the action, flooded with light from the sun or from hidden sources. The themes that were addressed included the victories of the Cultural Revolution; heroic images of workers, peasants and soldiers; successes in industry and agriculture, etcetera.

The visual arts mainly functioned to communicate the correct ideological standpoint and corresponding behaviour, along the lines 'tested' by the PLA. Only a narrow

BELOW LEFT: 'The growth of all
things depends on the sun'
(*Wanwu shengzhang kao
taiyang*), early 1970s.
BELOW RIGHT: 'New spring in
Yan'an' *(Yan'an xin chun)*, early
1970s.

OVERLEAF LEFT: 'Training crack
troops in the coldest time of the
year' *(Shu jiu lian jingbing)*,
early 1970s.
OVERLEAF RIGHT: 'New household in the mountain village'
(Shancun xinhu), early 1970s.

range of subjects was considered ideologically safe, and art was politicized and stereotyped to the extreme. For the first time, propaganda art became the most favoured vehicle for the transmission of party ideology. Works of art (oil paintings, water colours, woodcuts, and others) were reproduced for the ubiquitous large-format posters, and printed in smaller formats for mass distribution. As in Soviet posters of the 1930s, ageless, larger-than-life peasants, soldiers, workers and educated youth in dynamic poses, functioned as abstractions and dominated all artis-

'Two poems [by Mao Zedong]'

(Ci liang shou), early 1970s.

tic expression as ideal types. These heroic figures were usually boldly outlined, while the colouring tended to be varied and gay, in a style known as *Zhongguo hua*. However, in order to portray every subject as a hero, the physical distinction between male and female bodies often disappeared, leading to figures with standard bodies, absurdly big hands and feet, and different, but stereotypical, heads. Given the frequent changes in the interpretation of what was deemed correct, these political posters were carefully studied by the people (accustomed as they had become to the use of codes and symbols in the media) for any subtle change of tone or ideology, redirection of the (sub)movement(s), and use of slogans. Their version of consensus, after all, generally was accepted as the correct one at any moment.

Content-wise, the figure of Mao Zedong and his thoughts played a dominant role, often to the exclusion of other subjects. He could be depicted as a benevolent father, bringing the Confucian mechanisms of popular obedience into play; 'Reporting to Chairman Mao' (see page 40), shows Mao wearing the red scarf of a League member, surrounded by peasant youth. Or he was portrayed as a wise statesman, an astute military leader or a great teacher, as in 'New spring in Yan'an' (see page 41) and 'Heart-to-heart talk' (page 40). To this end, artists repre-

sented him in the vein of the statues of Lenin, which started to appear in the early 1920s in the Soviet Union. Another group of posters visually recounted the more illustrious of his historical deeds. The more the personality cult around Mao intensified, the more god-like and divorced from the masses he became in the portrayals. This is taken to extreme heights in 'The growth of all things depends on the sun' (page 41), in which Mao, surrounded by peasants standing in a cotton field, literally functions as the sun. The presence of his official portrait in every home, and the rituals enacted in front of it, showed many similarities with the traditional cult of the Kitchen God.

Those posters that did not feature Mao were devoted almost exclusively to idealized visualizations of life in the countryside, but as seen through an urban lens, reminiscent of the Soviet Union in the 1930s. 'The Commune's Fishpond' (see pages 12-13), 'The Brigade's Ducks' (page 50), and 'Brigade Chicken Farm' (page 51), a triptych created by the Huxian painters, are well-known examples. Such prints generally showed the successes of mechanized agriculture and water conservation, as in 'Contemporary Yu Gongs draw a new picture' (page 47) and 'Happy to see that pulling up seedlings no longer requires bending the waist' (page 48). Other examples include 'Commune's Spring' (page 49), 'Spring rain' (page 48), and 'Not depending on the sky' (page 59). Other themes included groups of peasants engaged in harvesting bumper crops (of corn, cotton, red peppers, cabbage, etcetera), as in 'It's always spring in the commune' (page 39), engaging in political study or participating in mass campaigns, as in 'Attending Party class' (page 48), which

BELOW LEFT: 'Two sisters' *(Jiemei liang)*, early 1970s.
BELOW RIGHT: 'Heart-and-soul' *(Quan xin quan yi)*, early 1970s.

shows a cadre lecturing while seated on a kang, with peasants and rusticated youth listening; and 'Electing a team leader' (page 47); or simply enjoying their improved lives, as in 'National Day in the Commune'

RIGHT PAGE, CLOCKWISE FROM TOP LEFT:

'Electing a team leader' (*Xuan duizhang*), early 1970s.

'Moving mountains to create fields' (*Yi shan zao tian*), 1977.

'Busy with a bumper harvest' (*Fengshou mang*), early 1970s.

'Contemporary Yu Gongs draw a new picture' (*Dangdai Yu Gong hui xintu*), one of two sheets, 1974.

(page 58), which shows a country fair, and 'Spreading out new clothes on a bumper harvest market' (page 48). Moreover, they paid great attention to the productive roles that women could play. The latter were frequently depicted engaging in pursuits that could be considered typically male, or as 'barefoot' doctors administering medicine in the countryside, as in 'Mountain village medical station' (page 53). 'I am a petrel' (page 52), depicting a female soldier in a tropical storm, installing telephone wires, is a typical example of this trend. Other materials

BELOW, CLOCKWISE FROM TOP
LEFT: 'Spreading out new clothes
on a bumper harvest market'
*(Fengshou changshang pi
xinzhuang)*, early 1970s.
'Happy to see that pulling up
seedlings no longer requires
bending the waist' *(Xikan
bayang bu wanyao)*, early 1970s.
'Spring rain' *(Chunyu)*, early
1970s.
'Attending Party class' *(Shang
dangke)*, 1974.

'Brigade Chicken Farm', 1973.

51

BELOW LEFT: 'I am a petrel' *(Wo shi haiyan)*, 1973.
BELOW RIGHT: 'Enrolling new students' *(Zhaosheng)*, 1977.

BELOW LEFT: 'The fragance of
flowers and fruit in the former
course of the Yellow River'
(*Huanghe gudao hua guoxiang*),
1973.
BELOW RIGHT: 'Mountain village
medical station' *(Shancun yiliaozhan)*, 1974.

LEFT: 'People and fish jump for
joy' *(Ren huan yu yue)*, 1978.
BELOW: 'Little swallows fly' *(Xiao
yan fei)*, 1976.

LEFT: 'Smash the Gang of Four'
(Da 'sirenbang'), 1978.
MIDDLE AND BELOW: Two popular cartoons criticizing policies of
the 'Gang of Four', ca. 1978.

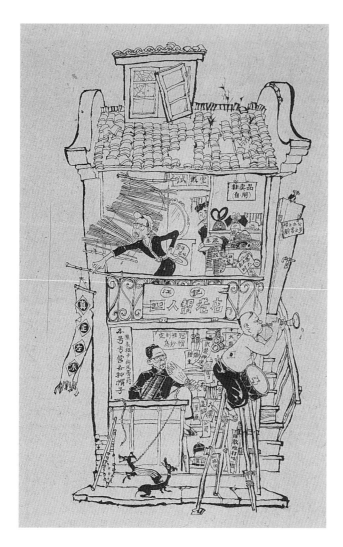

were devoted to the contributions to agriculture of rusticated students. 'Enrolling new students' (see page 52) shows three students, in the left corner, welcoming a colleague from the provincial agricultural college, while a Party cadre and a team leader look on.

Amateur artists from among the workers and peasants were given nation-wide attention and support. The most well-known were the peasant-painters from Huxian, Shaanxi Province, who gained international acclaim for their naive, colourful style of painting, and the workers from Shanghai, Yangquan and Lüda, who mounted a successful exhibition in 1975. Although these amateurs were promoted as representatives of the innate creative genius of the masses, it was later admitted that they had received extensive professional help and assistance in 'the composition of their pictures, as well as with the conception, presentation and skilful rendering' of their work. Various books and journals that supplied information on how to represent human beings, agricultural machinery, etcetera, were published. Without doubt, these publications functioned as sources of inspiration for the amateur artists. They contained concise close-ups of workers, peasants and soldiers, young or old, male or female, at work or engaged in some other meaningful activity. Sometimes examples were drawn from posters that had already been published, and were intended to provide good representations of human beings in art. In all probability, these source-books were responsible for the stereotypical quality of the visual propaganda of this period.

BELOW: Examples of representations of human beings, from a sourcebook providing details of propaganda posters, after 'Selection of images and workers, peasants and soldiers; vols.2 and 3' *(Gongnongbing xingxiang xuan;* Tianjin renmin meishu chubanshe, eds.), 1975.

OVERLEAF LEFT: 'National Day in the Commune' *(Gongshede jieri),* early 1970s.
OVERLEAF RIGHT: 'Not depending on the sky' *(Bu kao tian),* early 1970s.

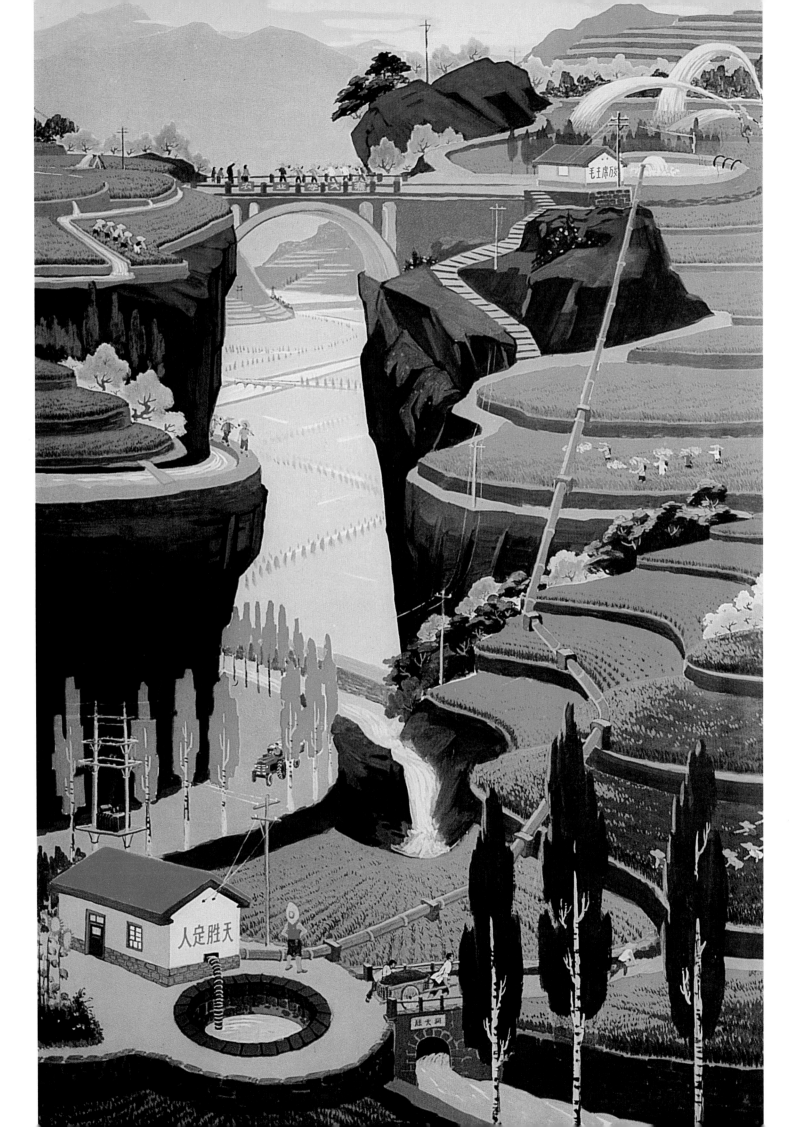

PROPAGANDA ART DURING HUA GUOFENG'S INTERREGNUM

After Mao's death in September 1976, his designated successor, Hua Guofeng, turned against Jiang Qing and what is contemporarily referred to as the Gang of Four. Supported by a temporary alliance of senior CCP and PLA leaders, Hua arrested them and their more famous followers. Hua, a relative newcomer to the centre of power, tried to mould his image in the example set by his predecessor. Hua did, however, attempt to modernize the economy, as spelled out in his ambitious 'Ten Year Plan 1976-1985', which was eventually shelved under pressure from the more pragmatic Deng Xiaoping. This plan called for large-scale imports of foreign technology, in order to shatter the Maoist fixation from preceding decades with self-reliance. In Hua's plans, however, modernization was almost completely limited to (heavy) industry, while the Four Modernizations centred around shifting priorities from industry to agriculture and from heavy industry to light industry.

As for the arts, not much changed. The poster style of the era was maintained, including the subjects that had become standard during the Cultural Revolution. 'Chairman Hua shows us the way' depicts Hua standing among bamboo with an elderly peasant who is quite reminiscent of the 'model' contained in the source-books for amateurs. The most notable change was that Hua took over the position previously reserved for Mao in works of art. In 'The revolution still has a helmsman', for example, Hua literally fills Mao's shoes. The people who are grouped together in the centre of the poster hold the official portrait of Hua aloft. Beneath this portrait, however, a grayish patch is visible. In the original design, this space was undoubtedly reserved for Mao's body.

A remarkable development in the years of Hua's reign was the leeway which visual artists were given for criticizing the Gang of Four; this freedom was manifested in the vengeance with which the 'Gang', arrested and awaiting trial, was lampooned and satirized in official publications and propaganda posters in the late 1970s. The representation of Jiang Qing as the 'White Bone Demon' of 'Journey to the West' *(Xiyouji)* fame in visual propaganda and in a number of comic dialogues *(xiangsheng)* created a target that easily could be recognized and criticized. The publication of the traditional-style 'Monkey thrice smashes the White Bone Demon' (see page 63) may have been accidental. 'Smash the Gang of Four' (page 56) provides an interesting example of the New Year pictures approach to this campaign.

Nonetheless, Hua's term of office witnessed the beginnings of a massive rehabilitation of artists and intellectuals who had been persecuted during the preceding 'ten years of chaos'. Due to the popularization of art work during the preceding 15 years,

people of all walks of life [had] now taken up brushes and paper, and other materials, and a broad segment of the population [was...] engaged in creative activity.

RIGHT: 'Monkey thrice smashes the White Bone Demon' (*Sun Wukong sanda baigujing*), 1977.
BELOW: 'Chairman Mao had a boundless confidence in Chairman Hua, the people and the army of the whole nation enthusiastically support Chairman Hua' (*Mao zhuxi wuliang xinren Hua zhuxi, quanguo junmin relie yonghu Hua zhuxi*), 1976.

金猴奮起千鈞棒玉宇澄清
万里埃 一九七六年冬趙宏本作

努力完成整党任务实现党

风根本好转

THE PROPAGANDA POSTER DURING THE FOUR MODERNIZATIONS ERA

THE FOUR MODERNIZATIONS ERA

POSTER ART AND THE FOUR MODERNIZATIONS

PAGE 64 - 65: 'Energetically complete the task of party rectification, bring about a basic turn for the better in party spirit' *(Nuli wancheng zhengdang renwu, shixian dangfeng genben haozhuan)*, 1984.

RIGHT, FROM LEFT TO RIGHT: 'Firmly uphold proletarian dictatorship' *(Bixu jianchi wuchan jieji zhuanzheng)*; 'Firmly uphold the socialist course' *(Bixu jianchi shehui zhuyi daolu)*; 'Firmly uphold Marxism-Leninism, Mao Zedong Thought' *(Bixu jianchi Ma Lie zhuyi Mao Zedong sixiang)*, all three 1984.

THE FOUR MODERNIZATIONS ERA

POLITICAL DEVELOPMENTS AFTER HUA GUOFENG'S INTERREGNUM

The CCP faced an enormous credibility gap as a result of its endorsement of policies such as the Great Leap Forward and the Cultural Revolution. The Four Modernizations era that followed Hua Guofeng's interregnum offered ample opportunities to make a clean break from these acknowledged political and economic mistakes. In the words of the late Hu Yaobang, former CCP General Secretary:

During the Cultural Revolution, we ruined our image as a Party.

The blame for the campaigns, particularly for the Cultural Revolution, could conveniently be laid at the doorstep of Deng Xiaoping's predecessors, in particular the Gang of Four. This enabled the CCP to approach the problems it faced with fresh ideas, thus allowing for a redefinition and revitalization of its leadership role. The CCP decided to de-emphasise the political struggle that had characterized its rule during the preceding two decades, and base its legitimacy to rule on its ability to modernize and to improve the Chinese economy, thereby improving the livelihood of the Chinese people.

An important aspect of the reform program was its aim to break the country's isolation, and to link up with global economic and industrial developments; this became known as the 'Open Door Policy', which had been presaged by Hua Guofeng's Ten Year Plan. The Open Door Policy enabled China to turn to the developed Western countries for advanced turn-key, or 'out of the box' technology in order to modernize the performance of its outdated industry, and to find international outlets for its industrial products. The income thus generated was to be invested in the productive sector of the national economy.

The subsequent influx of foreign businessmen and tourists, enabled the Chinese people to personally gain a deeper knowledge of the world beyond their borders. This process was facilitated by the informal penetration of non-specialized, non-technical culture. Furthermore, the success of the modernization program led to an enormous growth in the individual ownership of radios and televisions.

In the political domain, the two most important domestic goals of the Four Modernizations program were the decrease of the actual power of the state (or the CCP) to control society, and the repudiation of certain funda-

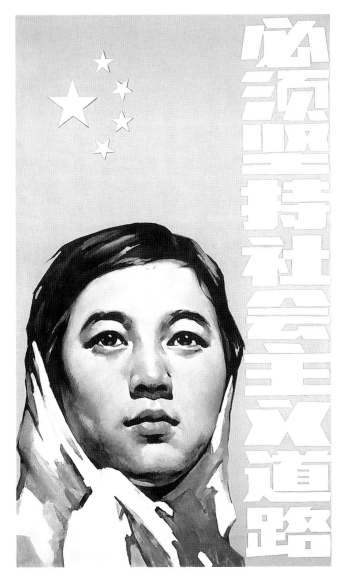

mental aspects of the Maoist ideology that had been religiously adhered to in the preceding decades. In concrete terms, this latter aspect meant not only a de-emphasis of political struggle, but also a de-emphasis of revolutionary purity, egalitarianism, and shunning contacts with the outside world. The pre-eminence of 'Redness' (political activism) over 'Expertise' (academic achievement) disappeared.

Although adherence to Mao Zedong Thought remained an important legitimizing factor for the CCP under Deng, it became quite clear from a very early stage that the orthodoxy represented by Mao's ideological heir would not, and could not, be treated with the previous reverence. Mao's contributions to the People's Republic of China were assessed in the early 1980s as being those of a 'great proletarian revolutionary, strategist and theorist', who had gone, or been led, astray in his later years. Yet the image of Mao as a wise leader continued to be held up.

Of course, the Four Modernizations period still witnessed

its share of political campaigns. Campaigns were waged to inculcate the 'Four Basic Principles', coined in March 1979 by Deng. They consisted of: adherence to CCP rule, to the socialist model of development, to Marxism-Leninism, and to the democratic dictatorship of the people. One campaign set out to combat 'spiritual pollution', and by doing so, attempted to keep the population at large, and intellectuals, writers and artists in particular, in line with the ideological demands formulated by the more conservative elements in the leadership. Another was aimed at resisting 'bourgeois liberalism', which called for a negation of the socialist system in favour of capitalism. The latter movement increased in intensity from its inception in 1987, and remained in force until the early 1990s. In all, five major purges in the sphere of politics and culture can be identified in the period between 1978 and 1988. Some elements of these campaigns did make their way into visual representations, although their representation in the field of visual propaganda was negligible when compared with the intensity of previous political campaigns, and their tone was relatively subdued. The main reason for this lies in the fact that the reforms, coupled with the various decentralizing policies that were formulated, made central control over society less effective, thus largely disabling the mechanisms of the propaganda system outlined in the previous chapter.

THE FOUR MODERNIZATIONS

The Four Modernizations were to take place in four sectors of the economy. Each had to be addressed differently by visual propaganda.

Agriculture

The first sector to undergo modernization was agriculture, imperative because over the decades it had been neglected in favour of industrialization. As a result, food production had only barely remained in step with population growth. A major step in the rural reforms was the decollectivization of agrarian production, in particular the disbanding of communes and the reintroduction of the household as the key unit of production and accounting. The political, economic and administrative functions formerly held by the communes were vested in the township governments which had been re-established. In an effort to more closely link productivity to income, various types of 'responsibility systems' were introduced, first on an experimental basis in the more marginal rural areas such as Anhui Province. However, as word of their success spread, they soon were adopted in all of rural China. The system most widely adopted was the 'household production contracting system', under which a household contracted for use of a plot of land, a piece of machinery, a workshop or enterprise for operating it. Land contracts specified a quota of particular crops to be grown, which had to be turned over partly as taxes and partly as a fee for land use. Everything produced above this quota could be sold on the private rural markets that were once again allowed. If unable to fulfil its contractual responsibilities, a household faced a fine.

These measures initially led to an enormous increase in food production. Combined with reforms in the countryside which allowed the peasantry to engage in other agriculture-related activities (such as setting up transport companies, building teams and rural industries), these policies made peasants (particularly those living in the peri-urban areas) the *nouveau riches* of the 1980s. Nonetheless, faced with severe unemployment that had previously been hidden, growing numbers of peasants flocked to the cities, where, as a 'floating population', they increasingly created social problems including crime.

Industry

In the early 1980s, there was a similar trend towards 'economic responsibility systems' in industry, as well as the introduction of market reforms and a closer linkage between productivity and income. Moreover, in order to modernize both production processes and the product mix, the Open Door Policy was to play an important role. By setting up 'Special Economic Zones' in Southern China (where bureaucratic interference, stifling rules and tax burdens were to be reduced), foreign companies

RIGHT: 'Chinese industry. The sun rises in the Eastern sky' (*Zhongguo gongye. Xuri dong-sheng*), February 1987.

were lured into cooperation with Chinese industrial complexes. Preferably, such cooperation would take the form of joint ventures, in which the Chinese side would contribute raw materials, soil, infrastructure and (cheap) labour, and the foreign partner would supply advanced technology, management and production processes. In a later stage, even wholly-owned foreign companies were allowed to profit from China's relatively cheap labour and less stringent environmental protection regulations.

Furthermore, following the example set by Hungary and other East European countries, enterprises and factory managers were to be given greater autonomy in decision-making, to the detriment of the mechanism of central planning, and in favour of scientific management and increased efficiency. As an incentive, enterprises were allowed to retain part of their profit for reinvestment in production, welfare or housing, or as bonus payments for the workers. Limited competition between enterprises was allowed, transcending the socialist emulation of the past.

With the downgrading of central planning, enterprises were made responsible for the direct marketing of their products. Moreover, they were given limited flexibility in labour management, enabling them to break 'iron rice-bowls' where and when they saw fit, in the name of increased efficiency.

National defence

The modernization of the military sector seemed to be seen strictly in terms of the upgrading of weaponry and an increase in professionalism and human efficiency. The need to modernize this sector forcefully hit home when the PLA suffered an unexpected drubbing during the 'punitive expedition' against Vietnam in 1979. However, military modernization had to take place alongside the development of agriculture and industry, and no special funds were earmarked for it. By 1981, the PLA budget had dropped sharply in comparison with earlier years, only to be even further reduced in the years to come.

China initially was forced to turn to the West in order to modernize the outdated weapons systems it had acquired from the Soviet Union in the 1950s. Only at a later stage was the PLA able to develop its own modernized weapons, on the basis of the knowledge gained through Western arms imports and reverse engineering of non-Chinese military technology.

The first budgetary measure was the reduction of the number of soldiers. A second budgetary measure was the streamlining of the defense industry. Lastly, in order to heighten professionalism in the Army, new attention was paid to the military expertise of the recruits of the officers' corps, rather than to their political reliability. This, amongst other things, meant doing away with the egalitarianism prevalent since the early 1960s, and resulted in the reintroduction of ranks and insignia, and a renewed attention to the curricula of cadets from the military acad-

LEFT: 'Love labour' (*Ai laodong*), 1983.

OVERLEAF, LEFT: 'Our future' (*Womende jianglai*), 1987.

OVERLEAF, RIGHT: 'Another leap in the history of Chinese medical science' (*Zhongguo yixue shishangde you yici feiyue*), 1987.

emies. Now, only the most motivated and best-educated recruits could be absorbed into its ranks, resulting in increased professionalism of the Army.

Science and technology

Although the science and technology sector ranked fourth in the modernization scheme, it was stressed from the beginning that success or failure of the complete scheme depended on the successful modernization of this sector. In a way, science and technology were regarded as magic wands that could be used to almost automatically transform, reform and modernize the economy. Already in 1977, Hua Guofeng had made it clear that science no longer had to be sacrificed for politics. Deng Xiaoping took this line of reasoning one step further by asserting that science and technology formed part of the productive forces, and not, as Mao had insisted, of the superstructure; thus the sector would no longer be subjected to the necessity of political struggle.

After the anti-intellectualism of the Cultural Revolution, the scientific and academic institutions had to be restored and rebuilt, so that activities could be resumed. The use of economic levers to regulate and stimulate academic activities, instead of administrative means, formed an important part of this. As part of the attempts to create horizontal links between ministries, administrative units and research institutes, even military scientific research was to be transferred to civilian use.

On a more practical level, science and technology were to be coordinated with the development of the economic and social spheres by creating links between the research and productive sectors. This meant a focus on applied research in agriculture and industry, which led to developments in genetic engineering, the sectors of energy, raw materials technology, computer science, and laser technology. As for the emphasis on productive technologies, their popularization was to be promoted, if necessary through a commoditization of knowledge. Attention was paid to advanced scientific experience of other countries, and to international academic trends and developments.

Both the educational system and its standards were restored after their complete disbandment during the Cultural Revolution. The newly-introduced examination system stressed academic excellence over political purity. In order to speed up the training of an indigenous scientific labour force, and to catch up with scientific developments abroad, large numbers of Chinese scientists and students were sent to Western countries to speed up their training in state-of-the-art research techniques. This, however, led to problems associated with the mechanism of enculturation. Through their stay abroad, Chinese scholars and students discovered alternative ways of organizing social reality, which affected their attitudes towards the political and social arrangements existing at home. Their casual assimilation of Western lifestyles, social tech-

公元12世纪 我国就已发明火
药箭
公元20世纪 我国成功地发射
世界先进水平的
运载火箭
公元21世纪 我国的火箭技术
拭目以待……

我们的过去
我们的现在
我们的将来

中国医学史上的又一次飞跃

- 微循环的发现
  与"修氏理论"
- 人工再造的成功
- 针灸的发展
  与突破

niques and expectations, both in a material and scientific sense, created problems upon their return. It was not conducive to their reintegration into Chinese society, because it confirmed the suspicions held against them by conservative Party officials.

Economic (re)construction, and the necessity of the Party's guidance in attaining modernization and prosperity, became the centrepieces of propaganda in the 1980s. As a result, little room was left for its original purpose, namely the continuing political socialization of the population. At the same time, the decrease in attention devoted to political subjects 'reduced the State's capacity to isolate, encapsulate, atomize, manipulate — and thereby dominate — society'. More was needed than a simple restructuring and rephrasing of well-worn elements of the messages that had been sent out over the decades. One consideration that called for a new approach to propaganda was the Chinese perception that behaviours can only become habit when performed over a long period of time. Patterns of past behaviour become fair predictors of future behaviour; stereotypes and stereotypical behaviour are much more easily aroused than eradicated. The 'ideological bonding' by, or the 'pernicious' influence of twenty years of hyperbolic propaganda of, for example, the Great Leap Forward and of the class-hate induction of the Cultural Revolution, and the concomitant behaviour that was a result of this, had to be wiped out.

Now that the war waged by the CCP against society had come to a halt, attention had to be devoted to the vari-

ous components of the modernization policy. One pressing question that had to be answered was why China, after thirty years of scientific socialist rule, was still backward compared with the Western world. This latter point forcefully hit home on the occasion of Deng Xiaoping's trip to the United States in 1979, when the Chinese people were confronted with 'educational' television programs. The spacious living arrangements, the number of consumer durables and the size of the cars owned by the American workers could only cause wonder among Chinese viewers. Decision-makers and power-holders at all levels had to be brought in line with the changed approach to development. This was attempted through consecutive campaigns which combined coercion, education and positive role models for emulation, to criticize the lingering influences of the Gang of Four and their own resistance to modernization.

It was not only necessary to take a fresh look at the way the new, result-oriented ideology of the Four Modernizations period was to be presented and portrayed, but also to decide toward which target groups utterances were to be directed. A fresh approach called for the creation of the 'Four Modernizations Man' living in a 'New Age'; at the same time, stress on serving the people and

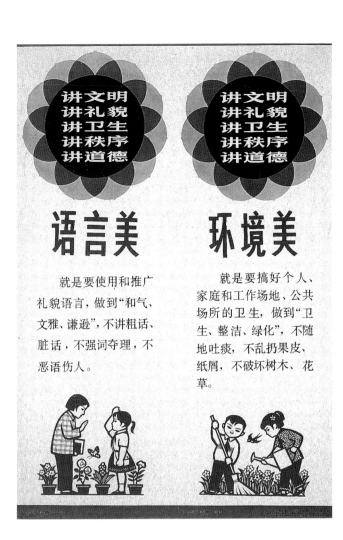

LEFT AND FAR LEFT: 'Five do's' and 'Four beauties' ('Wujiang' 'Simei'), 1983.

socialism remained an important function of literary and artistic propaganda. The fact that increased exposure to international mass media made the population more knowledgeable than ever before, made a reappraisal of the methods and contents of propaganda all the more imperative. As one editorial office responsible for printed propaganda put it, it was now necessary to 'use real (*shishizaizaide*) examples' of desired behaviour.

Moreover, the possible negative side-effects of the modernization process in society called for the inculcation of new popular values and attitudes, which made the clearing of the channels of communication between leaders and people an extremely urgent prerequisite. The popular 'crisis of faith', or 'crisis of trust', towards the CCP that was clearly felt among the population, had to be addressed and, where possible, combatted. This crisis had not only resulted in apathy towards the policy process and outright scorn towards the CCP and its members, but also in a quest to find solace in other belief systems, such as religion, or in 'plain old material acquisition'.

The lack of popular faith towards the CCP was formed by public perceptions of corruption and nepotism among its officials and their preoccupation with their own (materi-

al) situations. In the early 1980s, both the trial against the Gang of Four, and the official reassessment of the historical role of Mao, had brought to light innumerable examples of cadres' abuse of power at various levels in the hierarchy. Also, the Open Door Policy and the attendant individual confrontation with what the outside world (in particular capitalist countries) really looked like, led to the loss of faith in socialism as an ideology. In order to regain credibility, relatively neutral and non-political subjects were now stressed. Patriotism and pride in national tradition and culture were considered to be more potent substitutes for the previous ideological propaganda of Marxism-Leninism, Mao Zedong Thought.

UNINTENDED EFFECTS OF THE MODERNIZATION POLICIES

In addition to promoting the policy goals and behaviours suitable to the Four Modernizations, posters had to respond to the problems which stemmed from these same policies. After initial successes in the introduction of the Four Modernizations in both rural and urban areas, unexpected and unforeseen negative side-effects had to be addressed and, if possible, combatted. First of all, a fear existed among the population that the reform policies would only be short-lived. Especially in the agricultural sector, this seriously hampered the overall effects of the newly-introduced production responsibility and contract systems. Despite assurances about the continuation of the reform, and the extension of the contract periods, people shirked from investing in the plots they had contracted, while attempting to extract the utmost.

RIGHT: 'Defending the Borders tenaciously' *(Gushou bianfang)*, 1989.

Secondly, the trend towards 'consumerism' (which had initially been officially advocated and which had become prevalent among the people) had to be cooled, and the rampant materialistic trend of 'looking toward money in everything' had to be checked. Coupled with this was the necessity to instill new love for things Chinese, and to oppose the general infatuation with things foreign, if only to deplete the stockpiles of goods in the warehouses of Chinese state industries. Thirdly, there existed a pervasive fear among people, particularly among urbanites, that they had done rather well, but should have done even better. The feeling among a large number of people that they had somehow missed out while others had succeeded, created widespread dissatisfaction.

This feeling of missing out led to an upsurge of crime throughout society. The popular feeling that safety in society was breaking down was partly exacerbated by such unknown social phenomena as unemployment and a floating population. The policy pronouncements that inequality in income distribution would be beneficial to overall development, were belied by the social reality of the increased occurrence of crimes against property. In fact, income inequality and the parallel inequality in ownership of consumer goods led to the wide-spread occurrence of crime and 'red-eye disease' *(hongyanbing)*, the colloquial term for envy.

These developments led to a number of normative sub-campaigns, clearly of an integrational bend, that were designed to contribute to the creation of a 'socialist spiritual civilization'; the Five Stresses — civilization, courtesy, sanitation, order, and ethics —, the Four Beauties — of mind, language, conduct and environment — (see the posters 'Five do's' and 'Four beauties' on pages 74 and 75) and the Three Ardent Loves — of the country, socialism and the CCP (see the posters on pages 66 and 67). New positive role models were created of successful private entrepreneurs who welcomed their newly-acquired economic and political freedom. The sub-campaigns did not succeed in allaying the growing unrest that had resulted from the rapid social changes following the successes in economic modernization; nor did they address the question of whether 'the institutions' (the Party, Army and State) needed changes along the same lines, or should continue to hold on to their time-honoured policies. In other words, although behavioural models on how to become economically successful were held up, behavioural indications for those who did not make out in this 'New Age', and explanations for, and behavioural modes towards, the often bewildering and unanticipated social changes taking place as a result of the Four Modernizations, were not forthcoming.

Moreover, the effectiveness of propaganda, in general, seemed to be diminishing. As a result of the intellectual emancipation that took place under the Open Door Policy, many people started to believe that they were subjected to endless government hyperbole that was designed to create an unrealistic, overly-positive picture of actual conditions. Although socialist ideals can be best represented by displaying the actual accomplishments of real people, those being confronted with the conspicuously didactic role models could not help but be amused by the government's naive attempts to get them to unquestioningly follow the examples.

固守边防

何永坤 作　　云南人民出版社出版　云南新华印刷厂印刷　云南省新华书店发行
1989年8月第一版第一次印刷　编号：8222·1776　定价：0.30元

POSTER ART AND THE FOUR MODERNIZATIONS

NEW TARGET GROUPS

The leadership no longer considered the bombardment of the population at large with visual propaganda to be as necessary as it had been in the past. On the contrary, in the second half of the 1980s, propaganda art in the streets was replaced by mere normative illustrations of social order, traffic safety, birth control, and advertising for Chinese and foreign products. The integration of China into the 'global village' of electronic media, a result of the increased exposure of the population to the international mass media, moreover, gave its people more alternative sources of information about their surroundings, and alternative belief systems. The State also had to deal with broadcasts that reported items the leadership deemed unfit for mass consumption; this was particularly the case with reports, usually in Chinese, but quite often also in English, that were broadcast by foreign radio stations such as the BBC World Service and the Voice of America. Remarkably enough, listening to these stations was not prohibited, as it offered people the chance to acquire knowledge of a foreign language.

The propaganda posters that continued to be produced seemed mainly to be aimed at primary school children, as yet untainted by the disruptive propaganda of the preceding periods. The reason for this can be found, of course, in the fact that youngsters are more impressionable and more likely to respond enthusiastically to pressures for attitudinal change. However, this generation of the 1980s saw through the political messages and no longer believed in the symbols generated by the CCP; young people were, in the last analysis, mainly concerned with themselves, and not with 'loving the people', or with 'building a socialist state'. But the goal of modernization by the year 2000 largely depended on youth, in particular urban, educated youth.

Another subject that had to be addressed was the social and political position of the intellectuals, who were supposed to play such a major and crucial role in the modernization process. The Party's policies towards intellectuals and scientists had been reformulated; with science and technology belonging to the productive forces, it logically followed that the people who were engaged in science and technology work belonged to the working class. In an atmosphere where scientists no longer needed to fear being labelled as enemies of the people after making 'mistakes', many of their representatives were rehabilitated, and their positional titles reinstated. Still, the leadership's promises for the improvement of the material well-being of intellectuals never seemed to materialize, and widespread discrimination, exclusion, and oppression of intellectuals continued to exist.

Intellectuals were seen as the linchpin around which the whole process of modernization revolved, without whose cooperation and input it would be impossible for the CCP to regain its former pre-eminent position. As a group that had known serious persecution in the past, but was now again to be stimulated into cooperation with the regime, soothing visual representations of its future were produced in an obvious effort to allay possible fears of a policy change. They became a regular subject of visual propaganda, and were pictured side-by-side with the former standard bearers of the People's Republic of China: peasants, workers and soldiers. An intellectual (wearing a white coat and glasses) can be seen on the 50 *yuan* RMB banknote released in 1980, acting as a reminder that intellectuals were once more looked upon with favour; until then, Chinese banknotes had featured toiling peasants and workers.

Although the CCP continued to impose its image of society (as well as its definitions of reality, truth and the meaning of life) on the nation, an unprecedented liberalization in the arts and visual propaganda took place in the period of the Four Modernizations. The slogan 'practice is the sole criterion of truth' became the new guiding principle for the pragmatic reform faction around Deng. A very important aspect was Deng's insistence that literature and the arts were no longer to be subjected to politics. At the same time, the call for the liberation of thought allowed the scope for literary and artistic creations to be widened, enabling intellectuals and artists in particular to explore terrains hitherto closed to them. Modernization, after all, also applied to the arts, and being 'modernized' entailed the necessity to entertain new ideas, new concepts and new qualities.

Works of art now could be created for audiences of intellectuals and cadres, although their traditional, basic orientation towards the workers, peasants and soldiers was to remain. The arts, as 'engineers of the soul', were, after all, still considered to be educational tools for instilling correct thoughts and attitudes in people. So not surpris-

ingly, despite the official order that writers and artists totally utilize their creative spirit, the arts still reflected the prevailing party 'spirit', in this period defined as contributing to the Four Modernizations and to socialism.

This implied the end of Socialist Realism as the sole principle of creation in Chinese art. An important new trend, not only in literature, film and drama, but also in painting and propaganda art, was the use of 'flashback' styles. The flashback, for example in 'scar-literature' and 'scar-art', allowed for the recounting of personal suffering as a result of the political misfortunes personally encountered during the political campaigns of the past two decades. 'Scar literature', or 'literature of the wounded', provided realistic accounts of the Cultural Revolution, and exposed the 'dark forces harming the masses'. It originally emerged as 'new wave' literature in 1977, and derived its later name from Lu Xinhua's story 'The Wounded', published in the late Summer of 1978. Such outpouring of pent-up resentment was officially tolerated, as the cathartic effect of venting bad feelings in order to feel better could be channelled into support for the new policies. This was facilitated by the simultaneous official re-evaluation of the Great Leap Forward and the Cultural Revolution, which allowed artists to portray the 'dark side' of society and the negative effects of some recent CCP-policies, instead of only paying attention to the glorious achievements brought about by the Party.

With Socialist Realism no longer proscribed, other realist or representational styles were tested. One style that rocked the world of painting was so-called 'New Realism', made up of Western-inspired Post-impressionism, Expressionism and even Symbolism, but without the

LEFT: 'Little guests in the Moon
Palace' (Yuegong xiao keren),
early 1970's.
BELOW: 'Little warriors' (Xiao
yongshi), 1986.

LEFT: 'Love the people' *(Ai ren-min)*, 1983.

RIGHT: 'We should do more and engage less in empty talk — Deng Xiaoping' *(Duogan shishi, shao shuo konghua — Deng Xiaoping)*, 1992.

FAR RIGHT: 'Our master planner' *(Womende zongshe jishi)*, 1992.

爱人民 AI REN MIN

typical elements of its Socialist Realist predecessor. Other artists made use of Photo-realism and Magic Realism, although their works did not always meet with a favourable response. It should be noted that the amalgamation of Chinese ink outline and Western colour shading, also known as *Zhongguo hua*, almost disappeared.

Abstract art continued to be misunderstood and unappreciated by most people, including the CCP-leadership, as can be gauged from the official warnings against the 'alienation of the masses' supposedly resulting from confrontation with abstract works. Despite this, a strong trend towards non-representational images became clearly discernible in the visual arts. Although people continued to be an important tool in bringing across the intended behavioural message, abstract elements were increasingly used. This, of course, was a departure from earlier practice, as discerning the intended meaning of the new visualizations demanded more intellectual effort than the cartoon-style propaganda of the preceding decades. Also, the increased use of the *pinyin* system of transcription on propaganda posters made the message more difficult to understand.

Although not necessarily in line with the aesthetic policy in force at the time, Western visual elements were introduced to portray the 'New Age' of visual and artistic styles that made their way into China as a result of the opening-up of the country. Both literature and the visual arts experimented with Western-style science fiction and Futurism. This usually was not done in an effort to create a critique of contemporary developments, as is often the case in the West, or to popularize science, as had been the Chinese practice until then. Instead, coinciding with the optimism of the gigantic projects and perspectives of the Second Great Leap Forward of the late 1970s, they were to serve as 'the talisman of instant modernization'. Moreover, they were intended, according to science fiction writer Zheng Wenguang, to

sing the praises of science [...], of the various beautiful things the labouring masses will create through their reliance on science, and of the basic struggle of our one billion people to realize the Four Modernizations. That is why, while science fiction usually describes the future, its basic reasons for doing so are highly significant for the present.

Particularly in propaganda art, this led to glimpses of a Chinese future that was crowded with icons of progress, technological innovation and development similar to what had been conceptualized in the West during the 1960s and 1970s. The future was symbolized by spacecraft (clearly modelled on the NASA Space Shuttle) hovering in the air, high-speed bullet-trains, highrise buildings, and freeways crowded with cars. 'Energetically complete the task of party rectification, bring about a basic turn for the better in party spirit' (see pages 64-65), shows such

多干实事，
少说空话。

邓小平

我们的
总设计师

glimpses of a horrific future to the left of the clenched fist of the figure dominating the poster. To the right of him, a pagoda, presumably the one at Yan'an, is visible.

The most remarkable aspect of these and other representations of the 'New Age' in China (which, in Western eyes, would be seen as an ecological nightmare) was the almost complete absence of specific Chinese symbols of progress that had previously been used. An earlier, rather childish example of the use of space travel is provided in 'Little guests in the Moon Palace' (see page 80), which shows little bare-armed and bare-legged children, escorted by stuffed animals, with space helmets on, travelling to and alighting on the moon to present the hare, pounding immortality elixir, with flowers. The future, as it was visualized in the 1980s, faithfully mirrored the globally-accepted, mainstream representation of what was to come in a world where science and technology reigned supreme. As such, the contents of propaganda were a far cry from the visualization of the agrarian utopia of the past decades. In this sense, China finally and irrevocably linked up with what the media philosopher Marshall McLuhan has termed the 'global village': the world as one community, with commonly-held desires and aspirations, often inspired by the electronic media. Moreover,

most propaganda prints of the 1980s were clearly urban-oriented and took the interiors of factories or city-scenes as their backdrop. It should also be pointed out that these prints devoted an increasing amount of space to slogans, which can be interpreted as proof of the new stress on education, as well as of the general intellectual development of the Chinese population.

As in the first three decades of the 20th century, advertising techniques made their way into the People's Republic of China through the Special Economic Zones in southern China, and the 'Open Cities' along the eastern seaboard designated for commercial contacts with the West. These exerted an enormous influence on the visual arts, in particular the application of design concepts and the use of photo-montage and mixed-media. One of the most remarkable examples of this use of mixed-media is 'Love the people' (see page 82), in which the background is composed of colour photographs of women engaged in traditional feminine pursuits such as child care and care for the elderly. This development in Chinese advertising and visualization techniques is particularly visible when one compares the aesthetic leap forward of the advertisements published in the official trade journal 'China's Foreign Trade' in the period between

Three posters from the commemorative series 'Ode to Socialism' (*Shehuizhuyi song*), 1989.
BELOW LEFT: 'The achievements in national defence and science and technology are glorious' (*Guofang, keji chengjiu huihang*).
BELOW RIGHT: 'Chinese agriculture takes on a new look' (*Zhongguo nongye mianmao yixin*).
RIGHT PAGE: 'Industry develops and changes with each passing day' (*Gongye fazhan rixin yueyi*).

1975 and 1980. Visual elements derived from advertising can also be seen in propaganda art, in particular on posters published in the period from 1982 through 1984, that call for more safety on the job and in traffic.

The visual propaganda employed in the One Child Campaign (started in 1979 to curb the projected problematic growth of the population), was an exception in more than one respect. In order to forcefully and successfully communicate the message that the offspring of a couple should be limited to one child, traditional visual elements

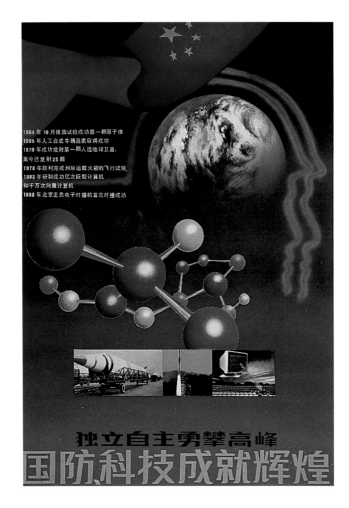

工业发展日新月异

到 1988 年工业固定资产比 1949 年增加 85 倍。
钢增加 375．1 倍 原煤增强 29．6 倍,
发电量增加125．8 倍

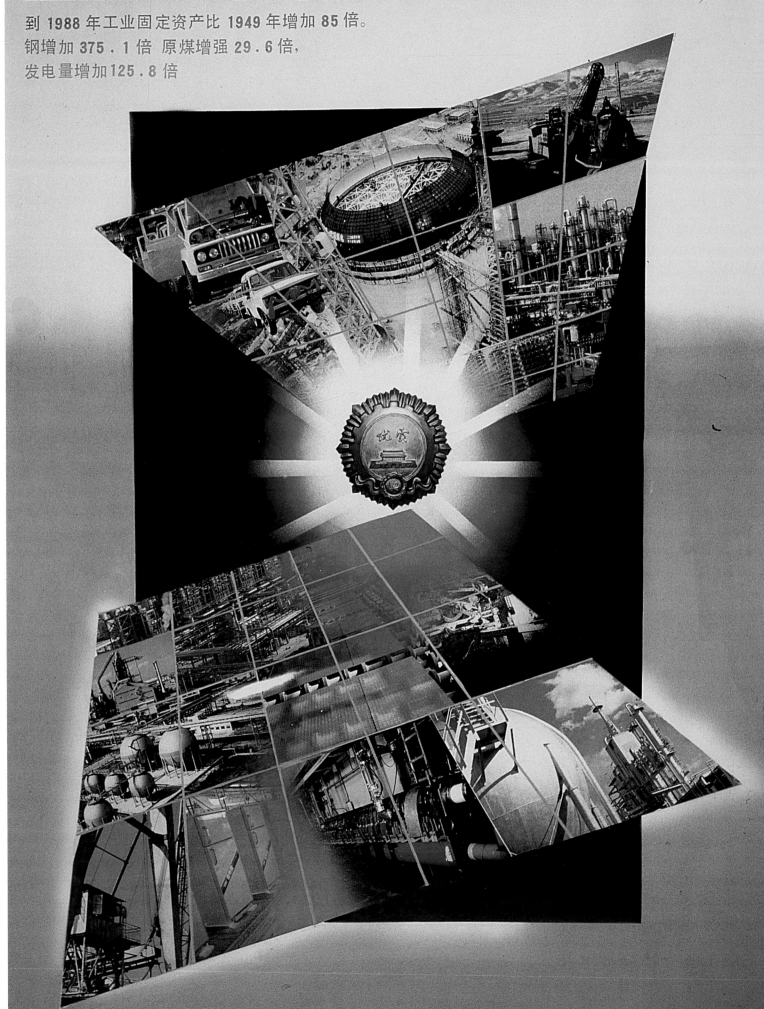

BELOW: 'Study Lu Xun's revolutionary spirit' *(Xuexi Lu Xunde
geming jingshen)*, 1978.

学习鲁迅的革命精神

aesthetic appeal for the people) were used. Pictures featuring chubby baby boys and golden carp attracted the attention of both rural and urban populations, whether or not they contained slogans to the effect that 'one is better'. Similarly, traditional New Year picture-inspired means of representation were mixed with more original Socialist Realist elements, and applied to romantic portraits; they featured certain well-loved historic CCP leaders such as Zhou Enlai and Zhu De, usually with small children or representatives of minority peoples, or historical personages such as Lu Xun who played an important role in the CCP struggle for state power (see page 86). While other political leaders, particularly the members of the new ruling elite (namely Deng Xiaoping, Hu Yaobang or Zhao Ziyang) were notably absent, the sugar-sweet portrayal of popular heroes from the past was clearly intended to bring back memories of the less disastrous elements and activities of CCP-rule. However, in November 1992, as a result of the growing personality cult around Deng, a poster was released bearing his portrait in simple black and white. Later, even some of Deng's more pithy utterances were reproduced on posters (see page 83).

Proof of the acceptance of the various Western styles in propaganda art by the political leadership lies in the fact that they continued to be employed, even after the Four Modernizations period had come to an end. Even in the era of 'reform and opening up' (1988-1992), which can generally be characterized as more politically conservative, works of propaganda art continued to prominently feature the futuristic imagery first introduced in 1978. Some convincing examples can be found in a poster series published in December 1989, in commemoration of the 40th anniversary of the establishment of the People's Republic of China, called 'Ode to Socialism' (see pages 84-85); and a series published in May 1991, to mark the 70th anniversary of the founding of the CCP, titled 'Celebrate the 70th anniversary of the founding of the Chinese Communist Party' (see pages 88-89).

THE 'NEW ARTISTS'

Although the indiscriminate borrowing and mixing of visual styles and graphic forms from the West often resulted in awkward hybrids, it is safe to say that the new inspiration led to an 'explosive diversification in the cultural products offered, including the revival of discredited works and genres' that had been popular before. Partly, this diversification can be seen as the symbolic manifestation of the more general cultural diversity which was encouraged by the reform program. But it could also be attributed to the massive rehabilitation of painters who had been discredited as 'rightists' during the Great Leap Forward and the Cultural Revolution. Many had been sent to rural areas to be 'reeducated' by the peasantry. After their teachers considered them to be sufficiently imbued with the 'revolutionary spirit and modes of thought' to become revolutionary art workers, they were often employed in designing propaganda murals, packaging or advertisements for the products of the fledgling rural industries. When they were finally allowed to return to their original occupations and work units (usually art schools, art associations or museums), they continued to create works of art, which, although strong-

光輝的业绩

LEFT: 'A glorious, outstanding achievement' (*Guanghuide yeji*).
RIGHT: 'Party, oh Party, beloved Party' (*Dang ah dang, qin'aide dang*).

Both posters are from the commemorative series 'Celebrate the 70th anniversary of the founding of the Chinese Communist Party' (*Qingzhu Zhongguo gongchandang jiandang 70 zhounian*), 1991.

ly influenced by their previous experience of painting in the Socialist Realist mode, also were heavily influenced by the new artistic techniques they learned in the countryside.

Other types of artists, who were far removed from the officially recognized art academies (which hierarchically fan down from Beijing) became active. Most of these 'new artists', who can be considered the representatives of an independent art movement, no longer wanted their art to convey political or moral messages. Among them is a group of sub-professional painters, made up of talented peasants and workers who paint in a naive way, or in deviant styles, inspired by their contacts with Western and overseas-Chinese mass culture. As they form no part of the bureaucratic structure of the arts world, and do not have to produce work on order, they have been able to deviate from the artistic requirements laid down by the centre. The volume of art supplies available in department stores, art specialty shops and corner stores, moreover, indicates that there is a vast number of such practising part-time and amateur painters.

The non-official artists started selling their works on the semi-legal art market that sprung up in the mid-1980s as a component of the free markets that were again allowed due to rural reforms. Later, these markets also spread to the urban areas, where they developed gradually into non-food markets. This 'commoditization' of art enabled some artists to break loose from the official patronage of cultocrats, who previously hampered their artistic endeavours.

The 'new artists' were often denigrated by the 'established' painters who worked in the 'velvet prisons' along the creative guidelines supplied by the government. In the eyes of the establishment painters, who considered themselves to be the guardians of the Chinese cultural traditions, the works of art created by those working outside of the confines of the academies did nothing but compromise the unique Chinese identity. Chinese identity should be defined as the concept of a unified and shared culture, based on notions of civility, conformity and order. The 'independents', on the other hand, did not try to conform, and looked for innovation instead. They sought inspiration in Western art and culture, in an attempt to counter what they saw as the impoverishment of form, technique, and content in the art of the 'official' painters. From the government's point of view, this gave rise to complaints about the vulgar tastes of the masses, and their willingness to pay for cultural products created and produced by artists outside of the state-system. More importantly, it gave rise to the development of a popular culture that was no longer guided or dominated by the CCP.

Another, younger group of artists consists of rusticated youth: high-school graduates who were sent to the countryside during the Cultural Revolution in order to steel their revolutionary commitment under the guidance of the peasantry. They have tried to make a living outside

of agriculture by creating non-controversial works of art; some of these feature traditional themes from pre-modern popular religion, such as the Kitchen God or the God of Wealth, thus filling a gap in the market not serviced by State publishing. An interesting mixture of traditional themes and political content, is 'Defending the Borders tenaciously' (see page 77), which depicts a soldier, with flowing cape and large ceremonial sword, on horseback. The poster clearly forms one half of a pair and is done in the style of the ancient Door Gods.

The fact that people are now able and allowed to buy works of art purely on the basis of aesthetic appeal or entertainment value, and not because they should be scrutinized for political content, has greatly added to the popular demand for art. Potential customers could be found among the many hotels and restaurants that have sprung up to cater to the local and foreign tourist boom, since they are in need of non-political artwork to decorate their lobbies and function rooms. The establishment of private companies and galleries to act as dealers for young artists, or as middlemen for foreigners who want to buy Chinese art outside official channels, has further stimulated the art market.

The continuing existence and further development of non-government controlled art has been facilitated by the 1988 decision of Wang Meng, then Minister of Culture, to allow artists to operate on a collective or private basis, while at the same time allowing for inter-artist competition.

SPECIAL EFFECTS

A number of special techniques have been employed for propaganda posters, often corresponding with the specific target groups toward which they were directed.

On a general level, it should be stated that the *gongbi*-style, the realistic style that is characterized by fine brushwork and close attention to detail that was prevalent in the posters of the Cultural Revolution fell into disuse in the Four Modernizations era, to be replaced by a more 'impressionistic' style resembling the traditional *xieyi*-style of representation, a sketchy style that uses freehand brushwork and which is characterized by vivid expression and bold outline. In line with this was a more subdued use of colours, in a clear departure from the bright pinks, reds, yellows, greens and blues so characteristic of the *Zhongguo hua*-style that had become the hallmark of the representational paintings during the first half of the 1970s. In this sense, the materials produced during the reign of Hua Guofeng, although hampered by during the reign of Hua Guofeng, although hampered by the same dualism that characterized the policies of the period, already give an intimation of changing aesthetics in propaganda posters.

Moreover, Socialist Realism as the dominant mode of representation lost its prominence, not only to other types of realistic representation, but also to Western-inspired styles. The influences emanating from advertisements making their way into China from the 'Special Economic Zones' and the 'Open Cities', whether Western-inspired or Western-produced, also clearly left an imprint on the popular aesthetic consciousness, calling for the introduction of mixed-media techniques and non-representative, or even abstract, visualizations in the design of posters.

On a more specific level, special techniques were employed to create resonance with the audience by linking or reinforcing audience predispositions. The use of traditional styles, themes and bright colours inspired by New Year Prints, for example, made their way into posters designed to spread the 'one-child' policy. Such depictions were typically appreciated for their contents, while their message might go unheeded. It is difficult to assume, however, that the failure of that specific campaign was a direct consequence of the way the messages were depicted.

Various systems of symbolic reward were established in the visual idiom of the period, while symbolic punishment was played down. Posters that stress the successes of the Four Modernizations Campaign by offering glimpses of the material well-being that can be in everybody's grasp as long as everyone works for it, limit themselves to the optimistic side, and gloss over the collective punishment that would most certainly result if the Four Modernizations failed to deliver: a return to poverty, deprivation and scarcity.

A closer link between reward and punishment can be found in the sizable body of posters designed for spreading legal knowledge among the people based on the newly-codified corpus of laws. The punishments meted out to those straying from the course, as spelled out in the illustrated law books and posters, are in line with the new laws and regulations, while those abiding by the law in the end get to partake of the fruits of a society that is slowly but surely reaching a stage of being moderately well-off.

The use of symbols of power was essentially limited to two types of propaganda. On the one hand, national symbols (the Great Wall), symbols of state power (the Gate of Heavenly Peace) and of the CCP (hammer and sickle) were reserved for the propaganda aimed at school children, in order to create and reinforce feelings of patriotism and sacrifice for the nation. On the other hand, similar symbols were used in those posters stressing the need to adhere to certain ideological precepts. The series produced to inculcate the Four Basic Principles is a typical case in point.

One symbol of national unity or state power that fell into disuse in the Four Modernizations era was the book, or document. In the preceding decades, books had been present in visual propaganda as the result of a radical attempt to turn a whole population into readers. It was held that by reading, the people would be politically influenced out of free will, and become motivated spokespersons for the socialist State. Specifically, persons

OVERLEAF LEFT: 'Create a new age of civilization' *(Kaichuang wenming xin shidai)*, 1983.
OVERLEAF RIGHT: 'Spread Spring all over the Divine Land — dedicated to those who contributed to the Four Modernizations' *(Saman Shenzhou chuchu chun - xian geiwei sihua zuo gong- xiande renmen)*, 1983.

alibi for their actions, or as a reward for specific behaviour, disappeared; the decisions of the Party, the National People's Congress or other policy-formulating bodies were no longer held aloft in mass scenes to reinforce or illustrate the deeper meaning of a visual representation. The popular practice during the Cultural Revolution of presenting meritorious persons with sets of the selected works of Mao Zedong, or similar sets of books or State documents, also disappeared completely.

A last special technique was the arousal of emotions, in particular those of nationalism and patriotism. This was brought about by resorting to two major types of stimuli. One was the repetitive insistence that the Four Modernizations were to make China 'rich and strong', thus enabling the nation to once more take its rightful and traditionally elevated position among the nations. Another was the recurring stress on the historical uniqueness of the Chinese people. The latter group of posters clearly was intended to nurture popular pride in the Chinese tradition and culture, and to contribute to the formation of the 'socialist spiritual culture' that was designed to combat the infatuation with things Western. This was done by pointing out the endeavours of the Chinese people, their creativity, or their art (in particular the Dunhuang cave paintings). The 'Flying Devis from Dunhuang' appeared in 'Create a new age of civilization' (see page 92). A Chinese girl painted (or airbrushed) in similar Dunhuang-style hovers over a modern sky-line done in abstract style, in 'Spread Spring all over the Divine Land — dedicated to those people who contributed to the Four Modernizations' (see page 93). Another topic was the centuries-old dedication to schol-

arly pursuits, and the scientific and scholarly accomplishments of representatives of the Chinese people. Li Shizhen, for example, was made the topic of one poster (see page 97) devoted to his compilation of the standard work *'Materia Medica'*.

'The Three heroes battle Lü Bu' (see page 95) is an example of a poster containing the appropriate educational stimuli of patriotism. Also published were 'comic strip' stories, usually made up of two sheets, which offered modernized visualizations of legends (see page 96).

PROPAGANDA AND 'SOCIALIST SPIRITUAL CIVILIZATION'

The official acceptance and continuous use by the CCP of Westernized visions of the future impeded the formation of a 'Socialist Spiritual Civilization'. The concept first was mentioned by Deng Xiaoping in December 1980, and has been on the CCP agenda ever since 1982. Broadly speaking, it should consist of the building of a material civilization and the raising of people's political consciousness and morality, as well as the fostering of revolutionary ideals, morality and discipline; all should reflect the demands of the 'New Age', but with communist ideology at its core. It is clearly an attempt to formulate a framework for a new social structure, in line with the new vision of a future that would be capable of enlisting mass support in order to combat the spread of undirected popular culture. Underlying this search for a modernized culture with Chinese characteristics, were broad questions such as

开创文明新时代

KAICHUANGWENMINGXINSHIDAI

撒满神州处处春

such as

what is the proper course for modern China [...and...] through what combination of Chinese identity and reform do we best preserve our self-respect.

This new cultural system was to reflect, and to be based on, the economic modernization process that changed society since 1978, as well as to combat (in the eyes of the leadership) the sleaziness and the negative social aspects of commercialism and consumerism.

Attempts to create this 'Socialist Spiritual Civilization' have, until now, failed to create visual propaganda which provides the clear instructions for popular performance, to which the Chinese people have grown so accustomed. As opposed to the reasonably predictable, single and simple propaganda messages of the preceding decades, the visual instructions for behaviour in the 1980s have become multi-layered and confusing, containing various conflicting attitudinal stimuli and instructions for behaviour. Getting rich, for example, was first hailed as a glorious undertaking with beneficial and educational effects, but has subsequently been deplored as the 'worship of money'. Another development prohibiting the formulation and propagation of comprehensive behavioural instructions has been the increasingly heterogeneous character of society, in which social, generational and occupational groups, even 'the masses', can no longer be treated as an undifferentiated whole. In the eyes of the social scientist Wang He, there exists a 'generation gap', resulting in vast discrepancies in interests, views, standards and even vocabulary and language among people with slightly more than a decade's difference in age. According to Wang, visual propaganda has stopped short of one of its ascribed goals, namely the

continual deepening of [the] people's understanding of modernization as well as the increasing scope of the reforms which have moved from simple technical importation to structural reforms, and now to a change in ideology and culture.

Moreover, if socialism, as it is defined by the CCP, is to guide the formation of this spiritual culture as the new controlling ideology, it seems a self-defeating process. The CCP and its ideology are, after all, increasingly seen as stumbling blocks for the Western-style modernization that more and more Chinese see as the ultimate goal. Over the years, a contradiction between the reform policies and Mao Zedong Thought has become apparent to the people, while impatience with the pace of reform is growing. Party rule and tight control over the modernization process, both in the economic and the political sphere, are considered impediments to the realization of the personal, usually material, desires of the population, often inspired by Westernized propaganda and direct contacts with Westerners and Western-made goods.

BELOW: 'The Three heroes battle
Lü Bu' (San ying zhan Lü
Bu), 1982.

李時珍

1518—1593

我国的医学家和药物学家·辑成"本草纲目"，

中载有中国药用植物1892种·11000多个单方。

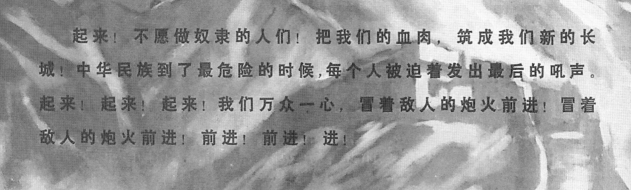

起来！不愿做奴隶的人们！把我们的血肉，筑成我们新的长城！中华民族到了最危险的时候,每个人被迫着发出最后的吼声。起来！起来！起来！我们万众一心，冒着敌人的炮火前进！冒着敌人的炮火前进！前进！前进！进！

万众一心向

WANZHONG YIXIN XIAN

前进

GQIANJIN

THE FUTURE SYMBOLIZED: PROPAGANDA POSTERS OF THE FOUR MODERNIZATIONS ERA

AN ANALYSIS OF GENERAL SUBJECTS

POLITICAL SUBJECTS
ECONOMIC SUBJECTS
SOCIAL SUBJECTS

AN ANALYSIS OF SPECIFIC TARGET GROUPS

YOUTH
MEN
WOMEN
INTELLECTUALS
PEASANTS
WORKERS
SOLDIERS
CADRES
MINORITIES

THE FUTURE VISUALIZED: AN ANALYSIS OF SYMBOLISM AND IMAGERY

PERSONAL APPEARANCE AND CLOTHING
SYMBOLS OF DEVELOPMENT
SPARE-TIME ACTIVITIES
GENDER REPRESENTATION AND MALE CHAUVINISM
SYMBOLS OF POLITICAL POWER
SYMBOLS OF MODERNITY
TRADITIONAL NEW YEAR PICTURES
THE USE OF COLOURS
VISUAL SYNTAX

PREVIOUS PAGE: 'The myriad masses move forward with one heart' *(Wanzhong yixin xiangqianjin)*, 1984.

RIGHT: 'Commemorate the day that Marx, the greatest proletarian instructor of the world, died 100 years ago' *(Jinian quan shijie wuchan jiejide weida daoshi Makesi shishi yibai zhounian)*, 1983.

RIGHT BELOW: 'Lenin loves children' *(Liening ai haizi)*, 1982.

OPPOSITE PAGE: 'Struggle in unity to contribute to the vigorous development of China' *(Tuanjie fendou wei zhenxing Zhonghua zuo gongxian)*, 1984.

AN ANALYSIS OF GENERAL SUBJECTS

POLITICAL SUBJECTS

Despite the decreased intrusion of politics into the private lives of the Chinese in the era of the Four Modernizations (with the possible exception of the One Child Campaign), political subjects continued to be featured in propaganda posters. After all, the various commemorative occasions marking the foundation of the Party, the PLA or the People's Republic of China, had to be accompanied by relevant visual propaganda. For example, a large poster was published in June 1984 to mark the 35th anniversary of the foundation of the People's Republic of China, and was titled 'Struggle in unity to contribute to the vigorous development of China' (see page 101). The poster features cameos of a female peasant, a male worker, and the atomic symbol surrounded by doves, against a Dunhuang-inspired background. Similar propaganda posters commemorated the founding fathers of the ideology shielded by the Four Basic Principles: Marx and Lenin. In 1983, a spate of posters was published commemorating Marx's death, for example 'Communism will certainly be realized — commemorate the day that Karl Marx died 100 years ago' (see page 102). Other examples of such posters are 'Commemorate the day that Marx, the greatest proletarian instructor of the world, died 100 years ago', and 'Lenin loves children'. The latter poster shows Lenin, with a kitten on his arm, surrounded by a group of caucasian children in front of a Christmas tree. According to the caption, which is belied by the modern interior and clothing,

1949　　1984

团结奋斗为振兴中华做贡献

LEFT: 'Communism will certainly be realized — commemorate the day that Karl Marx died 100 years ago' (*Gongchan zhuyi yiding yao shixian - Jinian Kaer. Makesi shishi yibai zhounian*), 1983.
BELOW LEFT: 'Comrade Mao Zedong, comrade Zhou Enlai, comrade Liu Shaoqi and comrade Zhu De together' (*Mao Zedong tongzhi, Zhou Enlai tongzhi, Liu Shaoqi tongzhi, Zhu De tongzhi zai yiqi*), 1982.
BELOW RIGHT: 'Chairman Mao Zedong and his comrades-in-arms' (*Mao Zedong zhuxi he tade zhanyou*), 1983.

this gathering took place shortly after the victory of the October Revolution. Such political subject matter was only used for specific events, and the pervasive presence of politics in posters did disappear.

Attempts to create leader-worship, as with Mao Zedong during the 1960s and the Cultural Revolution, and with Hua Guofeng in the late 1970s, disappeared completely. In line with Deng's dictum that leaders and their glorious deeds should remain in the background, and with the clear aim of bolstering the flagging support for the CCP, the stress was on political subjects that portrayed the glorious deeds of the past (in particular those of the formative, pre-1949 period), and of glorious, departed leaders (in particular Zhou Enlai). An example of such posters, 'Comrades Zhou Enlai and Deng Yingchao' (see page 103), pictured Zhou and Deng posing in front of a Southern Chinese landscape. No posters published in the

1980s showed the contemporary representatives of the leadership, be they Deng Xiaoping, Chen Yun, Hu Yaobang, or Zhao Ziyang. In an obvious attempt to demonstrate the legitimacy of the Deng-line, however, the older leaders, including Deng and Chen, did appear in posters featuring group photographs or paintings of the CCP-leadership of the 1950s (including Mao Zedong, Zhou Enlai, Liu Shaoqi and Zhu De). In these posters, Deng and Chen are often given a higher profile and position than history would suggest. 'Chairman Mao Zedong and his comrades-in-arms' is an artist's rendition of the well-known photograph (to which Deng Xiaoping and Chen Yun have been added) of the reception of Zhou Enlai at Beijing airport in the 1950s (see below).

Posters continued to be used to concretely demonstrate how the Party's more abstract policy pronouncements (exhortations to love socialism or the collective, for

LEFT: Zhu De, 1982.
BELOW LEFT: 'Comrades Zhou
Enlai and Deng Yingchao' *(Zhou
Enlai he Deng Yingchao tongzhi)*,
1983.
BELOW RIGHT: 'Premier Zhou has
come to the training field' *(Zhou
zongli laidaole xunlianchang)*,
1978.

people of the whole country unite to struggle for the creation of a completely new situation of socialist modernized construction' (see page 108). This was a concrete expression of the awareness among CCP leaders that class harmony and class unity existed and that it was no longer necessary to call for unity among the nationalities. After all,

[w]hile Mao knew how to bring the classes together to liberate China from Japanese invasion and imperialist aggression, Deng knows how to put together a new coalition of classes to modernize China's backward economy.

example) should be interpreted. It should be noted that political subjects such as the Four Modernizations and the Four Basic Principles were usually envisioned to have validity for a longer period of time. Incidental campaigns, or short-term policies, were increasingly presented through television.

What largely disappeared over the years were the group scenes which portrayed all demographic and occupational groups of the Chinese population as one big, happy family, enthusiastically marching with the rhythm of the new policies. A late exception to this trend was 'The

LEFT: 'Ceremony proclaiming the founding of the State' *(Kaiguo Dadian)*, 1990.

RIGHT: 'People's heroes' *(Renmin gongchen)*, 1984.

BELOW: 'Achievements and happiness throughout the ages' *(Gongye qianqiu xingfu wandai)*, 1990

BOTTOM: 'Discussing great plans together' *(Gongshang daji)*, 1985.

人民利益高于一切

LEFT: 'We are the hope of the mother country' *(Women shi zuguode xiwang)*, 1985.

BELOW LEFT: 'The people's interest is placed above everything else' *(Renmin liyi gao yu yiqie)*, 1983.

BELOW: 'The national flag is hoisted in our hearts' *(Guoqi zai women xinzhong shengqi)*, 1984.

PAGE 107 TOP LEFT: 'A courtyard full of Spring colours' *(Manyuan chunse)*, 1977.

PAGE 107 TOP RIGHT: 'Culture, courtesy, greening, beautification' *(Wenming limao lühua meihua)*, 1982.

PAGE 107 BOTTOM LEFT: 'We love the nation' *(Women ai zuguo)*, 1985.

PAGE 107 BOTTOM RIGHT: 'Cherish greening, treasure old and famous trees' *(Aihu lühua, zhenxi gushu mingmu)*, 1983.

文明礼貌 绿化美化　WEMINGLIMAOLUHUAMEIHUA

爱护绿化 珍惜古树名木

A similar stress on the glorious deeds of bygone days and leaders marked a number of posters featuring the PLA. Particularly noteworthy is the series depicting the 'Nine Marshals' (Zhu De, Liu Bocheng, Peng Dehuai, He Long, Ye Jianying, Chen Yi, Nie Rongzhen, Xu Xiangqian and Luo Ronghuan) in both a group scene, 'People's heroes' (see page 105), and in individual poses reminiscent of classic Western paintings of noblemen on horseback (see page 103). Lin Biao, who fell from grace in the early 1970s is, of course, excluded. It is not clear whether such materials were published for general consumption, for a limited PLA audience, or for use in PLA veterans' homes. The posters that depicted relations between the people and the PLA as being like 'lip and teeth,' a theme common during the Cultural Revolution and the Hua Guofeng era, almost completely disappeared. 'A courtyard full of Spring colours' (see page 107), for example, depicts PLA soldiers of both genders preparing an art exhibition assisted by peasants. The posters addressing devotion to the mother country use army-related imagery, usually a combination of a soldier in uniform, with the Great Wall as a backdrop (see page 109).

The Communist Youth League received increasing attention. The depiction of the various activities organized by the Communist Youth League in the 1980s, however, had little in common with the posters of earlier times. The Youth Leaguers who were active in the modernization era no longer had to recite political statements, but officiated at flag-raising ceremonies. 'The national flag is hoisted in our hearts' (see page 106) is a photograph of a flag-raising ceremony in front of Tian'anmen Gate, attended by League members. 'We love the nation' (see page 107) provides a more childish depiction of such a ceremony taking place in a schoolyard.

Other posters showed them actively taking part in the various patriotic and Greening of China Campaigns that were organized from the mid-1980s on; in particular, 'Culture, courtesy, greening, beautification' (see page 107), and 'Cherish greening, treasure old and famous trees' (see page 107). In other cases, they were depicted as standard-bearers of the revolution. 'The people's interest is placed above everything else' (see page 106), for example, depicts a League member saluting, with in the background cameos of models such as Zhou Enlai, Lei Feng and Zhang Haidi. In general it can be said that youth continued to be seen and presented as the *spes patriae*, as is nicely demonstrated by 'We are the hope of the mother country' (see page 106).

ECONOMIC SUBJECTS

The propaganda of the Four Modernizations saw a clear reorientation from the countryside to the urban areas. Successful peasants who had succeeded in putting the reforms to their personal advantage were no longer models. It seemed that the propagation of these aspects was best left to other media, such as newspapers directed to a rural readership, or word of mouth. The neglect of communal facilities, such as irrigation systems, public roads and rural welfare, which resulted from the trend of 'going it alone', was not addressed.

Although the agricultural reforms initially formed the backbone of the modernization process, the economic subjects depicted in the propaganda of the era were

BELOW LEFT: 'Create a great new situation in socialist modernized construction' (*Kaichuang shehui zhuyi xiandaihua jianshede weida xin jumian*), mid-1980s.

BELOW RIGHT: 'Foster a correct spirit, resist the evil spirit, resist corruption, never get involved with it' (*Fuzhi zhengqi, dizhi waiqi, ju fushi, yong buzhan*), from the series 'Regulations for staff and workers' (*Zhigong shouze*), 1983.

largely industrial. 'Create a great new situation in socialist modernized construction', for example, depicts a male intellectual, soldier, worker, and female peasant, in 'modernized China', with skyscrapers, fly-overs, space craft launching pads and a bullet-train against an abundant grain harvest in the background. One of the most striking posters featuring infrastructural themes is 'Long live the People's Republic of China' (pages 114-115), in which visual elements derived from Western science-fiction are employed. Interestingly, despite the surge of private entrepreneurship in the first half of the 1980s, and its beneficial effect of absorbing the labour surplus, this was

BELOW: 'Becoming more prosperous every day' (Zhengzheng
rikang), early 1970s.

BELOW: 'On the banks of the
Yangzi river, Daqing blooms'
(*Yangzijiangpan Daqing hua*),
early 1970s.

中华人民共

LEFT: 'Be careful not to stab your foot' (*Dangxin chuojiao*), 1984.

BELOW: 'Take strict precautions against traffic accidents' (*Yanfang chehuo*), 1984.

OVERLEAF, LEFT: 'Be careful around live wires' (*Dangxin chudian*), 1981.

OVERLEAF, RIGHT: 'Be careful around dangerous machinery' (*Dangxin jixie shangren*), 1984.

not considered a subject that had to be addressed in visual propaganda. This was no doubt a result of the propagation of the Four Basic Principles, which, theoretically at least, could not countenance the successes of economic activities taking place outside of the domain of State control.

Although the number of visual materials devoted to economic subjects decreased during the 1980s, four developments in the representation of these subjects can be discerned. First of all, industrial production was no longer visualized as a 'battle' that had to be waged by the workers, by sacrifice of life and limbs. Instead, increasing attention was being paid to the hazards of certain production processes and activities, and safety on the work floor in general became a subject to which a whole body of posters was devoted. These include 'Be careful not to stab your foot' (see page 116), 'Take strict precautions against traffic accidents' (see page 117), 'Be careful around live wires' (see page 118), 'Be careful around dangerous machinery' (see page 119) and 'Guard against injuries while hoisting' (see page 120). 'Prevention of fires and explosions' (see page 121) is a graphic warning against laxness with fire. It is interesting to note that in posters devoted to industrial production, the peaked cap, formerly the trademark of the Chinese worker, was replaced by the hard hat. This can be seen as a symbol of modernity, but also as the result of adherence to safety rules.

Secondly, with the increase of the individual responsibility of shop stewards and factory managers for production, visual propaganda aimed at the prevention of corrupt behaviour on their part was developed. The eighth of the

poster series 'Regulations for staff and workers', depicts a cadre resolutely refusing to accept bottles of alcohol and ginseng cigarettes, with the caption 'foster a correct spirit, resist the evil spirit, resist corruption, never get involved with it' (see page 111).

搞好安全用电 保障生命和生产的安全

当心触电

DANG XIN CHU DIAN

当心机械伤人

机械的传动部分要安装防护装置。运转中的机械严禁检修。不准戴手套操作机床。

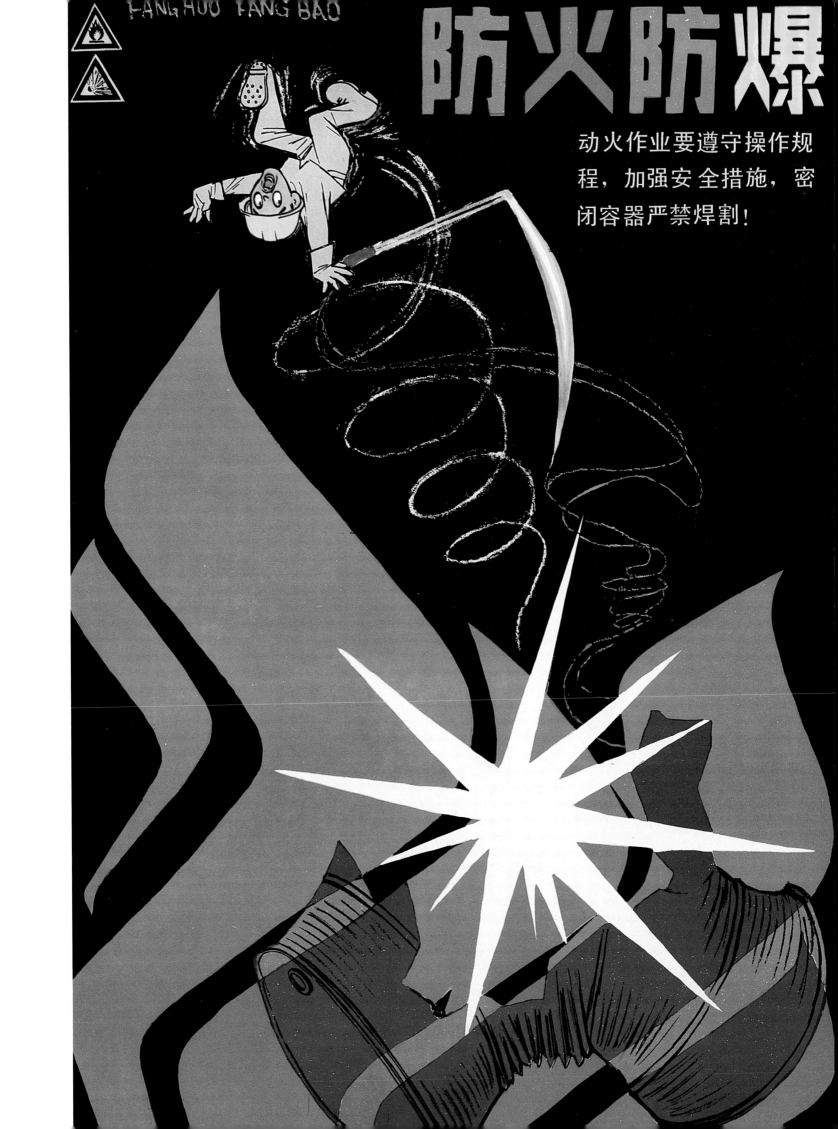

PREVIOUS PAGE, LEFT: 'Guard against injuries while hoisting' (*Jinfang qinzhong shanghai*), 1984.

PREVIOUS PAGE, RIGHT: 'Prevention of fires and explosions' (*Fanghuo fangbao*), 1984.

BELOW: 'Protect environmental hygiene' (*Baochi huanjing weisheng*), 1983.

RIGHT: 'Make the mother country green' (*Lühua zuguo*), 1982.

cheaper production methods, more efficient methods of production, etc.

Fourthly, from the mid-1980s on, the initial infatuation with industrialization and all-out development that marked the visual propaganda of the Hua Guofeng era, was gradually replaced by a concern for the detrimental ecological and environmental effects of modernization. The same applies to the use of industrial imagery in general: bellowing smokestacks, an image that was frequently used in earlier times, apparently were no longer needed as proof of the message that socialism worked. Scenes such as the one entitled 'On the banks of the Yangzi river, Daqing blooms' (see page 113), with a petrochemical complex presented in the style of a traditional Chinese landscape, were no longer produced. The growing concern for the environment was demonstrated by the publication of a number of posters that called on the population to contribute to the Greening of China Campaigns. 'Make the mother country green' (see page 123) and 'The whole people plant trees and put rivers and mountains in order' (see page 124), the first of a four-poster series, may serve as an example for the new ecological awareness. It remains doubtful whether these really contributed to a deeper understanding of what was at stake.

Thirdly, a new type of economic model was introduced for emulation. These models no longer had to sacrifice themselves in the ongoing production struggle to achieve the ultimate success of the Four Modernizations, but they were admired for their contributions to this process:

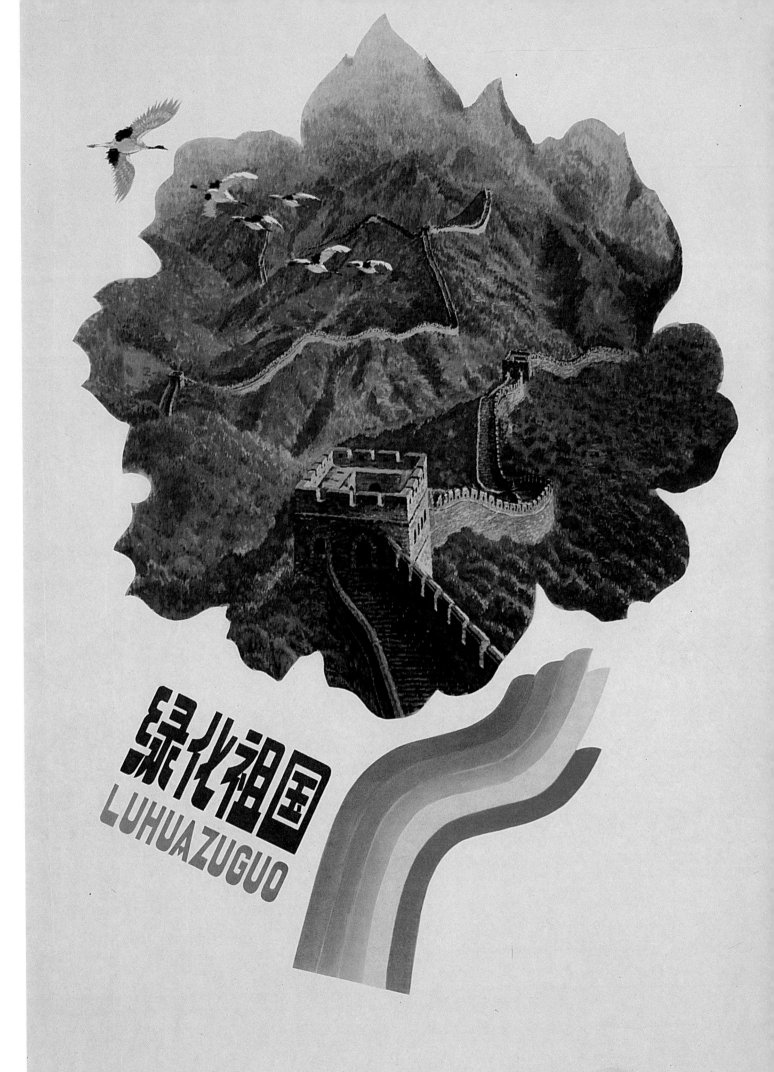

绿化祖国
LUHUAZUGUO

绿 化 祖 国

张长青 作

四川人民出版社出版 四川省新华书店发行 七二三四工厂印刷
1982年12月第一版 1982年12月第一次印刷 印数1～15,000

书号: 8118·1390 定价: 0.18元

全民植树 治理河山

上海市园林局绿化宣传站　周瑞庄作

LEFT: 'The whole people plant
trees and put rivers and mountains in order' *(Quanmin zhishu,
zhili heshan),* 1983.

BELOW: 'Observe social order -
pay attention to boarding trains
in a civilized way' *(Zunshou shehui zhixiu - jiangjiu wenming
chengche),* 1981.

SOCIAL SUBJECTS

Five social themes can be identified as being visualized most in the first half of the 1980s. The first called on the people to adhere to the policy of population control. Posters that explained the mechanism of human reproduction, and methods to limit one's off-spring to a single child, were produced for use in glass display cases erected in streets or for community rooms. Examples of such educational posters — which include explanations about what a woman feels when she is pregnant, the use of condoms, etc. — are the 'posters popularizing the science of family planning' (see page 126). Posters featuring chubby babies and traditional icons of abundance were clearly based on New Year prints and had the obvious implication that circumstances would be better for all involved, in particular in urban areas, when only one child was born per family. In that sense, elements of modernity started creeping into traditional scenes, such as high-rise buildings, and modern interiors, as in 'In the heyday of the year of the dragon plump babies are born' (see page 127).

The second group of posters propagated the new body of laws that was promulgated in order to create socialist legality. A number of multiple-sheet educational 'comic strip' posters was published, both in colour and black-and-white to increase popular understanding of the new laws and regulations (see pages 161 and 194). These strips often recounted true events of the recent past. Of these laws, the newly-formulated rules for the protection of the rights of women and children were portrayed most frequently, shedding light on a dark aspect of Chinese

society. It seems that despite past pronouncements to the contrary, and despite the professed equality of all, the official guarantee of the social position of these two demographic groups needed extra attention. These posters leave no doubt about the fact that women and

BELOW LEFT: 'Posters popularizing the science of family planning' (*Jihua shengyu kepu
huabao*).

BELOW RIGHT: Zhang Haidi, 1984.

RIGHT: 'In the heyday of the year
of the dragon plump babies are
born' *(Shengshi longnian yu
pang wa)*, 1987.

children continued to be victimized by males. As a whole, the body of posters related to this subject functions as a catalogue of male chauvinist, male 'feudal,' or simply male criminal behaviour.

The third most frequently depicted theme was made up of posters that called for orderly, disciplined and civilized behaviour in all aspects of daily life, as in 'Observe social order — pay attention to boarding trains in a civilized way' (see page 125). 'Take strict precautions against traffic accidents' (see page 117) is a very graphic reminder of the need to observe safety in traffic. Other posters were directed against behaviour that was not necessarily criminal, but that could be considered to endanger public security. Depending on the age of the target group(s), these attitudinal stimuli ranged from indications of basic social skills, i.e. how to cross a busy thoroughfare, to the general reminder to obey the police.

The fourth theme stressed the value of learning, intellec-

tual pursuit and love of study. Although this stimulus was applied to all age groups, vocational school students and university students logically were considered to be important recipients of this message. In propaganda addressed to workers, but not the peasantry, these values were represented in posters that stressed the necessity of contributions of science and technology, and of 'low-tech' inputs from the work floor, for the success of the modernization process. One poster of the series 'Regulations for staff and workers' for example, calls for energetic study, and an improvement of the political, cultural, scientific-technological, and vocational levels of the persons addressed. Although this latter aspect was a continuation of earlier propaganda practice, the fact that technology transfer was often taking place in the successful rural industries was not visualized at all.

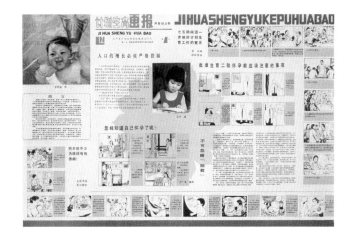

BELOW LEFT: 'Make many contributions to the Four Modernizations in the same manner as Jiang Zhuying' (*Xiang Jiang Zhuying neiyang wei Sihua duozuo gongxian*), 1983.
BELOW RIGHT: Qian Xuesen, 1990.

In posters aimed at intellectuals, the representation of elderly male intellectuals of the past played an important role. The optics specialist Jiang Zhuying, who died in 1982, served as an important intellectual model in the early 1980s (see below). Later, Qian Xuesen, one of China's principal nuclear scientists, became the most well-known intellectual appearing in propaganda posters. The attention devoted to learning was all the more salient in propaganda directed at the PLA, given the fact that education had become one of the most important grounds for promotion within the ranks of the military; professionalization of the PLA was to end the focus on

political trustworthiness that had existed in the past. The stress on the necessity of contributions to science and technology was designed to have an obvious educational effect on cadres. After all, in the past they used to spurn learning and intellectuals, either because of the danger scientific knowledge could pose to the cadres' position, or because policy pronouncements stated that 'revisionist' behaviour existed among (a small group of) intellectuals. Even in the modernization decade, such cadre behaviour persisted.

The fifth major theme was patriotism, and in the posters addressing this theme were the promptings to work hard to reclaim the paramount international position as a result of the successful modernization process, and the satisfaction everybody could derive from this, clearly spelled out. It should be noted that as modernization progressed over the years, in the process of which more and more aspects of social life were changed or influenced, and a general feeling of inadequacy, cloaked in a love for things foreign, became more widespread and apparent, these themes became to be portrayed more frequently.

In order to convincingly portray a number of the subjects mentioned above, models of accepted social and even cultural behaviour were employed, who were relatively prominent in some aspect, but not as perfect and free from shortcomings and errors as previous role models. These new heroes, reflecting the trend toward diversity and pluralism that became the undercurrent in the China of the 1980s, strove to improve their country and its international position; they valued learning; they contributed greatly to the urgent task of building a socialist

spiritual civilization; and, significantly, they did not necessarily belong any longer to the former 'mainstream', namely, workers, peasants or soldiers, but could also be intellectuals.

In a low-key fashion, primary school children continued

LEFT: 'China's healthy sons soar over the five regions and six continents' *(Zhongguo jian'er tengfei wu liu zhou)*, 1987.

RIGHT: 'Chinese braves for the first time trail the Changjiang' *(Zhonghua yongshi shou piao Changjiang)*, 1987.

to be called upon to learn from Lei Feng ('Uncle Lei') for basic social morality, whereas the 'modernized models' seemed to be mostly directed towards adolescents and young adults, to graft onto the basic concepts of obedience and discipline inculcated by posters extolling Lei Feng. An example from the Lei Feng posters directed towards primary school children is 'Learn from Uncle Lei Feng, strive to become a red-flowered youth' (see page 129). It is interesting to note the large number of girls featured in this type of poster.

The model status of Zhang Haidi, widely publicized in print and in propaganda posters from 1983 on, is a case in point (see page 126). As a self-taught paraplegic, not only did she function as a model because of her intellectual accomplishments or her devotion to serving others, but also, in the words of the political scientist Alan P.L. Liu,

In Lei Feng, Chinese youths had to reach for communism. In Zhang Haidi, communism reaches for Chinese youths.

Her depiction that a disabled person could still function normally in Chinese society, and even contribute to its modernization, was also clearly intended for all those who were maimed and crippled during China's 'punitive expedition' against its southern neighbour Vietnam in 1979. The attention suddenly given to invalids might even be linked to Deng Xiaoping's son, Deng Pufang, who ended up in a wheelchair as a result of Red Guard interrogations. Persons such as Zhang Haidi did not necessarily have to be martyrs for the revolutionary cause or pay with their lives in order to attain model status. They simply were visualized in their 'daily' activities, which were clearly designed to make people feel proud of being a woman, or Chinese.

Other convincing examples are successful Chinese athletes, as depicted in 'China's healthy sons soar over the five regions and six continents' (see above), or a group of youngsters who trailed the Yangzi River's course from source to end, immortalized in 'Chinese braves for the first time trail the Changjiang' (see page 131).

中华勇士首漂长江

公元1986年6月到11月，中华民族的英雄儿女，以非凡的勇敢、坚毅和智慧，首次实现了对长江全程——6300公里，落差5400米——的非机动连续漂流，其中包括地球上最深的"魔鬼大峡"——虎跳峡。

这是人类对大自然的一次伟大的征服，这是人类对人本身一次自觉而深刻的认识。人类将永远记住这光辉的日子和勇士们的英名。

BELOW: 'Observe traffic regulations, safeguard public order' *(Zunshou jiaotong guize, weihu gonggong zhixu)*, 1987.

AN ANALYSIS OF SPECIFIC TARGET GROUPS

Traditionally, propaganda in China has been directed towards a mass audience; the modernization decade, however, saw the formation of an audience which was increasingly diverse. Aside from the small proportion of propaganda directed towards the population as a whole, usually of a political nature, specific propaganda subjects were designed in the 1980s for most of the demographic and occupational groups that comprise the Chinese population. It goes without saying that propaganda directed towards primary school children can also influence adult behaviour, or that women can internalize behavioural stimuli that, for all intents and purposes, seem to be directed towards males. The following analysis deals with the groups that have been identified as target audiences, and with the specific subjects that have been directed toward them.

YOUTH

Youth were clearly identified as the group that was to make the modernization process succeed by the year 2000, and as such, it became the most important target audience for visual propaganda in the 1980s. As a reflection of the growing diversity of the population, the propaganda directed at youngsters had a distinct, three-pronged approach: primary school youth, adolescents, and university students.

Studying the examples set by Lei Feng and other models remained a constant element, but was no longer taken seriously in an era in which 'getting rich first' was one of

the most important, recurring exhortations from the government. The participation of youth of all ages in political activities, or in mass campaigns with a clearly political tone, largely disappeared from visual propaganda after the 'smashing of the Gang of Four'.

LEFT: 'Practising hygiene from an early age' (*Cong xiao jiang weisheng*), 1982

BELOW LEFT: 'Pay attention to hygiene, take precautions against disease' (*Jiangjiu weisheng yufang jibing*), 1983.

BELOW RIGHT: 'Honour teachers, honour elders' (*Zunjing laoshi, zunjing zhanbei*), 1987.

OVERLEAF: 'I love my China, I love my Great Wall' (*Ai wo Zhonghua, ai wo changcheng*), 1985.

JIANG JIU WEI SHENG YU FANG JI BING

尊敬老师 尊敬长辈 ZUNJINGLAOSHI ZUNJING ZHANGBEI

Still, posters directed towards primary school children are mostly replete with symbols of state and political authority (the Great Wall, the national flag, etcetera), as in 'I love my China, I love my Great Wall' (see page 135-136), and 'Everywhere in the Mother country is my home — strike root and flower in those places that need it most' (see page 150), which features a girl with non-Han features, with the Great Wall in the background. A remarkable poster is 'I strive to bring glory to the mother country' (see page 138), which portrays four little girls and a

BELOW LEFT: 'Foster good habits, hobbies and interests from an early age on' *(Cong xiao yangcheng haode xiguan, aihao, qingqu)*, 1985.

BELOW RIGHT: 'I have put on the red scarf' *(Wo daishangle hong lingjin)*, 1983.

boy, dressed as ping-pong player, volleyball player, archer, swimmer and gymnast respectively, all sports in which Chinese athletes earned medals. Other posters give indications of courteous behaviour, as in propaganda prints that call for respect for school teachers and dis-ciplined behaviour in class. 'Honour teachers, honour elders' (see page 133), from the ten-poster set 'Propaganda posters on Primary School Pupils' Behavioral Standard' reminds youngsters to honour (elderly) authority figures. Paying attention to elementary

BELOW: 'Books are a source of
knowledge' (*Shuben shi zhishide
yuanquan*), 1985.

hygiene remained, as in the past, a message eminently
directed towards this age group. 'Practising hygiene from
an early age' (see page 133) and 'Pay attention to
hygiene, take precautions against disease' (see page 133)
both show small children washing hands, but they seem
to hail from different worlds: the former depicts three
children (two girls, one boy) neatly soaping their hands,
whereas the latter shows a boy and a girl boisterously
washing their hands against a collage of images.

Children also are impressed with the necessity of engaging in wholesome spare time activities, as is testified by
'Let youthful beauty glitter in behaviour' (see page 178)
which depicts vignettes of, among others, youth helping
the elderly, beating up criminals, and studying Lei Feng.
Young children also play an important part in posters
that call for cleaning up the environment, whether on a

BELOW LEFT: 'Celebrate International Children's Day June 1' (Qingzhu liu yi guoji ertongjie), 1979.

BELOW RIGHT: 'I strive to bring glory to the mother country' (Wo wei zuguo zheng guangrong), 1986.

RIGHT: 'Respect social morality' (Yao zunzhong shehui gongde), 1984.

national scale or in their own surrounding. An example of the latter is 'Respect social morality' (see page 139), which shows a little girl diligently picking up banana peels, scattered mindlessly by a young couple in the background.

Some posters were published to support the social posi-

tion and welfare of children, in particular girls, under the new laws. These posters nonetheless have not succeeded in eradicating such phenomena as child labour, child brides, and others. Others were published to mark the yearly celebration of International Children's day on June 1. Such materials, with an international flavour, usually

要尊重社会公德

青年朋友们·热爱书籍吧

书籍是知识的窗户

LEFT: 'Books are a window on
knowledge — Young friends,
enthusiastically love books'
(Shuji shi zhishide chuanghu -
Qingnian pengyoumen, re'ai
shuji ba), 1984.

feature representations of different ethnic groups.
'Celebrate International Children's Day June 1' (see page
138), for example, shows an Asian and African boy and a
Caucasian girl, comparable to ethnic groupings encoun-
tered in the posters marking the international 'Decade for
Women' (see page 146).

Vocational school students and university students are
usually called upon to study hard and thereby devote
themselves to the mother country by contributing their
newly acquired knowledge to modernization. Examples
— employing mixed-media design and portraying clearly
Westernized 'pretty girls' — are 'Books are a window on
knowledge — Young friends, enthusiastically love books'
(see page 140) and 'Books are a source of knowledge'
(see page 137).

The calls to leave the urban centres and to give one's
knowledge full play in the less-developed rural or marginal areas continued. In these posters, girls generally
were featured in scenes that called on them to move to
the countryside, while boys were visualized in the exhortations to apply their knowledge to the development of
industry in marginal border areas.

Students were also portrayed while actively taking part in
environmental campaigns, usually visualized as tree-
planting activities. An interesting aspect of these posters
is that the majority of them feature female students.

MEN

Most of the propaganda of the 1980s that was directed
towards the male part of the Chinese population had a
somewhat negative ring to it. This was due to the fact
that themes were chosen in order to discourage the continuation of undesirable behaviour, whether in a legal
sense or in the production process.

A number of reasons can be brought forward for this
development. One is the diminished use of the military
romanticism that formerly was associated with agricultural and industrial production, calling for dramatic visualizations of superhuman effort. A second reason could be
that private enterprise started to replace the Army as a
career opportunity in the 1980s. Another reason is the
disappearance of the cadre, traditionally a man's role,
from propaganda posters.

Most propaganda featuring men was designed to change
some aspects of their behaviour. Materials that were
designed to spread legal knowledge generally paint evil
men as the perpetrators. The series 'Legal system propaganda show window' (see page 161) shows men invariably victimizing women, young and old alike, either for
material gain or for carnal pleasure. Posters calling for
safety in factories and on workfloors usually show the
gruesome results of men not adhering to the rules.

Aside from the above examples, it is hard to pinpoint
specific messages that were intended for men. In propaganda aimed at inculcating disciplined and civilized
behaviour, men and women are depicted in equal numbers. In posters with political contents, men predominate
over women, who usually are only represented by a sin-

WO WEI ZU GUO XIAN BAO ZANG 我为祖国献宝藏

三、热爱本职，学赶先进，提高质量，讲究效率。

PREVIOUS PAGE, LEFT: 'I contribute precious deposits to the mother country' (*Wo wei zuguo xian baozang*), 1979.
PREVIOUS PAGE, RIGHT: 'Warmly love one's job, study to catch up with the advanced, raise quality, practice efficiency' (*Re'ai benzhi, xue ganxianjin, tigao zhiliang, jiangjiu xiaolü*), 1983.
RIGHT: 'Firmly protect the legal rights and interests of women and children' (*Jianjue weihu funü ertongde hefa liyi*), 1983.

gle female peasant. Generally, however, the presence of men, whether as the extremely motivated, self-sacrificing workers or peasants of the past or as an undifferentiated group providing a backdrop for the central image, declined in favour of the representation of women.

WOMEN

A striking development in the propaganda of this decade is that women in general have returned to their more traditional roles of servants or waitresses, mothers and child-rearers. Apparently, the need was no longer felt to urge women to break through the traditional assumptions of gender inferiority. In posters that feature both genders, the male's relative superiority of status over females is not expressed in any difference in size: man and woman stand equally tall.

Women were no longer depicted as trailblazers, or as engaging in 'male' pursuits in production. An obvious exception is 'I contribute precious deposits to the mother country' (see page 142), which depicts a female miner. The textile industry, with images of women engaged in spinning and reeling yarn, remained an exception to this general trend, as can be seen in 'Warmly love one's job, study to catch up with the advanced, raise quality, practice efficiency' (see page 143), the third poster of the series 'Regulations for staff and workers', devoted to a scene in a spinning shop with three women.

Instead, women returned to the stove, to the restaurant, to the day-care centre, or to the nursing profession, as in 'Treat and nurse with the best of care' (see page 149), all activities that traditionally were considered to be more feminine. A similar female occupation is shown in 'Warmly love the collective, work hard at economizing, take loving care of public property, participate actively in management' (see page 145), the second poster of the series 'Regulations for staff and workers', which depicts a ticket-seller repairing a bus seat. This development reflects a reality in which 'factory work has become less attractive, commercial and service work more attractive' for women.

The posters accompanying the courtesy-campaigns of the early 1980s, in particular, featured women who worked in service trades, exhorting them to be more customer-friendly and to adopt a fair attitude towards customers. 'Serve customers in a cultured, civilized and enthusiastic manner' (see page 148) and 'Treat customers politely, be enthusiastic and attentive, engage in trade in a cultured way' (see page 147) visualize women selling pies and serving food. Other posters showed women who were engaged in activities related to the welfare of children and the elderly; it is interesting to note that the task of supporting the aged, seen of old as the filial obligation of sons, is now relegated to women. Even girls were prepared for the supportive role they were to play in the future; this can be seen from the girl repairing a boy's t-shirt in 'Helping a little schoolmate' (see page 145).

This redefinition of the image of women — as non-threatening to male activities and positions — tallied well with the general tone of posters propagating legal knowledge, in particular those related to the protection of the position and the welfare of women (and children), in which 'evil men' were shown to commit the heinous acts that were now proscribed. The protection of these rights

BELOW LEFT: 'Helping a little schoolmate' *(Bangzhu xiao tongxue)*, 1982.
BELOW RIGHT: 'Warmly love the collective, work hard at economizing, take loving care of public property, participate actively in management' *(Re'ai jiti, qinjian jieyue, aihu gongwu, jiji canjia guanli)*, 1983.

OVERLEAF LEFT: 'The U.N. International Decade for Women — Equality, Development, Peace' *(Lianheguo guoji funü shinian - pingdeng, fazhan, heping)*, 1985.
OVERLEAF RIGHT: 'Treat customers politely, be enthusiastic and attentive, engage in trade in a cultured way' *(Limao daike, reqing zhoudao, wenming jingshang)*, 1983.

二、热爱集体,勤俭节约,爱护公物,积极参加管理。

was the theme of a substantial number of posters produced in the period 1978-1988. The facial representation of women became softer and more Eurasian, which could be a reflection of the increased attention that was paid to personal appearance. It furthermore points to the reappearance of the icon of the 'pretty girl' in propaganda, a development that also occurred during the relative political relaxation of the early 1960s.

礼貌待客 热情周到 文明经商

PREVIOUS PAGE, LEFT: 'Serve customers in a cultured, civilized
and enthusiastic manner'
*(Wenming limao reqing wei guke
fuwu)*, 1982.

PREVIOUS PAGE, RIGHT: 'Treat
and nurse with the best of care'
(Jingxin zhiliao, jingxin huli),
1983.

BELOW: 'Everywhere in the
Mother country is my home —
strike root and flower in those
places that need it most' *(Zuguo
chuchu shi wo jia — zai zui
xuyaode difang shenggen
kaifang)*, 1984.

posters of the 1980s, whether designed for the One Child
Campaign or not, were female.

Special posters were published in 1985 to mark the closing of the international 'Decade for Women.' China
donated to the voluntary fund of this movement, which
was sponsored by the United Nations, while the
Women's Federation was responsible for organizing
activities. As can be seen in 'The U.N. International
Decade for Women — Equality, Development, Peace'
(see page 146), these posters show the profiles of
Negroid, Caucasian and Asian women.

INTELLECTUALS

Wearing the white coats and spectacles reminiscent of
the medical specialist of Western advertising, intellectuals
usually are shown together with workers, peasants and
soldiers in propaganda devoted to political subjects. This
clearly is done in order to stress their regained position
in Chinese society. Other representations show them at
work, contributing to the development of the country
and the successes of the modernization process. Such
visualizations obviously were intended to convey to the
intellectuals that the policies favouring their contributions
and those that were aimed at improving their status and
social position would be a permanent element of the
Four Modernizations.

Intellectuals, as a group witnessed perhaps the most
remarkable change in the manner in which they were
portrayed in visual propaganda. Following their elevation
to 'mental workers', thus joining the ranks of peasants,
workers and soldiers as the occupational and demo-

One further important point should be mentioned here.
In order to break through the traditional perception that
girls contributed less to a family's general well-being than
boys, the majority of babies and children portrayed in the

BELOW: 'Register of heroes of
Four Modernizations' construction' *(Sihua jianshe
yingxiongbu)*, 1983.

graphic groups that formed the foundation of the People's Republic of China, they were no longer portrayed as persons scheming and conniving to overthrow the dictatorship of the proletariat, from which they had been excluded in the past. Instead, they were now seen as a productive group, in line with the major contributions they were expected to make to the successes of the Four Modernizations.

As such, the intellectual, frequently seen juggling the atomic symbol, became an important element of the visual propaganda of the 1980s. The contents of the visual messages in which they appeared were manifold: on the one hand, they were clearly employed in an attempt to convince other intellectuals who still harboured doubts towards the new policies, that the political climate had definitely changed in their favour. On the other hand, intellectuals were often visualized as the trailblazers of the modernization effort. In this capacity, intellectuals regularly appeared as role models for educated youth, or as examples of the innate intellectual creativity of the Chinese people. The most interesting example of this can be found in posters that portray intellectual models in the manner of the traditional door gods, namely two by two, as in the 'Register of heroes of Four Modernizations' construction' (see page 151).

Although the reform policies clearly favoured intellectuals, there was a marked tendency among lower-level cadres to sabotage government plans designed to improve their material well-being. Despite this, no propaganda posters appeared that stressed the necessity to comply with policies that were designed to improve the lot of the new 'mental workers'. It was left to newspaper cartoonists to criticize lagging cadres.

PEASANTS

An interesting development took place with the large rural audience of propaganda. As a group, the peasantry largely disappeared from visual propaganda, in line with the general urban reorientation which took place in the political domain. In itself, this is an interesting development: the initial successes of the modernization program all took place in the countryside, where the peasantry was the first to embrace the opportunities provided by the new policies, without any 'interference' by visual propaganda. One of the few exceptions is 'The countryside is reformed, the situation pleases the people' (see page 153). The peasantry that did appear in visual propaganda was most often represented by females.

Strangely absent in the propaganda prints are visual elements showing the successful application of the 'responsibility system' in the countryside, which initially served as a motor for the reforms in other sectors; or the improvements in rural living conditions, and the changed look of the rural areas that was the result of all this. Other themes that were not addressed by propaganda were the exhortations featured in policy pronouncements to become rich first, or to 'leave the soil' and engage in agriculturally related industrial activities and similar new phenomena in the countryside.

Peasants clearly did not need visualized attitudinal promptings or behavioural stimuli to see that decollectivization of the rural areas was in their best (material) interest. Nor could they be bothered by exhortations to get rich first, as they were already in the process of doing so. It is remarkable, however, that the phenomenon of the so-called '10,000 yuan households' that started appearing in the countryside was never propagated in visual propaganda, although these households did have obvious behavioural model qualities that could be emulated on the basis of the adagium 'let some get rich first in order to pull the others along'. The possibilities for emulating this particular model were not necessarily limited to the rural population; it had validity for urbanites

engaging in whatever form of private enterprise as well. However, this phenomenon was propagated in printed propaganda, particularly newspapers and journals that specifically were published for the rural population.

In the same vein, it is strange that no attention was paid to the importance of the input of science and technology in agriculture, an element regularly featured during the Gang of Four era. One would think that at a time when increased harvests and improved production contributed to the material well-being of the peasantry, visual propaganda would be produced that prominently featured advanced agricultural techniques and alternative economic activities in the countryside, such as the township enterprises.

Various explanations can be given for the relative absence of the peasantry from visual propaganda. Problems existed within the CCP-leadership as to whether and how individual rural enterprise and income inequality should be stimulated by visual propaganda. Furthermore, such portrayals could lead to jealousy and raise expectations among peasants living in marginal, or in non-peri-urban areas. Finally, these visualizations would lead to the distorted perception that 'going it alone' would lead automatically to becoming a '10,000 yuan household'.

WORKERS

In line with the general demilitarization of visual propaganda that took place in the 1980s, the portrayal of workers in the forefront of production struggles, a theme that was so common in the preceding decades, almost completely disappeared. Workers continued to be featured as one of the pillars of society, and as supporters of Party policy. In these prints, they were usually flanked by peasants, soldiers and intellectuals. Such groupings, however, were nothing but a weak echo of previous propaganda practices, where the solidarity between workers and peasants in the political and productive struggles was stressed time and again.

Propaganda posters in the 1980s no longer called on workers to sacrifice their health, or their lives, for the reconstruction of the Chinese industry, although reconstruction as such remained an important propaganda topic. Productive behaviour is largely absent in the visualizations, rather remarkable as increased production, and efficiency in particular, were intrinsic goals of the modernization process. Instead, workers as an occupational group are increasingly shown while adhering to the new rules and regulations promulgated for the work place. This is visualized in 'Observe discipline and be law abiding, be honest in performing one's official duties, rigorously implement rules and regulations', the fifth poster of the series 'Regulations for staff and workers', which depicts a male worker with the slogan 'safe production' embroidered on his jacket, showing his work permit while entering a factory.

Other new themes that were addressed were the criminal

BELOW LEFT: 'Observe discipline
and be law abiding, be honest in
performing one's official duties,
rigorously implement rules and
regulations' (*Zunji shoufa, lianjie
fenggong, yan'ge zhixing
guizhang zhidu*), 1983.
BELOW RIGHT: 'Offer high-quality
goods to the people' (*Yi youzhi
chanpin xiangei renmin*), 1981.

behaviour of producers of shoddy goods. This is spelled out explicitly in 'Offer high-quality goods to the people', by showing synthetic fibres, thermos bottle, bicycle, sewing machine and shirt, adorned with a quality mark, held up by two (female) hands. Other posters admonished workers who were susceptible to bribes, and workers who abused their position to gain access to scarce goods for re-sale on the black market. As such, they provide us with interesting glimpses of the way in which Chinese society developed.

BELOW LEFT: 'People's Liberation
Army' (*Jiefangjun*), 1980.
BELOW RIGHT: 'Bright and brave'
(*Yingzi sashuang*), 1982.

SOLDIERS

While the improved international standing of China led to a situation where the defence of the mother country lost a great deal of its urgency, soldiers as a target group of propaganda prints largely disappeared.

An exception to this general trend was the continued republication of scenes from the revolutionary past. In these visualizations, PLA-veterans or soldiers usually were presented together with the veteran CCP-leaders.

The PLA was depicted no longer as the Great Iron Wall defending the mother country and the revolution, even though that aspect of its activities remained. A rather late occurrence of this theme can be found in 'Sacred mission' (see page 109). An earlier, and more aggressive poster, showing MIG-pilots running to their machines for attack, is 'Train rigorously, do good in preparing to counter a war of aggression' (see page 157).

Soldiers as subjects of visual propaganda gradually disappeared in the 1980s, after the abundant attention that had been devoted to them in the preceding decades, usually in the form of military models such as Lei Feng, Ouyang Hai, and others. Their solidarity with workers and peasants (and now with intellectuals as well) was no longer visualized.

The PLA also lost much of its model status among the population, with the exception of youth. In printed propaganda, the glorious tradition of the PLA and its commitment to the Four Modernizations continued to be stressed, but visualizations of peace-time reconstruction were not forthcoming.

The remaining attention came in two forms, both reflecting the desire for the professionalization of the Army. A number of posters appeared depicting the representatives, male and female, of the various components of the PLA (Army, Navy, Air Force) in their respective uniforms.

BELOW: 'Train rigorously, do good in preparing to counter a war of aggression' *(Yange xunlian, zuohao fan qinlüe zhanzhengde zhunbei)*, 1978.

BELOW LEFT: 'Great war exercise'
(*Junshi da yanxi*), 1986.
BELOW RIGHT: 'A grand occasion
during National Day in the
Capital' *(Shoudu jieri
shengkuang)*, 1986.

RIGHT: 'Everybody observes
order, everybody pays attention
to social morality' *(Gege zunshou
zhixu, renren zhuyi shehui
gongde)*, 1983.

'People's Liberation Army' (see page 156) features a male sailor, soldier and pilot, in the uniforms used before the modernization of the system of ranks. 'Bright and brave' (see page 156) on the other hand, depicts a female soldier, sailor and pilot, and a member of the people's militia.

Another group of posters was published that stressed the alertness and fighting spirit of the PLA. These posters featured highly idealized scenes from war games. Air and ground manoeuvres and grenade launchers are the subject of 'Great war exercise'. Military parades on Tian'anmen Square also demonstrate the Army's readiness, as in 'A grand occasion during National Day in the Capital'.

A large part of the attention formerly lavished on the PLA and militias as guardians of social order was refocussed in the 1980s on the police. Representatives of the police appear in all posters devoted to spreading legal awareness among the population, most often depicted while administering justice. A third group of propaganda posters, moreover, visualizes police activities related to the maintenance of order in the street, by showing a well-trained force actively engaged in preserving social order. 'Everybody observes order, everybody pays attention to social morality' (see page 159), for example, depicts a policeman, offset against high-rise buildings, controlling traffic.

Other activities of the police force involve the ferreting out of spies and the arrest of 'ordinary' criminals. As can be seen in 'Sternly attack criminal activities' (see page 160), the faces of the criminals usually are done in the traditional greenish ashen colour known from Peking Opera. Policemen in action sometimes strike poses reminiscent of the martial posturing of peasants, workers and soldiers in the propaganda posters of the past. These materials can be seen as an attempt to put the people's minds at rest by showing that the government was taking steps against the increase in criminal activities.

个个遵守秩序 人人注意社会公德

BELOW: 'Sternly attack criminal activities' *(Yanli daji xingshi fanzui huodong)*, 1983.

BELOW: 'Who has murdered her?'
Fazhi xuanchuan chuchuang (Shi
shei haisile ta?), 1983.

CADRES

With agricultural decollectivization and the diminishing role and importance of the Party secretary in the various sectors of production, the occupational group of the cadres almost completely disappeared as a target of propaganda prints in the 1980s. This constitutes a clear break with the past, when many role models for cadres were provided.

In the era of reform, cadres often were seen by the pub-

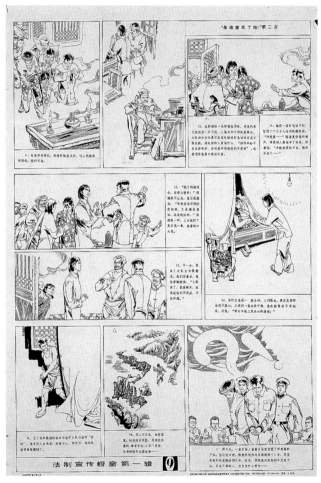

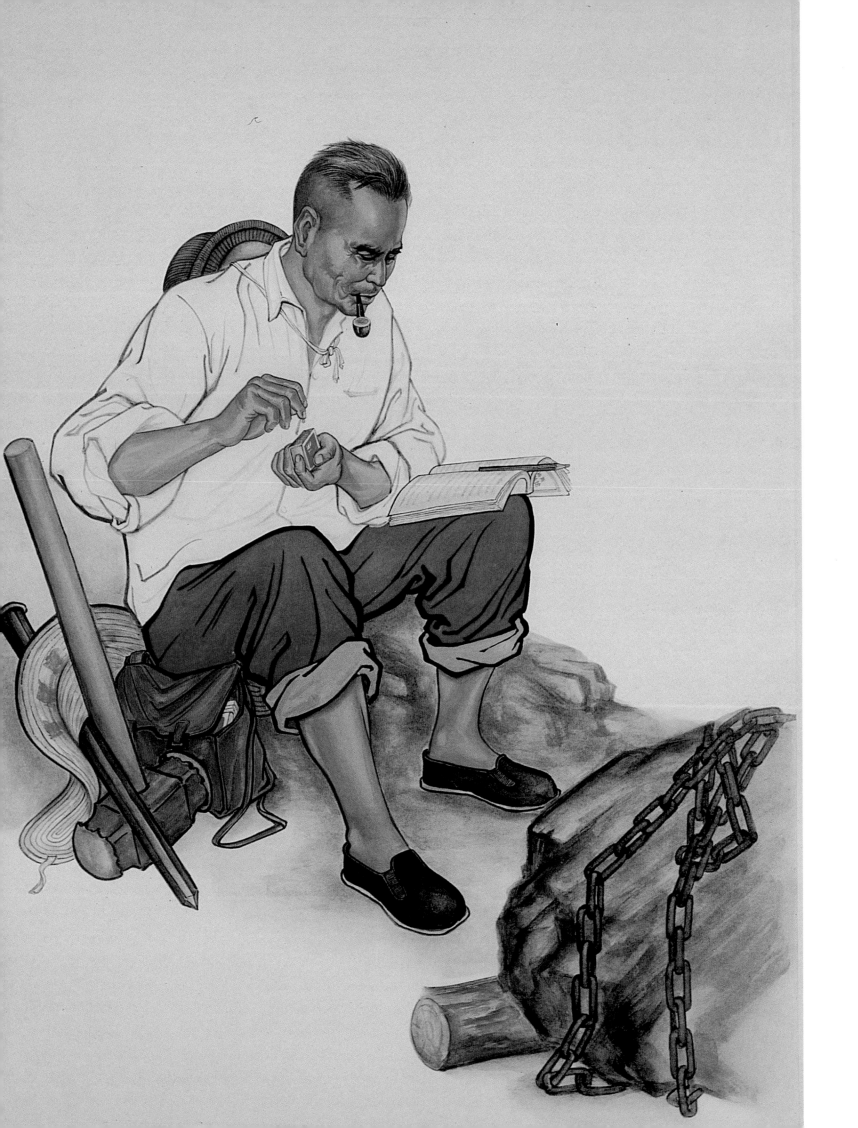

LEFT: 'Old party secretary' *(Lao shuji)*, 1974.

RIGHT TOP: 'Auntie has also come to bring zanba' *(Ayi you song zanba laile)*, early 1970s.

RIGHT MIDDLE: 'Representatives of brother nationalities visit a textile machinery plant' *(Xiongdi minzu daibiao canguan fangjichang)*, early 1970s.

RIGHT BOTTOM: 'The grasslands are connected with Beijing' *(Caoyuan lian Beijing)*, 1977.

lic as forces thwarting modernization, as they were associated with bad performance in the past. However, a few posters could be interpreted as being directed towards cadres who are unfamiliar with, or unaccustomed to, the side-effects of modernization. This is done with the clear purpose of setting their minds at rest, and to educate them about what popular behaviour is permissible in the 'new age'.

Some posters designed for the spreading of legal knowledge feature cadres who are prosecuted because of power abuse. The black-and-white double-poster 'Who has murdered her?' (see page 161), recounts the case of a rural cadre pressuring a 15-year old girl into marrying him.

MINORITIES

Although Han-chauvinism continued to exist unabated during the modernization era, the production of posters designed to contribute to the integration of minorities with the dominant ethnic group greatly diminished. Posters such as 'Fraternal love as in one family' (see page 166), which depicts representatives of various minorities in their national dress embracing, and 'Love Socialism' (see page 168), which shows social, ethnic and demographic groups dancing around the base of a monolith crowned with hammer and sickle, with the motto 'people are the masters of the country' *(Renmin shi guojiade zhuren)*, were exceptions.

There no longer seemed to be a need to represent minorities being treated in hospital by Han nurses, or on fact-finding tours in factories where they were guided by

163

BELOW LEFT: 'Embroidering a silk
banner with words of gold'
(Xiu jin bian), 1978.
BELOW RIGHT: 'The flower of
Dazhai is in full bloom on the
plateau' (Gaoyuan shengkai
Dazhai hua), early 1970s.

RIGHT: 'The 1936 meeting of Zhu
De and Living Buddha Geda'
(Yijiusanliunian Zhu De huijian
Geda Huofo), 1982.

fraternal Han workers. Examples of such revolutionary
materials from the late 1970s are 'Representatives of
brother nationalities visit a textile machinery plant' (see
page 163) and 'Auntie has also come to bring zanba' (see
page 163).

The late 1970s also witnessed the production of a number of posters depicting the minorities' joy with the tangible fruits of development, such as wireless radios and
electricity, as in 'The grasslands are connected with
Beijing' (see page 163), in which Mongolian children are
listening to a transistor radio. This type of poster, too,
ceased to be published in the 1980s, perhaps an indication of the leadership's worries about raising unrealistic
expectations among the minorities. The poster 'Border
cavalry' (see page 167) shows a female representative of
a minority in national dress astride a white horse while
shooting a Chinese AK-47, an example of an apparent
change in attitude towards minorities.

BELOW: 'Fraternal love as in one family' *(Tuanjie you'ai yijia qin)*, 1980.

RIGHT: 'Border cavalry' *(Bianjiang tieqi)*, 1978.

LEFT: 'Love Socialism' (Ai shehui
zhuyi), 1983.

OVERLEAF LEFT: 'Have ideals'
(You lixiang), 1986.
OVERLEAF RIGHT: 'Have morality'
(You daode), 1986.

THE FUTURE VISUALIZED: AN ANALYSIS OF SYMBOLISM AND IMAGERY

Paintings are meant to be viewed as symbols, and their characteristic themes [...] betoken not only themselves, but also something beyond themselves: they mean something.

By extending the intention of this quotation to include all visual representations, a number of posters will be analysed here for their 'symbolic language,' the symbolism and imagery that were applied in visual propaganda with the intention of preparing the people for the new role the CCP had designed for itself in the modernization decade and for the modernization policies.

During the Yan'an era, the CCP already decided to appropriate New Year pictures for propaganda purposes. This was done by first selecting artistic and aesthetic forms that the people had grown accustomed to, by filling these with new, revolutionary content, and by appropriately refashioning the contents as a whole. An unintented effect of this was that an artistic and cultural dilemma was created that has not been solved until today.

The revolutionary artists who congregated in Yan'an disdained these old forms of culture they saw among the people, as they were more dedicated to the cultural cosmopolitanism which had flourished in the urban areas during the 1930s. Moreover, in the eyes of the artists, these traditional art forms were considered to be too intimately connected with religious observances and elements of 'feudal', Confucian superstition. They were not altogether wrong with this observation: as we have seen, New Year pictures derived from 'paper gods' and other forms of utilitarian-magic art, and they continued to play a major role in family ritual and as votive prints. The traditional designers of New Year pictures likewise had adhered to the use of symbols and imagery reflecting old stereotypes which were rooted in the Confucian interpretations of approved behaviour in society

When New Year pictures were enlisted to serve as media for propaganda, and were secularized by injecting new and confusing elements into an existing system of symbols, the hybrid forms that guided their design could only form an uneasy compromise between the urban and rural assessment of traditional culture. The CCP-produced New Year pictures were much too 'Chinese' and vulgar to please intellectuals and the urbanites who considered themselves to be more sophisticated. The target group, the masses, on the other hand, found them too Westernized and over-simplified to be of great interest. This may account for the fact that Japanese visual war propaganda was so successful in China. The Japanese made use of symbols and images in a way that was much closer to the expectations and aesthetic experiences of the peasantry.

Another reason for the lack of peasant appreciation of these new, CCP-inspired New Year pictures may have been the fact that the peasantry, or the New Year pictures designers among them, were never called upon to collaborate actively in their production. This creative work was largely limited to art students and cadres. Thus, propaganda art was more or less forced on them. David Holm's excellent research on the development of new *yangge*-dance has borne out that by actively participating in this new form of traditional, heavily politicized

做有理想 有道德 有文化 有纪律的一代新人

有理想
YOULIXIANG

做有理想 有道德 有文化 有纪律的一代新人

有道德 youdaode

BELOW: 'Support the army and give preferential treatment to families of revolutionary army men and martyrs' *(Yongjun youshu)*, 1983.

dance, the peasantry was able to assimilate the new contents and thereby creatively integrate them with traditional notions. The only instance where the population, including the peasants, was stimulated to spontaneously produce art that could be used for propaganda purposes, was during the Great Leap Forward. Other popular

artists, such as the Huxian painters, were supported by the State.

'New' New Year pictures, then, only existed for political reasons. They could replace traditional New Year pictures because the CCP succeeded in shutting the latter out by means of its monopoly of the media. This explains why propaganda posters could be seen in individual homes in the first decades of CCP-rule. It also explains why other visual materials that contained more traditionally significant symbolic contents, started to replace them as soon as they became available on the free markets in rural and urban areas in the 1980s. In urban settings in particular, the visual links with the state, the party or the workplace have disappeared. Thus, it appears that specific traditional visual elements from New Year pictures, although having been appropriated by the CCP to propagandize socialist principles instead of playing a religious role, or merely conveying auspicious wishes, continue to remain a constant within the Chinese visual tradition.

An example of a poster close to the New Year picture tradition, using old forms and new contents, is 'Support the army and give preferential treatment to families of revolutionary army men and martyrs', which pictures a lion dance. This tradition, however, increasingly has been freed from the dominance over traditional culture that the CCP established in the days of Yan'an.

With the mechanisms of mass mobilization phased out in favour of social order and discipline, propaganda posters no longer featured mass scenes and production battles, whether in industry or agriculture. Instead, they became individualized, showing single persons or, when more than one person is involved, nuclear groupings such as

BELOW LEFT: 'Youthful dancesteps' *(Qingchun wubu)*, 1983.
BELOW RIGHT: 'Scattering
fragrance among the people'
(Fangxiang sa renjian), 1987.

the family. The most important change in visual propaganda in general, however, was the shift from urgings to act to urgings to think. In this, we can witness a change in CCP focus from striving to create some sort of orthopraxy, correct behaviour, to some sort of orthodoxy, correct thought. After all, there is a world of difference between propaganda that tells the people to go all-out for improved production, bumper harvests, studying Mao Zedong Thought, or from learning from the model production brigades of the *Dazhai* and *Daqing* types, on the one hand; and propaganda that calls on people to develop good habits, hobbies and interests, to pay attention to

BELOW LEFT: 'Make our cities
even more beautiful' *(Rang wode
chengshi geng meihao)*, 1982.
BELOW RIGHT: 'Love science,
explore diligently' *(Ai kexue, qin
tansuo)*, 1985.

RIGHT: 'Build up a good
physique, steel the will, to contribute strength to the realization
of the Four Modernizations'
*(Duanlian shenti, duanlian
yizhi, wei shixian sige xiandaihua gongxian liliang)*, 1979.

social morality, or to develop a socialist spiritual culture, on the other. The former type of propaganda, with its concretely defined goals, supplies clear-cut indications of behaviour, whereas the latter can only indicate, in the vaguest possible terms, what these qualities of thought are supposed to entail. One of the most explicit examples of such vague propaganda is the four-poster series 'Have ideals', 'Have morality' (see pages 170-171), 'Have

锻炼身体
锻炼意志
为实现四个现代化贡献力量

BELOW: 'Spring of science'
(Kexuede chuntian), 1979.
RIGHT: Western-style painting of
bathing beauties fot the 1981
calendar, published by
Sichuansheng Nanchong diqu
gongyi meishu yanjiusuo, 1981.
RIGHT BELOW: 'Young girl' (Shao
nü), 1985.

科 学 的 春 天

1980

culture' and 'Have discipline' (see pages 200-201). Although the images may have an aesthetic appeal to the viewer, they contain no indication whatsoever as to the way in which these ideals, morality, culture and discipline could be attained.

Posters were largely employed in the 1980s to show the achieved bounties of development, and to depict a satisfied population at rest. These developmental rewards were to function as a two-edged sword: on the one hand, they showed the concrete achievements of modernization as they would accrue to the population as a whole; on the other hand, these bounties were clearly

1985

intended to show the people what the results of their own efforts and support for the CCP's policies would be. These posters can be best termed as glimpses of 'living in a material world'. These glimpses do not necessarily form the main theme of a propaganda poster, as doing so might inspire people to engage in blind consumerism; rather, as a backdrop to the main action or activities portrayed, they function as a forceful reminder of the tangible results that lie in store for everybody who actively supports modernization. As such, they can be found in practically all posters devoted to modernization. More specific examples are provided in 'Youthful dancesteps'

BELOW: 'Marry late, conceive late'
(*Wanhun, wanyu*), 1988 calendar.
RIGHT: 'Let youthful beauty glitter
in behaviour' (*Rang qingchun
mei zai xingwei zhong shan
guang*), 1982.

(see page 173), and 'Scattering fragrance among the people' (see page 173), which depicts a woman in dress
astride a red motorcycle, delivering potted plants.

《晚婚、晚育》 ● 控制人口数量的基本要求是：晚婚、晚育。

1988
NIANLI

·辽宁省联合制作计划生育宣传品编绘委员会出版

编辑、设计：王广博 摄影：马杰

PERSONAL APPEARANCE AND CLOTHING

The first hint of the improvement in living conditions is
the development, both in material, design, cut and
colour, of the clothes that people, in particular women,
wear in posters. It is an obvious artistic recreation of the
greater diversity in clothing that was one of the first concrete indications of changing society. Gone are the blue,
grey or black uni-sex 'Mao-suits' that in the past demonstrated the people's proletarian outlook; in their place are
wind-breakers, track-suits, even turtle-neck sweaters for
men, and more feminine dresses and skirts for women.
Gone are the chopped hair styles and ponytails of past
posters, making way for coiffures that are permed or
styled in other fanciful ways.

Clearly, women started to devote greater care to their
appearance. They are still rosy-cheeked, as in the earlier
prints, but no longer in the tradition of Peking Opera
make-up. The women of the 1980s use eye-liner, lipstick,
rouge, and other types of make-up, including those that
clearly reflect the urban female's preference for a pale
look. This must be seen as a clear sign of the increased
interest in personal beauty in society. Stanley Rosen
relates that most single women in Harbin spent at least
half their income on clothing, accessories, cosmetics and

LEFT: 'New hand' *(Xin shou)*, early 1970s.

ond half of the 1980s. The 1980 calendar 'Spring of science' features the wildly popular peacock dance and the atomic symbol; the 1985 calendar, 'Young girl' features a girl from Hong Kong, and the 1981 calendar shows a Western-style painting of bathing beauties.

SYMBOLS OF DEVELOPMENT

A new development is the depiction of interiors of dwellings, and the careful way in which this is done. Previously, poster backgrounds were made up of factory interiors, public reading rooms, class rooms, or rural scenes in the open air. Coupled with this is increasing attention for items that make life more pleasant: sofas and radio-cassette recorders have become the standard elements that are depicted in every household. Indeed, the latter item became the most explicit symbol of modernization in the early 1980s; it was not only the first electronic medium that was made widely available to the people from the late 1970s on, it also became a standard part of the people's daily belongings.

Interestingly, the radio-cassette player was used to create the same effect as the printed word, whether in the form of books, newspapers, comic strips, or in the poster art of the Cultural Revolution. This might be proof of the shift in the communication strategy on the part of the CCP, from trying to turn the people into avid readers of (official) documents to turning them into subconscious consumers of a steady flow of approved information through the broadcasting media. With the disappearance of the printed word, the umbilical cord established in the Yan'an days, to link visual propaganda with literacy cam-

hair-styling. The apparent preference for a more Eurasian look, as featured in a large number of posters, may be interpreted as a reflection of the urban social reality of the 1980s; increasing numbers of women had cosmetic surgery, a process by which part of the upper eyelid was excised and a silicon strip was inserted into the nose.

A combination of a female beauty and the trend towards beautification can be found in 'Make our cities even more beautiful' (see page 174), which shows a pretty girl, with flying cranes, skyscrapers and an old temple in the background. Other examples are the two pretty girls studying butterflies in 'Love science, explore diligently' (see page 174), and also 'Culture, courtesy, greening, beautification' (see page 107).

This trend was clearly started with the depiction of women in demure swimming suits in 'Build up a good physique, steel the will, to contribute strength to the realization of the Four Modernizations' (see page 175). It is further supported by developments in the cheap, single-sheet calendars (see pages 176-177) that have been published in poster format in the 1980s. Political subject matter, while still visible in the 1980 calendar, has been completely replaced by photographs of actresses in the sec-

paigns was cut. While the radio-cassette player can be seen as an embodiment of successful modernization, it should be pointed out that the television set, despite its increased usage for propaganda purposes, is not represented in posters.

As an extra detail, the return to the Chinese interior of the potted plant and the flower vase, no longer considered signs of bourgeois living, should be mentioned.

In the few instances where the interiors of factories and workshops have been visualized, these have been modernized as well.

The increased freedom of movement that resulted from the withdrawal of scrutiny and control by the CCP from the daily lives of the people and the reform measures, led to an increase in the ownership of motorbikes and mopeds, and later of cars. These means of transport largely have replaced the bicycle and the tractor of the earlier prints. In cases where this ownership is not personalized, the representation of crowded highways clearly gives the impression that motorized personal transport will be within everyone's reach within the near future.

SPARE-TIME ACTIVITIES

An increase is discernible in the attention that propaganda posters of the 1980s pay to the propagation of 'wholesome' spare-time activities; adolescents are the most obvious targets for this type of propaganda, which is

slightly reminiscent of the Boy Scout ethos. Of course, with political study as a spare-time activity on the decline, other sound activities had to be found. Such activities can be characterized as various ways of 'serving the people', including cleaning up, helping the elderly, making music and planting trees, but also apprehending criminals. 'Let youthful beauty glitter in behaviour' (see page 178) features some of these activities in the background of an adolscent wearing a turtle-neck sweater.

Showing the people at rest, enjoying the fruits of development, or simply having fun, did not mean that posters no longer showed people engaged in labour. Some role models, often intellectuals, were still depicted as giving more than their best to society. Jiang Zhuying, for example, an intellectual who was so committed to the modernization of his country that he died from exhaustion while propelling the nation forward, is visualized while hunched over a work bench in 'Make many contributions to the Four Modernizations in the same manner as Jiang Zhuying' (see page 128). The various women who are portrayed in tertiary sector work, whether as sales persons or as nurses or teachers, on the other hand, do not give the impression of being overly fatigued, or harassed by the demands of their customers or charges. Indeed, their relaxed posture was necessary to illustrate the civilized and courteous behaviour that was to be endorsed.

All this is a far cry from the propaganda materials published earlier. Although the peasants and workers in Cultural Revolution propaganda also were depicted as taking pleasure in their work, they were usually exhorted to give their utmost. The rewards — bumper harvests of corn, steel quotas that were overfulfilled — generally

BELOW TOP: 'The production brigade's reading room' *(Dadui tushushi)*, 1974.

BELOW MIDDLE: 'Busy practising martial arts on Lake Baiyangdian' *(Baiyangdianshang lian wumang)*, 1976.

BELOW BOTTOM: 'Young eagles on Mount Swallow' *(Yanshan chuying)*, 1976.

RIGHT: 'Common aspirations' *(Gongtongde xinyuan)*, 1977.

were shown in these same images, a clear echo of traditional New Year pictures. In no instance, however, did people actually die from their work; nor did they have to be admonished to improve the quality of their work, as became the practice later. In those very few instances where people were shown at rest in the earlier materials, they were still always shown while engaging, as a group, in some form of meaningful activity. These activities could include taking part in socialist competitive sports meets, or in communal newspaper reading, or engaging in some sort of community activity, such as singing the praise of socialism, as can be seen in the Cultural Revolution poster 'Socialism is fine' (see page 183). The fact that the countryside practically disappeared as a setting for the posters of the 1980s, of course, contributed to the decrease in the number of labour-representations. The waitress and nurse posters in particular, calling for a more customer-friendly, fair attitude, are among the most convincing indications that propaganda art had acquired a more attitudinal character.

BELOW LEFT: 'Socialism is fine'
(Shehuizhuyi hao), early 1970s.
BELOW RIGHT: 'Today we are on
duty' *(Jintian women zhiri)*,
1979.

GENDER REPRESENTATION AND MALE CHAUVINISM

Cultural Revolution posters tended to show women as peasants, thereby linking them with fertility; others showed them at work in textile industries, traditionally seen as places of women's labour. Persons in positions of authority, whether as rural cadres or as foremen in the factories, usually were visualized as men; the appearance of women in cadre-functions is exceptional.

As pointed out before, women and girls became the most frequently portrayed group of characters in the 1980s, coinciding with attempts to combat male chauvinism and safeguard the rights of women and children. However, despite the calls in the printed media in the 1980s for a more balanced representation of women in leading bodies and functions, and despite the propagation of such models of female independence as Zhang Haidi, women in leading positions, whether in production or in politics, were not visualized in propaganda posters. Instead, women continued to be represented as peasants.

The frequent visualization of young girls is rooted in other causes. First and foremost, and in line with the One Child Campaign, is the attempt to convince the people that female offspring can have the same emotional value as male offspring. As the image of the young girl is a traditional element from New Year pictures, this meant a return to one of the roots of the propaganda poster.

SYMBOLS OF POLITICAL POWER

Deng Xiaoping's decision to do away with the leader worship of the past posed a problem for the propaganda organizations in terms of the visualization of political power, and therefore of the visualization of the Party itself. This was exacerbated by the fact that the 'grass-

roots level representative' of the Party, the cadre, also largely had disappeared as a symbol of CCP power.

The only exception to Deng's veto on leader portraits seemed to be the countenance of Zhou Enlai. This no

doubt was caused by the fact that the Chinese people considered Zhou as their most beloved leader, a belief that continues today. When Deng rose to power for a third time in the second half of the 1970s, he had clearly styled himself as a co-worker, and therefore the most logical successor, of Zhou. Furthermore, after the excesses and tragedies of the Cultural Revolution, Zhou was seen as a representative of a more human type of socialism than the ideological variety that was advocated by Mao. This echoes the 'good prime minister'-syndrome from traditional China. Of course, in selected places the image of Mao, whether in painted or sculpted form, remained in use, Mao's portrait overlooking Tian'anmen Square probably being the most well-known example.

Now that Mao Zedong, or his writings and quotations, no longer could function as the embodiment of the CCP and its power, new symbolism had to be adopted. In general, a similar effect was sought by using abstract symbols of power: these usually consisted of the images of the 'founding fathers' of socialism or of the People's Republic of China, ranging from Marx, Engels, Lenin, Stalin, and Sun Yatsen to Mao; the emblem of the State (Tian'anmen); the 'logo' of the CCP (hammer and sickle); and the symbol of the nation (five yellow stars on a red background). These elements were used in all visual materials that propagated adherence to some durable, political norm, thus clearly establishing a link between the behaviour sought and the organization that originated that norm. The substitution of the symbol of the founding father by those of the nation-state can also be seen as a reflection of the propagation of nationalism rather than communism as the source of regime legitimacy.

BELOW: 'Take part in labour
enthusiastically, cherish the fruits
of labour' *(Jiji canjia laodong,
aixi laodong chengguo)*, 1982.

积 极 参 加 劳 动，爱 惜 劳 动 成 果。

中学生守则之五

Another form of symbolism that was employed to demonstrate the continuity between the revolutionary struggles of the past and the current economic struggles, and the decisive role the CCP played in these struggles, was the use of history. This was not an altogether new practice: already in Yan'an, CCP artists had used the his-

torical scene, based on the New Year pictures opera print, to commemorate revolutionary events. Vignettes of historical events since the founding of the CCP usually ranged from the May Fourth Movement of 1919 to the War of Liberation of 1945-1949. See as an example the large-format 'To love the country one must first know its

BELOW LEFT: 'Pay attention to
sanitation and hygiene, beautify
the environment of schoolyards'
(*Zhuyi qingjie weisheng meihua
xiaoyuan huanjing*), 1987

ZHUYIQINGJIEWEISHENG MEIHUAXIAOYUANHUANJING

history — the deeper the knowledge, the more eager the love' (page 185). The more the economy flourished, and the CCP's power waned, the more use was made of this 'symbolic capital' — the 'accumulated prestige and honor' in Pierre Bourdieu's words — that had been built up during the Long March and the Yan'an period. Already in 1935, Mao Zedong had designated the Long March as a propaganda item

As an added difficulty, the topic of cleaner politics had to be addressed. It came as a direct result of the attempts to present the new, more benign face of the Party, as well as to break through the popular apathy towards the CCP and its policies. The metaphor that is used most frequently to signify this more sensible approach to politics, or a clean break with past political practices, is that of window cleaning. The implication of this is obvious: after the darkness and political unpredictability of the past, everybody, including the Party, should start with a clean slate to let the sunshine in. The activity itself usually is done by women dressed in the white uniform identified with nursing or the service sector. The use of the colour white for the uniform, of course, may also have been chosen deliberately to indicate innocence. In a large number of posters of the early 1980s, window cleaning takes place. Examples are, 'Today we are on duty' (see page 183), which depicts red-scarfed primary school students cleaning windows, and 'Take part in labour enthusiastically, cherish the fruits of labour' (see page 186). 'Love hygiene, stress civilization' (see page 184) also features a woman cleaning windows, while on the other side of the glass, people engage in their daily activities.

BELOW: 'Great struggle against
crooked valleys and rivers'
(Dazhan quyuhe), 1975.

SYMBOLS OF MODERNITY

As mentioned earlier, imagery inspired by Western science-fiction became a constant element in propaganda posters to symbolize modernity. Spacecraft in particular seemed to be ascribed with modernizing qualities that were to strike a chord with the people, while the use of building imagery (construction cranes, highrise buildings, and others) was a clear reference to the new policies promising change and prosperity, improving rural and urban living conditions and the changing skylines that became visible all over the country.

It has already been argued that these symbols were instrumental in changing the visual language of propaganda prints from rural, utopian visualizations of the future to a more urban perspective. 'The bustling Nanjing Lu of Shanghai' (see page 190), showing Western and African visitors, is a fine example, although the density of traffic is rather under-represented.

One observation must be made here. In early posters and the Cultural Revolution materials that were set in the countryside, the people could usually be seen as being actively involved in creating this rosy future as it was envisaged by the CCP: the peasants enjoying the fruits of the mechanization of agriculture, for example, were shown operating agricultural machinery, thus making a

188

BELOW: 'New appearance of the
harbour' *(Haigang xinmao)*,
1977.

BELOW: 'The bustling Nanjing Lu
of Shanghai' *(Fanhuade
Shanghai Nanjing Lu)*, 1989.

fully mechanized agricultural industry of the future tangible for spectators. The same can be said about the numerous posters extolling the benefits of irrigation and water conservancy in general. They all indicated to their target groups, in a romanticized but nonetheless very basic way, how irrigation and water conservancy could be managed by everyone. Thus, the materials gave clear prescriptions for the improvement of agricultural production (see page 188).

In the case of the symbolic use of spacecraft and building, on the other hand, it is remarkable that these only function as settings, or backdrops, for the messages of economic development that the posters of the 1980s contain. No materials have been published that show the people themselves actually engaged in building activities, or, for that matter, in the process of operating spacecraft. Of course, by using these visual elements in the sense of a far, but not unattainable future, by placing them outside the central action itself, the posters take on a truly utopian quality.

TRADITIONAL NEW YEAR PICTURES

In previous chapters, a case was made for the continuation of New Year picture symbolism, for example in posters that urged the people to adhere to the population policies of the CCP. In particular, the chubby baby boys holding carps, denoting male offspring and abundance, encapsulated traditional ideals of wealth, happiness and longevity. Babies continue to be visualized, with protective charms around their necks; clutching peaches of immortality, or surrounded by magpies and mandarin ducks. However, in an effort to counter female infanticide, they increasingly are portrayed as girls.

Also, various visual elements of economic development start to creep into the New Year picture type of poster designs; this trend starts with highrise buildings in the background, as in 'In the heyday of the year of the dragon plump babies are born' (see page 127). The climax in this development is no doubt reached in the bi-lingual series containing 'Do a good job in family planning to promote economic development' (see page 192-193). In these posters, all traditional visual elements have been replaced by modern imagery: highrise buildings, space ships, atomic symbols and remote controls. An element that these posters have in common is the dove; this bird is not presented as the traditional emblem of long life, but as the internationally accepted icon of peace. Given this shift from traditional symbols to more modern ones, one must wonder what this will imply for the votive aspects of New Year pictures that played such a major role in the development and popularity of the genre.

The dissident poet Duoduo (pseudonym of Li Shizhen)

OVERLEAF: 'Do a good job in
family planning to promote economic development' *(Gaohao
jihua shengyu, cujin jingji
fazhan)*, 1986

has observed, in the context of his review of an exhibition of Chinese avant garde painting in Rotterdam in
1993, that Chinese society is evolving from one which
was politicized to the extreme, into one in which money
governs everything. According to him, political symbols
increasingly are replaced by financial imagery. Although
this may seem to be a new direction that the New Year
picture is taking, in reality this is no novelty: money symbolism had already crept into traditional New Year pictures, as a reflection of the fact that commerce had
become an avenue for upward mobility in pre-modern
China.

When we look at the non-political traditional New Year
pictures that have been produced in the 1990s, for example 'The gods of wealth enter the home from everywhere, wealth, treasures and peace beckon' (see page
195), Duoduo's remarks are borne out by the composition. The *San Xing*, the gods of happiness (Tian Guan,
the 'Heavenly Official'), emolument (represented by
Zhou Wen Wang) and longevity (in the archetypical form
of the bald-headed Shou Gong), looking young and vigorous, holding their various symbols of rank, dominate
the top half of the picture. The He-He twins, symbolizing
good fortune, marital harmony and wealth, hold up a
copper pot with the text 'becoming rich' in characters.
The attention of the spectator is drawn to the contents of
this copper pot, which is located conveniently in the centre of the print: stacks of 50 and 100 *yuan* RMB bills, and
a sizable stack of American $100 bills.

THE USE OF COLOURS

One of the main features of New Year pictures has
always been that they brought some colour and bright-
ness to their surroundings, and colour symbolism traditionally plays an important part in Chinese culture. For
the 'new' New Year pictures this symbolism was appropriated, and adapted to suit the CCP's purposes.
Communism employed red worldwide as a result of the
traditional properties ascribed to this colour. In Russia it
stood for beauty, while in China it was seen as a 'life-giv-
ing' colour. It is also the colour of wealth, and functions
as the emblem of joy, for festive occasions, or for
expelling pernicious influences. The CCP used red to
denote joy, but also to symbolize itself, and some of its
publications. The 'Little Red Book' of the Cultural
Revolution is a nice illustration of the creative mixture of
traditional (joyous, driving away negative influences) and
modern (revolutionary, progressive) connotations of the
colour red. Also, during the 1980s, red was reserved for
political purposes and the depiction of joyous occasions.
In general, visual propaganda of the Four Modernizations
era was characterized by less strident colouring than the
single-line, flat-colouring of the *Zhongguo hua* style of
the preceding decades. The propaganda of the Cultural
Revolution, in particular, was marked by the frequent
and abundant application of rice-roots green, magenta
and cyclamen. It was precisely the darkness and gloominess with which the peasantry so strongly disagreed
when Western-inspired woodblock prints were introduced in the 1930s; the same criticism was levelled
against the first works of Soviet Socialist Realist art when

搞好计划生育

BELOW: 'Son lives in the Golden Bell Hall, mother dwells in the sheepfold' *(Zi zhu jinluandian, mu qi muyangjuan)*, 1983.

RIGHT: 'The gods of wealth enter the home from everywhere, wealth, treasures and peace beckon' *(Lulu caishen jin jia-men, zhao cai zhao bao zhao ping'an)*, 1993.

colouring, it is interesting to note that quite a few materials published in the 1980s were still in simple black-and-white. The posters published by the Falü chubanshe to spread the popular knowledge and understanding of the newly codified body of laws, for example, were almost exclusively executed in a monochrome cartoon-style. This style, with its quirky close-ups and meticulous attention to the depiction of non-peopled spaces, is reminiscent of the Corto Maltese stories by the French cartoonist Hugo Pratt. This is particularly the case with the two-sheet set 'Son lives in the Golden Bell Hall, mother dwells in the sheepfold'. These two posters recount the story of a son living the good life in a spacious appartment, no doubt as a result of the modernization policies, while he neglects his mother who is forced to live in a stable.

VISUAL SYNTAX

The poster 'I'm enthusiastic and fair, I hope to see you everyday' (see page 196) published in 1984, clearly during a drive to urge workers in the service sector to be more customer-oriented, is made of a rather simple design, compared with the other materials that have been presented here. The poster is dominated by a woman wearing an apron bearing the number 015, while weighing tangerines, against a white background. Judging by the realistic style in which this shop assistant and her facial expression are visualized, the print could easily have been produced in Eastern Europe. It is difficult to say whether the shop assistant is employed in a state enterprise or whether she is a private entrepreneur. The

they were introduced after 1945. According to one Chinese author, the demands emanating from the countryside for the use of more 'elegant' colours, were a reflection of the increased living standards.

Given the traditional Chinese appreciation of bright

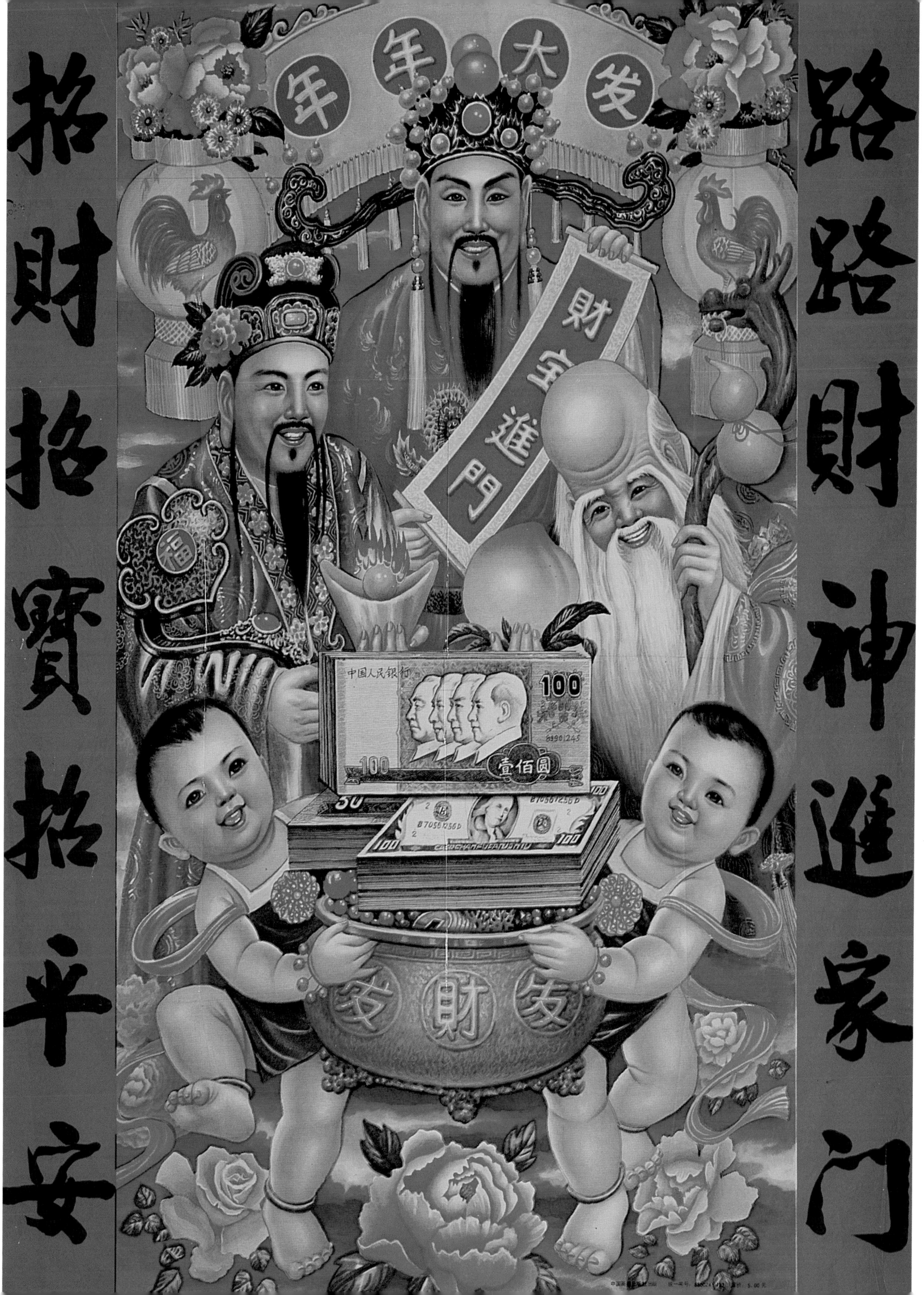

年年大发
路路財神進家门
招財招寶招平安
財宝進門
中国人民银行
100
壹佰圆
安財安

PREVIOUS PAGE LEFT: 'I'm enthusiastic and fair, I hope to see you
everyday' *(Reqing gongping
xiwang tiantian jiandao nin)*,
1984.
PREVIOUS PAGE RIGHT: 'Selling
the fruits of a bumper harvest in
a friendly manner' *(Shanshou
fengshou guo)*, 1978.
BELOW: 'Bette[r] birth and
upbringing, sturdily growing'
*(Yousheng youyu, zhuozhuang
chengzhang)*, 1986.

RIGHT: 'The fish is fat and big'
(Yu er fei you da), early 1970s.

number on the apron would suggest employment in a
state enterprise; however, the scales she uses to weigh
her tangerines, indicating the fairness of the transaction,
are used frequently in free markets. The 'message' of this
poster is contained in the text, which is provided in both

characters and *pinyin* transcription; this demands more
of an effort from the viewer to understand what is
demanded. The smile on the woman's face and the scales
which she uses provide a visual indication of this message. In general, it can be said that the intention of the
poster, namely that without enthusiasm and fairness on
the part of the sales woman, customers will not be
attracted, can be easily understood.

When we compare this poster with 'Selling the fruits of a
bumper harvest in a friendly manner' (see page 197),
published some months before the adoption of the Four
Modernizations program in 1978, a number of differences
become apparent. On the whole, this poster contains
considerably more visual indications of the message that
is presented. Most remarkable is the Socialist Realist,
somewhat dreamlike quality the image exudes, a result
that is enhanced by the soft colours which have been
used. 'Selling the fruits' is obviously located in a state
enterprise, as indicated by the slogans on the wall
('*Zhudong, reqing, naixin, zhoudao*,' or 'Initiative,
enthusiasm, patience, being considerate'), the sophisticated weighing apparatus and the way the fruit is stocked.
As in 'I'm enthusiastic and fair', this poster is dominated
by a saleswoman, dressed in a white coat. The abundance of fruit in the fore- and background of the composition, however, draws the attention of the viewer more
to the 'bumper harvest-element' that is provided in the
more modestly present text. Although the image of the
demurely smiling woman is employed to show the
friendly manner in which these fruits should be sold, she
seems to function more as a conduit between the abundance of fruit resulting from the bumper harvest, and the

BELOW: 'Have discipline' *(You jilü)*, 1986.

做有理想 有道德 有文化 有纪律的一代新人

有纪律

YOUJILU

The poster 'Bette[r] birth and upbringing, sturdily growing' (see page 198), produced after 1986 to support the One Child Campaign, makes use of visual elements that largely correspond with the traditional concepts and symbolism surrounding childbirth as they are employed in New Year pictures, although it does so in a rather clumsy way. The message of the poster is given both in characters and (misspelled) English, which demands even more of an intellectual effort from the recipient than a *pinyin* transcription.

The traditional visual elements used include the little apron that the baby boy wears, the 'tiger slippers', as well as the amulets around his neck and his left wrist. He moreover has a red spot painted on his forehead as protection against disease. However, he is not smiling, nor is he chubby, as babies are supposed to be, and instead of holding a fish *(yu*, a homophone of the word *yu* denoting abundance), he holds a rather skinny toy panda. Other auspicious symbolism is missing. The dominant colour is blue, a hue considered to be ambiguous, and the auspicious red is almost completely absent. On the whole, the image creates a rather subdued mood. It is hard to say how such a poster can contribute to popular conformity with the message.

The difference between this print and an earlier one, 'The fish is fat and big' (see page 199), is striking. Most remarkable is the exuberance and happiness emanating from the earlier poster. This in itself gives the image the joyous quality that is ascribed to New Year pictures. The baby, in full frontal nudity, may lack a red spot on his forehead, and he has no amulets for magical protection, but he is happy. Moreover, he has succeeded in hooking

prospective customer. The consumer, as a member of the people, can rightfully claim his share of this harvest. The friendly treatment of the customer that this poster calls for, then, is not obligatory and is not seen as boosting the sales of the fruit on display.

the fish of abundance in a pool of lotus flower *(lian)*, meaning 'May you have abundance *(yu)* year in and year out *(lian).*' Adding the slogan 'Better birth and upbringing, sturdily growing' would have created a much more forceful attitudinal indication than the one given in the 'Better birth' poster.

The vagueness and ambiguity of those posters that call for a change of thinking have been pointed out before. In the case of 'Have culture' (see page 201), it is absolutely unclear how the addressee of the message is supposed to acquire the quality that is endorsed. The centre of the poster is dominated by the likeness of a good-looking girl who clearly is not Chinese. The right hand, which supports her chin, holds a fountainpen, indicating that she is, or aspires to be, an intellectual. To the right of her, a rocket is ascending in the sky. To her left, the Great Wall is visible, while a flock of cranes, the symbol of accumulated wisdom, flies over it. The composition of the image seems to be mirrored: instead of looking towards the future, as represented by the rocket, the girl gazes toward the past, as embodied by the Great Wall.

Because behavioural indications are lacking in the image, the intended message of the poster must be found in the text. Below, 'have culture' is provided in both characters and *pinyin* transcription. The text is augmented by an exhortation at the top of the poster 'to become a generation of New Men having ideals, morality, culture and discipline.' But again, no indication is given how these qualities could be acquired.

The image of the companion poster, 'Have discipline' (see page 200), is slightly more forthcoming. The central

element is made up of the silhouettes of a student, a worker and a miner. The indications of a disciplined lifestyle are provided by the huge clock above the centre, showing eight o'clock, and fighter planes flying in formation. The texts in the poster, below and on top, contain

201

RIGHT: 'Let our lives have more order' (*Rang womende shenghuo geng you zhixu*), 1983.

the same elements as the 'have culture' poster. Nonetheless, neither of these two posters contain any concrete indications of how their suggestions can be implemented.

The poster 'Let our lives have more order' (see page 203) can be characterized as a more enigmatic example from the 1980s. Given the CCP-leadership's stress on order, the slogan of this poster, given in both characters and *pinyin* transcription, seems to turn this regime-directed attitudinal stimulus into a popular request. The image, however, supports this request in no clear way whatsoever. From the gloomy lower left corner, a nuclear family (father, mother and daughter) walks over a pedestrian crossing towards the brightly-lit horizon in the upper right corner. This horizon is dominated by brightly coloured circles. Do they represent the future? In that case, propaganda artists have done a better job in visualizing it elsewhere, as we have seen in the preceding chapters. Is it the glitter of Beijing, or another urban centre? This is highly unlikely, as the leadership attempts to divert the population flow away from the big cities and toward the rural townships. Could these circles serve as an artist's impression of traffic lights, as the colours red, yellow and green can be vaguely made out? If so, the concept of 'order' is very narrowly defined and echoes calls for the basic social skills which is enstilled in primary-school youth. The analysis of this poster, and the two preceding ones, indicates that general political and behavioural indications, aimed at changing thought rather than behaviour, have become increasingly difficult to depict.

202

EPILOGUE:
THE DECLINE OF THE
PROPAGANDA POSTER

ELECTRONIC MEDIA
THE EFFECT OF PROPAGANDA IN THE 1980s
THE EMERGENCE OF NEW PROPAGANDA AND
COUNTER PROPAGANDA
DILEMMAS IN THE PROPAGANDA OF THE 1990s

PREVIOUS PAGE: 'Study comrade
Lei Feng' *(Xiang Lei Feng tongzhi
xuexi)*, 1990.

ELECTRONIC MEDIA

In the Four Modernizations era, propaganda posters lost the predominance they enjoyed during the preceding three decades. What were the reasons for the gradual disappearance of the propaganda poster from the *Xinhua* bookstores in the second half of the 1980s? The main explanation for this development can be found in the fact that the popular ownership of electronic media increased as a result of higher standards of living. Television in particular made the world visible to a society that had lived in isolation since the founding of the People's Republic. It became the principal symbol of prosperity and of one's success at taking part in the process of modernization The number of television sets in China grew dramatically, from 10 million in March 1982, to 116 million by late 1988.

Electronic media, including audio and video tapes, have become the real mass media of the modernized China of the 1980s, particularly in the urban areas. They provide society with a mass culture that is shaped by foreign television programmes, film, music and other media materials, and that represents, as one author states, the people's revulsion against excessive politicization and regimentation.

The state, too, switched its attention to the use of electronic media for propaganda purposes. It has attempted to use them to unify the people, preserve CCP authority, and fulfil the promises of reform. Radio and television, moreover, were expected to help cultivate that elusive 'spiritual civilization' that was geared to modern times, by providing mass recreational activity, and by supply-

ing entertainment that is in 'good taste' and that reinforces state ideology and morality. Television programming reflects the emphasis on propaganda, instruction, education and national culture previously applied to the more traditional printed media, and this has turned the medium into the face and voice of the government.

Propaganda originating from the electronic media can be geared more quickly to changing circumstances, as it does not require a great deal of time for design, production, distribution, etc., as is the case with posters. In a climate of possible swings in prevailing policies, which might make posters obsolete as soon as they appear on the market, it may be seen as more effective to present the message via the electronic media.

However, it is safe to say that television, as a 'mind opener', has radically undermined the government. The stream of cultural imagery that has entered China since 1979 has produced a formidable and irreversible corpus of alternative visions and a diversity of cultural and political sentiments. Television programmes do not have a single meaning, connotation or objectively definable significance. Instead, they are polysemic, and pregnant with meanings, guaranteeing that a uniform ideology cannot be maintained. Moreover, television identifies, emphasizes and symbolizes certain fundamental contradictions and shortcomings of Chinese society. The commercials that are broadcast on Chinese television in particular often stand in contrast to reality, contributing to the people's confusion, frustration and dissatisfaction.

The most important question regarding propaganda in general is, of course, whether or not its purpose has been fulfilled. In most State-socialist societies, propaganda and education are intimately linked, making it practically impossible to ascertain the positive or negative effects of a single form of propaganda. Furthermore, Chinese society is a blatantly prescriptive one. It is not only through the electronic and printed media that a steady stream of suggestions, directives and announcements are constantly issued in the name of the CCP and the State; these exhortations are augmented by comparable ones which are transmitted through the more traditional and localized media of the neighbourhood posters, billboards and blackboards.

Another complication is the lack of Chinese research data into audience reactions. Despite the political calls for 'seeking truth from facts', audience research, and studies of propaganda effects in particular, are still in their infancy. Statistical research in the social sciences was taken up only in the mid-1980s, and involves politically non-threatening topics such as studies into changes in consumer behaviour, improvements in living conditions and marriage customs. Even then, studies have mainly been used to demonstrate the correctness of policy directives currently in force, and not for objective research of their viability.

In general, it can be said that the Four Modernizations was not a decade-long campaign that was tightly focused on a single goal. It was rather a series of campaigns that were integrated within a comprehensive framework, namely the rehabilitation of the economy after the disastrous policies of the Great Leap Forward and the Cultural Revolution. The successful overhaul of the economy also was to lead to a positive re-evaluation of the leading role of the CCP. The ideology of the Four Modernizations Campaign, a sub-set of Marxism-Leninism, Mao Zedong Thought, was to serve manifold aspects of reform and modernization.

Most importantly, there was the necessity to win the people over to the new approach to China's development, an approach that clearly deviated from the strategies that had been followed in the past. This not only involved the creation of support at all levels of society, but also an attempt to eradicate the lingering influence of previous slogans and inculcated modes of thought and behaviour. Propaganda, therefore, had to be appealing to the intellect, rather than to sentiment.

There are numerous indications that point to the existence of factional struggle within the CCP over policy, and examples of such occurances in the modernization decade. Although consequently denied by the leadership on the basis of its unwillingness to acknowledge the legitimacy of intra-elite conflicts of interest, there is clear proof of the existence of both a reformist and a conservative faction. The propaganda apparatus, functioning under the Central Committee of the CCP, should be as susceptible to factional struggle as any other part of the Chinese political structure. This is borne out by experiences in the past, when the media, which fall under the jurisdiction of the Propaganda Department, were used in factional conflicts.

It would be tempting to assume that the different factions

were able to devise propaganda policies supporting their respective political platforms, which would lead to the production of propaganda that is fundamentally different in both form and content. The propaganda of the 1980s that had a more integrational character, then, could be attributed to the reformist faction, while the conservatives, by falling back on the use of icons that were associated with a more militant past, could be seen as advocating propaganda that had a clearly agitational character.

When analyzing the posters that were published in the 1980s, in particular those that explicitly propagate political messages, the reappearance of Lei Feng during the periods when the campaigns against 'spiritual pollution' and 'bourgeois liberalization' were started, can be seen as a clear indication of a 'conservative' reaction to the policies as they were advocated by the reformists. Posters with more traditionally politicized contents were produced after the Tian'anmen Incident of June 1989, and most certainly the reissue of Lei Feng materials in the 1990s, which made clear to the people that the relative relaxation of the past years was halted. An example of such a post-Tian'anmen Lei Feng issue is 'Study comrade Lei Feng' which also contains an inscription by Mao (see pages 204-205).

Judging from the intra-Party criticisms that were voiced after the suppression of the student protests in June 1989, it is clear that the more conservative factions disagreed with the depoliticized and de-ideologized contents of propaganda of the preceding decade. The conservatives considered this to be partially responsible for the chaos that was said to have emanated from the neglect of polit-ical and ideological education, and subsequently for the events leading up to the Tian'anmen Incident.

THE EMERGENCE OF NEW PROPAGANDA MEDIA AND COUNTER PROPAGANDA

Until the mid-1980s, all printed media and the dissemination of all information used to be held under central control. Then, as a result of the modernization programme, great numbers of journals and newspapers, often published by economic research institutes and other non-State run organizations, started flooding the market, reducing the rigid hold which the Propaganda Department had on the media. These publications could be devoted to specialized technical or economic information for specific sections of the audience, or they regaled the population with gossip, hearsay, and racy topics, including love stories and sex. Nonetheless, the stress on order that prevailed during the decade precluded any attempts to question the legitimacy, positions and interests of the Communist Party. In such an atmosphere, counter-propaganda in whatever form could only exist underground.

In the second half of the 1980s, the people started using ephemeral means such as graffiti to protest certain negative developments that were encountered in society as a result of the modernization policies, such as the phenomenon of 'backdoor-ism' *(zou houmen)* and the increasingly widespread corrupt behaviour on the part of officials and cadres *(guandao)*. The general orientation of the modernization programme, and its perceived benefits, however, were never questioned.

Only during the student demonstrations which took place in Beijing and other urban centres in Spring and early Summer 1989, did ad hoc student groups produce pamphlets, essays, cartoons, caricatures and posters which countered the policies and the diminished amount of visual propaganda published by the leadership. These were widely visible and contributed to a mobilization of urbanites who expressed their dissatisfaction with inflation, official corruption, power abuse and the unresponsiveness of the leadership to their complaints.

Particularly in Southern China, an 'informal penetration' by Hong Kong popular culture took place through the electronic media. Through pop music and radio and television programmes, picked up by aerials or satellite dishes, the Chinese population got a taste of the 'good life' under capitalism. In the eyes of the CCP-leadership, the political awakening of the Hong Kong population, and the calls for increased democracy that were heard ever louder after 1989, posed a greater threat. After all, after Chinese sovereignty over the area has been reasserted in 1997, and the colony has become a Special Administrative Region with a large degree of autonomy, a democratic Hong Kong would have an enormous political, and potentially dangerous, influence on the rest of the country. It could thwart the CCP-attempts to keep Southern China, and its successful Special Economic Zones in particular, under central leadership.

DILEMMAS IN THE PROPAGANDA ART OF THE 1990s

Why has the CCP let the propaganda poster fall into disuse? The production of posters could have been trans-formed, for instance, into one providing public information messages to address the negative social developments that started springing up in society as a result of the modernization process. However, contrary to the propaganda produced in the printed media, no posters were published to indicate to the people that their moving illegally from the countryside to the large cities would not yield employment opportunities, or to warn against the health hazards of prostitution. Although not necessarily in terms of actual contents, inspiration for such a redirection of visual propaganda messages could have been found in other Chinese communities such as Singapore and Hong Kong. In the latter city, the medium has been used over the years to inform the population of various developments, such as posters calling on people born in a certain year to have their identification papers renewed. Medical information can be found in posters in glass showcases all over the territory, warning against the dangers of smoking and the necessity to practice safe sex, and social information is contained in posters warning against the use of drugs and against the dangers of joining Triads, especially for youngsters.

In the Soviet Union — generally one of the models used by the CCP — after Mikhael Gorbachev succeeded in pushing through his reform-oriented policies in the latter half of 1980s, the twin slogans of *glasnost* (openness) and *perestroika* (reform), allowed the one-dimensional conception of the political poster to disappear and made way for a more sophisticated expression of non-government directed views. The 'liberation' of the political poster from government interference under the Gorbachev leadership, turned it from a medium with

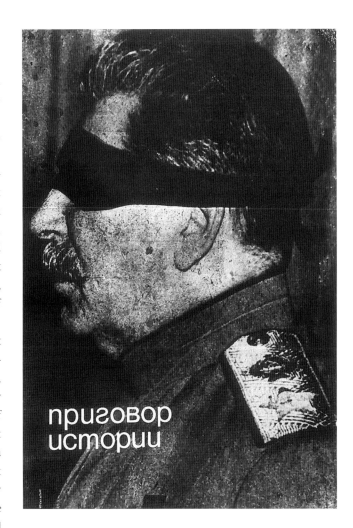

BELOW: 'The verdict of history' (1988), after Yegorov and Litvinov, *Posters of glasnost and perestroika.*

specified political contents into one that contained social comments and addressed issues concerning everyone. Instead of the mass-produced, didactic and triumphal propaganda of the past, posters were now employed to tell people the truth about their society and history. Moreover, their contents became more intellectualized as opposed to the previous infantilization of the population. This resulted in extremely outspoken posters that criticized various aspects of Soviet society. The subjects that were featured in these *glasnost* posters included criticism of political leaders from past and present (not only Lenin, Stalin and Brezhnev, but also Gorbachev himself), and the stranglehold in which the state bureaucracy kept reforms. 'The verdict of history (1988)', for example, reflected the mounting calls in 1988 for a 'public trial' of the Great Leader (Stalin).

The Four Basic Principles were the main reason that Chinese poster artists could not follow a similar development. The unassailable character of CCP-rule, socialism, ideology and democratic dictatorship preempted any Chinese attempts to form a truly Chinese equivalent of *glasnost* in artistic expression. One must conclude that devoting attention to unpleasant social phenomena would have run counter to one of the principles that form the core of the use of the media in China; that by upholding the fundamental power and authority of the CCP, an imaginary world has to be created that is filled with symbols, slogans and code words, but only weakly penetrated by reality.

Yet, by opening its doors, China and its people became acquainted with and plugged into the largely Western-inspired desires and aspirations for a better future, as shared by the world community. Gone is the 'splendid isolation' that marked the imperial era, or the utopia of agrarian self-sufficiency that was visualized and lauded in the 1950s and 1960s. Judging by the recurring elements in the imagery that was used in the 1980s, the days of the information society and automation had arrived in China.

An abundance of competing images originating from abroad has shown the people that other ideologies may be more successful, and less demanding, in bringing about this modernization as it is envisioned. The Party has not been able to visualize appropriate, indigenous behavioural stimuli for a society in the throes of modernization, and has limited itself, in an echo of the Confucian tradition, to calling indirectly for obedience, austerity and discipline, against a modernized background.

Clearly, visual propaganda of the Four Modernizations lost contact with the population, despite the fact that attempts were made to counter this trend by catering more than ever to popular tastes. What was produced had less and less to do with whether propaganda should be used for popularization or raising standards. What do we make, for example, of the new-style, traditional New Year pictures as they have been produced in the early 1990s, posters that feature the traditional element of wealth by depicting American banknotes? The CCP-leadership basically struggled, and continues to do so, with the dilemma of how the population should be socialized, to support communist values and the continuing political and social dominance of the Party.

From the experiences that have been gained since June 1989, it is obvious that this fundamental dilemma still has not been solved by the CCP. It continues to define the population's well-being largely in terms of its obedience to Party-rule rather than anything else, and to see a social atmosphere conducive to the successful implementation of the policies of modernization as something that is dependent on its own ability to maintain order. It would appear that the population is no longer buying that message, at least not in the form of propaganda posters.

NOTES

PAGE 10

ALL-ROUND MODERNIZATION: Hua Kuo-feng (Hua Guofeng), 'Unite and Strive to Build A Modern, Powerful Socialist Country! — Report on the Work of the Government delivered at the First Session of the Fifth National People's Congress on February 26, 1978', *Documents of the First Session of the Fifth National People's Congress of the People's Republic of China*, pp. 1-118. Quotes are from pages 35 and 36.

FUQIANG: Hu Yaobang, 'On the Party's Journalism Work', Brantly Womack (ed.), *Media and the Chinese Public: A Survey of the Beijing Media Audience*, p. 198. James Lull, *China Turned On: Television, Reform, and Resistance* (London, New York: Routledge, 1991), p. 5. Lucian W. Pye, 'Communication and Political Culture in China', Godwin C. Chu and Francis L.K. Hsu (eds.), *Moving a Mountain; Cultural Change in China*, pp. 165, 168.

PAGE 11

VOICE OF CHINA: Lull, *China Turned On*, pp. 1, 17, 131. Deborah Davis, 'My Mother's House', Perry Link, Richard Madsen, Paul G. Pickowicz, *Unofficial China — Popular Culture and Thought in the People's Republic*, p. 92. Lowell Dittmer, 'China's "Opening to the Outside World": The Cultural Dimension', *Journal of Northeast Asian Studies*, Vol. 6, No. 2 (Summer 1987), pp. 7, 8. The diversification of society is clearly described in Zhang Xinxin and Sang Ye, *Chinese Profiles*; more official accounts are in Liu Bingwen and Xiong Lei (eds.), *Portraits of Ordinary Chinese* (Beijing: Foreign Languages Press, 1990). The regular reports written by Orville Schell provide another source of information. See for example *To Get Rich is Glorious — China in the 80s and Discos and Democracy — China in the Throes of Reform*.

PAGE 14

COMMUNIST UTOPIA: David S.G. Goodman, *Beijing Street Voices — The Poetry and Politics of China's Democracy Movement*, p. 1.

BILLBOARDS: John Gittings, *China Changes Face — The Road from Revolution 1949-1989*, p. 254; Randall Stross, 'The Return of Advertising in China: A Survey of the Ideological Reversal', *The China Quarterly*, No. 123 (September 1990), pp. 485-502. Examples from 1981 can be found in Franc Palaia, *Great Walls of China*.

PAGE 18

CLUSTERING: Donald J. Munro, *The Concept of Man in Contemporary China*, pp. 26-27; and 'Belief Control: the Psychological and Ethical Foundations', Amy Auerbacher Wilson, Sidney L. Greenblatt and Richard W. Wilson (eds.), *Deviance and Social Control in Chinese Society*, pp. 22, 24. Lucian W. Pye, *The Spirit of Chinese Politics; a Psychocultural Study of the Authority Crisis in Political Development*, p. 15.

PAGE 19

FATHER-FIGURE: K.C. Chang, *Art, Myth and Ritual; The Path to Political Authority in Ancient China*, pp. 34-35. Michael Harris Bond and Kwang-kuo Hwang, 'The Social Psychology of Chinese People', Michael Harris Bond (ed.), *The Psychology of the Chinese People*, p. 215.

DATONG: Chang, *Art, Myth and Ritual*, p. 33. Fred C. Hung, 'Appendix A: Some Observations on Confucian Ideology', Godwin C. Chu and Francis L.K. Hsu (eds.), *Moving a Mountain; Cultural Change in China*, p. 421; Scott Minick and Jiao Ping, *Chinese Graphic Design in the Twentieth Century*, pp. 11-12.

CONFUCIANISM: Shryock, *The Origin and Development of the State Cult of Confucius*. Ambrose Y.C. King and Michael H. Bond, 'The Confucian Paradigm of Man: A Sociological View', Wen-Shing Tseng and David Y.H. Wu (eds.), *Chinese Culture and Mental Health*, p. 30. Kwang-kuo Hwang, 'A Psychological Perspective of Chinese Interpersonal Morality', Carl-Albrecht Seyschab, Armin Sievers and Slawoj Szynkiewicz (eds.), *Society, Culture, and Patterns of Behaviour*, p. 14; Pye, *The Spirit of Chinese Politics*, p. 87.

EDUCATION: Munro, *The Concept of Man in Contemporary China*, pp. 24-25, 84; Tu Wei-ming, 'Confucianism: Symbol and Substance in Recent Times', Wilson, Wilson and Greenblatt (eds.), *Value Change in Chinese Society*, p. 43.

PAGE 20

DAFANG: Pye, *The Spirit of Chinese Politics*, p. 93. Rodney L. Taylor, *The Way of Heaven — An Introduction to the Confucian Religious Life*, p. 11. Susan Mann, 'Widows in the Kinship, Class, and Community Structures of Qing Dynasty China', *Journal of Asian Studies*, Vol. 46, No. 1 (February 1987), pp. 37, 40-41.

GRAMMATOCRACY: David Johnson, 'Communication, Class, and Consciousness in Late Imperial China', David Johnson, Andrew J. Nathan and Evelyn S. Rawski (eds.), *Popular Culture in Late Imperial China*, pp. 47-48.

XIANGYUE: Burch, 'Models as Agents', p. 126; and Munro, *The Concept of Man*, p. 138. Hsiao Kung-chuan, *Rural China; Imperial Control in the Nineteenth Century*, p. 195. For the revival of the 'village compact' (*xianggui minyue*) during the 'Four Modernizations', designed to broaden democratic participation at the local level, see Ann Anagnost, 'Socialist Ethics and the Legal System', Jeffrey N. Wasserstrom and Elizabeth J. Perry (eds.), *Popular Protest and Political Culture in Modern China: Learning from 1989*, pp. 177-205.

CONFUCIAN ETHIC: The Six Maxims were: 1. Perform filial duties to one's parents; 2. Honour and respect one's elders and superiors; 3. Maintain harmonious relationships with one's neighbours; 4. Instruct and discipline one's sons and grandsons; 5. Let each work peacefully for one's own livelihood; 6. Do not commit wrongful deeds. The Sacred Edict was essentially an elaboration of the Six Maxims, but placed more emphasis on the prevention of unlawful and anti-social behaviour. The Amplified Instructions strengthened the role of the rural police system, the *baojia*. See Hsiao, *Rural China*, pp. 186-189, 194-195.

PAGE 21

'EXPLANATIONS': Mair mentions the *Shengyu tujie* [Illustrated explanation of the Sacred Edict] by Zhong Huamin, 1587; the *Shengyu xiangjie* [Illustrated explanations of the Sacred Edict] by Liang Yannian, 1681; and the *Shengyu tuxiang yanyi* [Illustrated explanation of the Sacred Edict] by Li Laizhang, c. 1704. 'Language and Ideology', pp. 327, 330, 333.

SCHOLAR-BUREAUCRATS: Bond and Hwang, 'The Social Psychology', p. 215.

CULTURAL INDOCTRINATION: James Hayes, 'Specialists and Written Materials in the Village World', Johnson, Nathan, Rawski (eds.), *Popular Culture in Late Imperial China*, p. 107.

PAGE 22

PICTURES OF TILLING: Minick and Jiao, *Chinese Graphic Design*, pp. 14-15. Laing, *The Winking Owl*, p. 8.

DIANSHIZHAI HUABAO: Laing, *The Winking Owl*, pp. 8-10.

DURING THE NEW YEAR FESTIVAL...: Wang Shucun, in Wang Shucun (ed.), *Ancient Chinese Woodblock New Year Prints*, p. 5.

PAGE 23

PEASANT POPULATION: Maria Rudova and Lev Menshikov (eds.), *Chinese Popular Prints*, p. 10; Zhang Yanyuan (Tang), Lidai minghuaji, quoted in Zhongguo meishu quanji bianji weiyuanhui (ed.), *Zhongguo meishu quanji, huihuabian 21 minjian nianhua* [Chinese fine arts collection, painting Vol. 21, popular New Year prints], p. 3.

...ARE SO CONVENTIONAL...: Daniel H. Kulp II, *Country Life in South China — The Sociology of Familism*, Vol. I: Phenix Village, Kwangtung, China (New York: Bureau of Publications, Teachers College, Columbia University, 1925; reprinted Taipei: Ch'eng-wen Publishing Co., 1966), p. 276.

ZHIHUA: Rudova, Menshikov (ed.), *Chinese Popular Prints*, pp. 5, 6, and the introduction to Wang Shucun (ed.), *Zhongguo minjian nianhua baitu* [100 Popular Chinese New Year Prints] (Beijing: Renmin meishu chubanshe, 1988); Holm, 'Art and Ideology', p. 157.

NIANHUA: Wang, *Ancient Chinese Woodblock New Year Prints*, pp. 1-3. Rudova and Menshikov (eds.), *Chinese Popular Prints*, p. 8. For popularity in urban areas, namely Peking, see Tun Li-ch'en, *Annual Customs and Festivals in Peking*, pp. 100-101; for rural areas, in particular in South China, see Kulp, *Country Life*, pp. 265, 269, 275.

PAGE 24

ART EDUCATION: Laing, *The Winking Owl*, pp. 7-8. According to Wang, *Zhongguo meishu quanji*, p. 21, Western techniques, introduced to the Qing court by Jesuits such as Matteo Ricci and Giuseppe Castiglione, slowly found their way into nianhua prints. Minick and Jiao, *Chinese Graphic Design*, pp. 17, 18.

IMPORTED TECHNIQUES: Mayching M. Kao, *China's Response to the West in Art: 1898-1937*, pp. 7, 129-32; Minick and Jiao, *Chinese Graphic Design*, p. 134.

VISUAL MATERIALS: Sherman Cochran, *Big Business in China — Sino-Foreign Rivalry in the Cigarette Industry, 1890-1930*, pp. 19, 35, 38, 198-199, describes, among other things, the advertising activities of the British American Tobacco Company. Kulp, *Country Life*, p. 265. Minick and Jiao, *Chinese Graphic Design*, pp. 17, 18

'NEW MAN': Donald J. Munro, 'The Malleability of Man in Chinese Marxism', *The China Quarterly*, No. 48 (October-December 1971), pp. 610-611.

PAGE 25

APPEAL TO REASON: Based on David Wedgwood Benn, *Persuasion & Soviet Politics*, pp. 55-56.

PAGE 26

ELEMENT OF PEDAGOGY: Wedgwood Benn, *Persuasion & Soviet Politics*, pp. 56-59, 221. Peter Kenez, *The Birth of the Propaganda State; Soviet Methods of Mass Mobilization, 1917-1929*, pp. 26, 121.
EMULATION: During the 'Cultural Revolution', Mao Zedong Thought was ascribed solely to Mao's genius. When his contributions were assessed in the 1980s, it was interpreted as the collective wisdom of China's veteran revolutionary leaders. The latter assessment is laid down in the Resolution on Certain Questions in the History of Our Party Since the Founding of the People's Republic of China, adopted by the Sixth Plenum of the Eleventh Central Committee of the CCP in 1981. See *Resolution on CPC History* (1949-81), pp. 11, 56-57.
MAO ZEDONG THOUGHT: Paul J. Hiniker, *Revolutionary Ideology & Chinese Reality — Dissonance under Mao*, p. 81. Lucian W. Pye, *The Mandarin and the Cadre: China's Political Cultures*, pp. 31-32. Munro, 'The Malleability of Man', p. 612; Burch, 'Models as Agents', p. 127; Bonnie S. McDougall, *Mao Zedong's 'Talks at the Yan'an Conference on Literature and Art': A Translation of the 1953 Text with Commentary*. Michigan Papers in Chinese Studies No. 39, p. 26.
NEWLY-ACQUIRED POWER: Liu Shaoqi, 'How to be a good Communist', *Three Essays on Party-Building*, pp. 6, 11-12. Pye, *The Mandarin and the Cadre*, p. 56. Munro, *The Concept of Man*, p. 176.
CONFRONTATION: Munro, *The Concept of Man*, pp. 139-140.
MAO'S OWN WORDS: As quoted in Chi P'ing, 'Attach Importance to the Role of Teachers by Negative Example', *Peking Review* (31 March 1972), p. 5.

PAGE 27

POWER OF IDEOLOGY: Hiniker, *Revolutionary Ideology*, pp. 67-68. According to Pye, the belief that the difficulties related to modernization can be overcome by eliminating some surface defects and allowing the basic virtues of the people to reassert themselves is based on a conviction that the precise qualities required for successful modernization were once a part of the Chinese heritage. Pye, *The Spirit of Chinese Politics*, pp. 58-59. Alan P.L. Liu, *Communications and National Integration in Communist China*, pp. 32, 55; Lucian W. Pye, 'Communication and Political Culture in China', Godwin C. Chu and Francis L.K. Hsu (eds.), *Moving a Mountain; Cultural Change in China*, p. 165.
STIMULI AND IMAGES: Munro, *The Concept of Man*, pp. 137, 140-142; Burch, 'Models as Agents', pp. 129-131; Pye, 'Communication and Political Culture', p. 166.
LARGER THAN LIFE: The observation of peers and the emulation of teachers or other models are considered pedagogic tools for learning. Robert A. LeVine and Merry I. White, *Human Conditions: The Cultural Basis of Educational Development*, pp. 163-164.
BEHAVIOURAL PROBLEM: Pye, *The Mandarin and the Cadre*, pp. 60, 65, 85, 90; Munro, *The Concept of Man*, p. 151. Burch, 'Models as Agents', p. 123.
TWO-WAY COMMUNICATION: Hiniker, *Revolutionary Ideology & Chinese Reality*, p. 49.
TAKE THE IDEAS…: Mao Zedong, 'Some Questions Concerning Methods of Leadership', *Selected Works of Mao Tse-Tung*, Vol. III, p. 119. See also Kuo Mo-Jo (Guo Moruo), 'Romanticism and Realism', *Peking Review* (15 July 1958), pp. 7-11.

PAGE 28

REWARD FOR A MODEL: Pye, *The Mandarin and the Cadre*, p. 60. See also Xing Fangqun, 'Guanyu xuanchuan xianjin renwu he xianjin dianxingde jidian yijian', p. 127.
SUCH EFFORTS: Lü Cheng, Zhang Zhuwu, Zhong Bihui, Su Xisheng, He Jinqing (eds.), *Dangde jianshe qishinian jishi 1919-1991*, pp. 19, 20, 36-37, 144, 158.

PAGE 29

RECTIFICATION: Frederick C. Teiwes, *Politics & Purges in China — Rectification and the Decline of Party Norms 1950-1965*, pp. 5, 18. Timothy Cheek, 'Redefining Propaganda: Debates on the Role of Journalism in Post-Mao Mainland China', *Issues & Studies*, February 1989, pp. 53, 56-57.
(SELF-)CRITICISM: Martin King Whyte, *Small Groups and Political Rituals in China*, p. 37. Teiwes, *Politics & Purges*, pp. 32, 33.
CCP'S MONOPOLY: Ibid., p. 48.

PAGE 30

MANAGEMENT OF CULTURE: James Lull, *China Turned On: Television, Reform, and Resistance*, pp. 31, 139, 142.
PROPAGANDA DEPARTMENT: Francis W. Houn, *To Change a Nation; Propaganda*

and Indoctrination in Communist China, pp. 23-25. Liu, *Communications and National Integration*, pp. 34, 38, 40, 43. Liu, *How China is Ruled*, p. 257.
PROPAGANDA DEVICES: Bruce Holbrook, *Mainland China's External Propaganda Values, 1958-1974: A Content Analysis of 'Peking Review'*. Lynn T. White III, 'Local Newspapers and Community Change, 1949-1969', in Chu and Hsu (eds.), *Moving a Mountain*, pp. 76-112. Eileen P. Blumenthal, *Models in Chinese Moral Education: Perspectives from Children's Books*. Charles P. Ridley, Paul H.B. Godwin and Dennis J. Doolin, *The Making of a Model Citizen in Communist China*. Joe C. Huang, *Heroes and Villains in Communist China; The Contemporary Chinese Novel as a Reflection of Life*. Joe C. Huang, 'Ideology and Confucian Ethics in the Characterization of Bad Women in Socialist Literature', Wilson, Greenblatt and Wilson (eds.), *Deviance and Social Control*, pp. 37-51. Parris H. Chang, 'Children's Literature and Political Socialization', in Chu and Hsu (eds.), *Moving a Mountain*, pp. 237-256. Ai-li Chin, 'Value Themes in Short Stories, 1976-1977', Chu and Hsu, *Moving a Mountain*, pp. 280-304. Stefan R. Landsberger, 'After the Bumper Harvest': China's Socialist Education Movement as seen through short stories from the Sixties, ZZOA Working Paper No. 46 (Amsterdam: University of Amsterdam, 1984). Donald C. Clarke, 'Political Power and Authority in Recent Chinese Literature', *The China Quarterly*, No. 102 (1986), pp. 234-252. Jay Leyda, *Dianying — Electric Shadows; An Account of Films and the Film Audience in China*. George S. Semsel (ed.), *Chinese Film; The State of the Art in the People's Republic*.
IDEALISTIC VISIONS: Lull, *China Turned On*, pp. 1, 18, 180.

PAGE 31

CONTROL OF THE MASS MEDIA: Liu, *How China is Ruled*, pp. 63-64.
NATIONAL FORM: Lucian W. Pye, *The Spirit of Chinese Politics; a Psychocultural Study of the Authority Crisis in Political Development*, p. 8. Minick and Jiao, *Chinese Graphic Design*, pp. 21, 22, 55; Ng, *The Russian hero*, pp. 32, 34.
MAY FOURTH MOVEMENT: Chow Tse-tung, *The May Fourth Movement — Intellectual Revolution in Modern China*, p. 1
DEFINED AS…: Chow, *The May Fourth Movement*, p. 5.
POPULAR RULE: Ng, *The Russian hero*, p. 39.
FUTURISM: Joan Lebold Cohen, *The New Chinese Painting 1949-1986*, p. 38. Minick and Jiao, *Chinese Graphic Design*, pp. 22-23, 44-51.

PAGE 32

SOCIAL RESPONSIBILITY: Minick and Jiao, *Chinese Graphic Design*, p. 26; Paul Pickowicz, *Marxist Literary Thought and China: A Conceptual Framework*. Studies in Chinese Terminology No. 18, p. 20.
WESTERN-STYLE PRINTS: Laing, *The Winking Owl*, pp. 11-12, 14; Minick and Jiao, *Chinese Graphic Design*, p. 91. Holm, 'Arts and Ideology', p. 94. Hans-Jürgen Cwik, 'Flut des Zorns' — die Bewegung des Neuen Holzschnittes', Jerg Haas et al., *Holz Schnitt im neuen China — Zeitgenössige Graphik aus der Volksrepublik China*, p. 79.
PESSIMISM: Laing, *The Winking Owl*, pp. 7, 11-12; Jerg Haas, 'Kontinuität und Bruch — Tradition und Moderne in der chinesischen Kunst', Haas et al., *Holz Schnitt im neuen China*, pp. 53, 56; Hans-Jürgen Cwik, 'Flut des Zorns', p. 80. Minick and Jiao, *Chinese Graphic Design*, pp. 26, 28-31, 36; Holm, 'Art and Ideology', p. 96.

PAGE 33

JUDGES OF HELL: Laing, *The Winking Owl*, p. 14; Holm, *Art and Ideology*, pp. 77-78.
PHOTO-MONTAGE: Minick and Jiao, *Chinese Graphic Design*, pp. 82-83; Laing, *The Winking Owl*, p. 13. Holm, *Art and Ideology*, p. 51.
A SEARCH WAS UNDERTAKEN: Holm, *Art and Ideology*, p. 78.

PAGE 34

MASS REPRODUCTION: Laing, *The Winking Owl*, pp. 13-16; Minick and Jiao, *Chinese Graphic Design*, pp. 89-90. Holm, 'Art and Ideology', p. 202.
EXPRESSIONIST WOODCUTS: Laing, *The Winking Owl*, p. 15; Holm, 'Art and Ideology', p. 109.
LEADER PORTRAIT: Holm, *Art and Ideology*, pp. 66-67; Holm, 'Art and Ideology', pp. 102-103, 185, 186, 309-310.
ORGANIZATION OF PROPAGANDA WORK: This section draws on David Holm, *Art and Ideology in Revolutionary China*, pp. 18-23. See also *Zhonggong dangshi zhuyao shijian jianjie*, pp. 187-191. For a translation and extensive discussion of the contents and the various versions of Mao's opening and closing remarks, see Bonnie S. McDougall, Mao Zedong's 'Talks at the Yan'an Conference on Literature and Art': A Translation of the 1953 Text with Commentary. Michigan Papers in Chinese Studies No. 39.
PRE-EXISTING VALUES: Holm, *Art and Ideology*, p. 20.

PAGE 35

CULTURAL DOGMA: McDougall, *Mao Zedong's 'Talks'*, p. 39. See also Arnold Chang, *Painting in the People's Republic of China: The Politics of Style*, p. 5.

LITERATURE AND ART...: McDougall, *Mao Zedong's 'Talks'*, p. 58.

IDIOM OF THE MASSES: Ng Mau-sang, *The Russian hero in modern Chinese fiction*, p. 276. Chang, *Painting in the People's Republic of China*, p. 6; McDougall, *Mao Zedong's 'Talks'*, pp. 67, 75.

SERVE POLITICS: Chang, *Painting in the People's Republic of China*, pp. 6, 7, 73-77. McDougall, *Mao Zedong's 'Talks'*, pp. 70-71. Holm, *Art and Ideology*, p. 91.

WHAT WE DEMAND...: McDougall, *Mao Zedong's 'Talks'*, p. 78.

OLD FORMS: Holm, *Art and Ideology*, pp. 333-334. David L. Holm, 'Art and Ideology in the Yenan Period, 1937-1945', pp. 38, 183, 184.

PAGE 36

RURAL SCENES: Scott Minick and Jiao Ping, *Chinese Graphic Design in the Twentieth Century*, pp. 92-93; Ellen Johnston Laing, *The Winking Owl: Art in the People's Republic of China*, pp. 15-16; Chang, *Painting in the People's Republic of China*, pp. 8-9; Holm, *Art and Ideology*, p. 94.

YAN'AN STYLE: Minick and Jiao, *Chinese Graphic Design*, p. 102; Laing, *The Winking Owl*, p. 16.

IT ENABLED...: Minick and Jiao, *Chinese Graphic Design*, p. 93; Laing, *The Winking Owl*, p. 16. McDougall, *Mao Zedong's 'Talks'*, p. 72; Chang, *Painting in the People's Republic of China*, pp. 10-11. Kao, *China's Response*, p. 195; Ma Ke, 'Jianguo shini-anlaide zhengzhi xuanchuanhua', p. 1.

DECLINE OF THE WOODCUTS: Minick and Jiao, *Chinese Graphic Design*, p. 98; Laing, *The Winking Owl*, pp. 17, 21. See also the various photographs made by Henri Cartier-Bresson in Nanjing and Shanghai in 1948-1949, reproduced in Robert Guillain, *L'autre Chine — Photographies de Henri Cartier-Bresson*.

PAGE 37

NEW MESSAGES: Laing, *The Winking Owl*, p. 20; Minick and Jiao, *Chinese Graphic Design*, p. 102. Chang, *Painting in the People's Republic of China*, p. 74.

NEW SOCIALIST WORLD: Laing, *The Winking Owl*, pp. 20, 21; Minick and Jiao, *Chinese Graphic Design*, p. 102. Howard L. Boorman, 'The Literary World of Mao Tse-tung', *The China Quarterly*, No. 13 (1963), p. 18. Ng, *The Russian hero*, p. 277. Zhang Xinxin and Sang Ye, *Chinese Profiles*, p. 226.

OUTSPOKEN CRITICS: For a more extensive discussion of the 'Hundred Flowers' and 'Anti-Rightist' campaigns, see, among others, Merle Goldman, *Literary Dissent in Communist China*, pp. 158-242; Bill Brugger, *Contemporary China*, pp. 152-159.

PAGE 38

REVOLUTIONARY REALISM: Kuo Mo-Jo (Guo Moruo), 'Romanticism and Realism', *Peking Review*, 15 July 1958, p. 11; Ng, *The Russian hero*, pp. 278-279; Minick and Jiao, *Chinese Graphic Design*, pp. 108-109. Cohen, *The New Chinese Painting*, p. 51.

INAPPROPRIATE GLOOMINESS: Cohen, *The New Chinese Painting*, p. 90.

IDEALIZATION: Minick and Jiao, *Chinese Graphic Design*, p. 106; see also pp. 110-111. Early examples of this 'Illustrator Realism' can be found in *Zhonghua renmin gongheguo fazhan guomin jingjide di'yige wunian jihua (1953-1957) tujie* and Tongsu duwu chubanshe (ed.), *Zhongguo gongchandang guanyu di'erge wunian jihuade jianyi huace*.

LABOUR EXPERIENCE: Minick and Jiao deplore the destruction of minority and folk traditions by the retraining processes to which many peasant artists were subject- ed. See *Chinese Graphic Design*, pp. 108-113; Laing, *The Winking Owl*, pp. 30-32. The peasant painters from Jiangsu in particular received national attention. p. 83.

PAGE 39

RAISING OF STANDARDS: Donald A. Gibbs, 'Shao Ch'üan-lin and the 'Middle Character' Controversy', Kai-yu Hsu (ed.), *Literature of the People's Republic of China*, pp. 642-652. Joe C. Huang, *Heroes and Villains in Communist China; The Contemporary Chinese Novel as a Reflection of Life*. Liang, *The Winking Owl*, p. 50. Chang, *Painting in the People's Republic of China*, pp. 74-75.

WESTERN TECHNIQUES: Minick and Jiao, *Chinese Graphic Design*, pp. 106-107, 114-115; Laing, *The Winking Owl*, pp. 37-38, 40-41, 45, 51.

THE PLA: C.S. Chen (ed.), *Rural People's Communes in Lien-chiang; Documents Concerning Communes in Lien-chiang County, Fukien Province, 1962-1963*. Richard Baum and Frederick C. Teiwes, *Ssu-Ch'ing: The Socialist Education Movement of 1962-1966* (China Research Monographs No. 2). Brugger, *Contemporary China*, pp. 241-280. Stefan R. Landsberger, *'After the Bumper Harvest': China's Socialist Education Movement as seen through short stories from the Sixties*, zzoa Working Paper No. 46.

PAGE 40

HYPERREALISTIC POLITICAL ART: Laing, *The Winking Owl*, pp. 54-56; Minick and Jiao, *Chinese Graphic Design*, p. 120.

JIANG QING: Jiang Qing's policies were laid down in the Summary of the Forum on the Work in Literature and Art in the Armed Forces with which Comrade Lin Piao entrusted Comrade Chiang Ch'ing.

THE THEMES THAT WERE ADDRESSED: Laing, *The Winking Owl*, pp. 71, 73-75; Minick and Jiao, *Chinese Graphic Design*, pp. 128-129.

PAGE 44

THEIR VERSION OF CONSENSUS: Bonnell, 'The Peasant Woman', p. 81. Minick and Jiao, *Chinese Graphic Design*, p. 120; Laing, *The Winking Owl*, pp. 64-65; Lucian W. Pye, 'Communication and Political Culture in China', Godwin C. Chu and Francis L.K. Hsu (eds.), *Moving a Mountain; Cultural Change in China*, pp. 157-167, 173-175.

KITCHEN GOD: James T. Myers, 'Religious Aspects of the Cult of Mao Tse-tung', *Current Scene*, Vol. X, No. 3 (10 March 1972), pp. 2, 7. Laing, *The Winking Owl*, pp. 66-67; Minick and Jiao, *Chinese Graphic Design*, pp. 124-125.

PAGE 56

SOURCE-BOOKS: Laing, *The Winking Owl*, pp. 82-84. Jutta Bewig, 'Huxian — die Heimat der Bauernmalerei', in Jutta Bewig (ed.), *Bauernmalerei aus Huxian*, pp. 15-18. Liu Zhide et al., *Huxian nongminhua. Huxian nongminhua*. Guowuyuan wenhuazu meishu zuopin zhengji xiaozu (ed.), *Shanghai, Yangquan, Lüda gongrenhua zhanlan zuopin xuanji*. Yangquanshi renmin wenhuaguan (eds.), *Yangquan gongren huaxuan*. Renmin meishu chubanshe (eds.), *Renwuhua xizuozuan*. Shanghai renmin chubanshe (eds.), *Renwuhua cankao ziliao*. Tianjin renmin meishu chubanshe (eds.), *Gongnongbing xingxiang xuan* Vols. 2 and 3. The journal *Meishu* published similar stereotypes in the early 1970s.

PAGE 61

SHIFTING PRIORITIES: Chu-yüan Cheng, 'The Modernization of Chinese Industry', Richard Baum (ed.), *China's Four Modernizations — The New Technological Revolution*, p. 41. Martin Lockett, 'The Urban Economy', Robert Benewick and Paul Wingrove (eds.), *Reforming the Revolution — China in Transition*, p. 114.

CRITICIZING THE GANG OF FOUR: Ningxia Huizu zizhiqu zhanlanguan (ed.), *Bokai 'Sirenbang' huapi* and Renmin ribao she (ed.), *Chu sihai manhua ji (er)*. For a discussion of the artistic freedom in the cartoons of the late 1970s, see Ralph C. Croizier, 'The Thorny Flowers of 1979: Political Cartoons and Liberalization in China', Bulletin of Concerned Asian Scholars (ed.), *China From Mao to Deng; The Politics and Economics of Socialist Development*, pp. 29-38. Perry Link, 'The Limits of Cultural Reform in Deng Xiaoping's China', *Modern China*, Vol. 13, No. 2 (April 1987), p. 157.

PEOPLE OF ALL WALKS...: Chang, *Painting in the People's Republic of China*, p. 75; Michael Sullivan, 'Painting with a New Brush: Art in Post-Mao China', Robert B. Oxnam and Richard C. Bush (eds.), *China Briefing*, 1980, p. 53.

PAGE 66

DURING THE CULTURAL REVOLUTION...: Hu Yaobang, 'On the Party's Journalism Work (1985)', Brantly Womack (ed.), *Media and the Chinese Public: A Survey of the Beijing Media Audience*, p. 179.

IMPROVING THE LIVELIHOOD: Peter R. Moody Jr., 'Spiritual Crisis in Contemporary China: Some Preliminary Explorations', *Issues & Studies*, June 1987, p. 41.

OWNERSHIP OF RADIOS: Minick and Jiao, *Chinese Graphic Design in the Twentieth Century*, pp. 131, 134; Lowell Dittmer, 'China's "Opening to the Outside World": The Cultural Dimension', *Journal of Northeast Asian Studies*, Vol. 6, No. 2 (Summer 1987), p. 7; James Lull, *China Turned On: Television, Reform, and Resistance*, pp. 17, 62, 64, 76-77, 154.

PAGE 67

PRE-EMINENCE: Michel Bonnin and Yves Chevrier, 'The Intellectual and The State: Social Dynamics of Intellectual Autonomy During the Post-Mao Era', *The China Quarterly*, No. 127 (September 1991), p. 573. Thomas B. Gold, 'Guerrilla Interviewing Among the Getihu', Perry Link, Richard Madsen and Paul G. Pickowicz (eds.), *Unofficial China — Popular Culture and Thought in the People's Republic*, pp. 175-176.

MAO'S CONTRIBUTIONS: *Resolution on CPC History (1949-81)*, pp. 46, 47, 56.

CONSERVATIVE ELEMENTS: In October 1983, Deng defined 'spiritual pollution' as 'disseminating all varieties of corrupt and decadent ideologies of the bourgeoisie and other exploiting classes and disseminating sentiments of distrust towards the socialist and communist cause and to the Communist Party leadership'. Thomas B.

Gold, 'Just in Time!', *Asian Survey*, Vol. xxiv, No. 9 (September 1984), p. 952.

RESISTING BOURGEOIS LIBERALISM: The task of the 'Anti-Bourgeois Liberalization Campaign' centred around the criticism of: American-style democracy; the capitalist system; the idea of all-round Westernization; and the Taiwanese experience. See An-chia Wu, 'The Anti-Bourgeois Liberalization Campaign: Its Background, Tasks and Impact', *Issues & Studies*, June 1987, p. 18.

FIVE MAJOR PURGES: These political campaigns took place in March 1979 (the anti-liberalization campaign and the promulgation of the 'Four Basic Principles'), in January 1980 (the attack on 'negative social effects'), in August 1981 (the campaign against the film *Kulian* [Unrequited Love], based on the novel by PLA writer Bai Hua), in October 1983 (the 'anti-spiritual pollution campaign'); and in January 1987 (the 'anti-bourgeois liberalization campaign'). See Geremie Barmé, 'The Chinese Velvet Prison: Culture in the "New Age", 1976-89', *Issues & Studies*, August 1989, p. 66.

PAGE 68

FOOD PRODUCTION: Based on Marc Blecher, 'The Reorganisation of the Countryside', Robert Benewick and Paul Wingrove (eds.), *Reforming the Revolution — China in Transition*, pp. 91-107.

QUOTA: Blecher, 'The Reorganisation of the Countryside', p. 96. Zhan Wu and Liu Wenpu, 'Agriculture', Yu Guangyuan (ed.), *China's Socialist Modernization*, pp. 225-234. Renmin ribao nongcunbu, 'Women dui nongcun shengchan zerenzhide xuanchuan', *Zhongguo xinwen nianjian 1983*, pp. 145-147.

PAGE 70

INCREASED EFFICIENCY: Lin Senmu, Zhou Shulian and Qi Mingchen, 'Industry and Transport', Yu (ed.), *China's Socialist Modernization*, pp. 323-328. Martin Lockett, 'The Urban Economy', Benewick and Wingrove (eds.), *Reforming the Revolution*, pp. 113-115.

PLA BUDGET: Lonnie D. Henley, 'China's Military Modernization: A Ten Year Assessment', Larry M. Wortzel (ed.), *China's Military Modernization — International Implications*, p. 98.

PRODUCTIVE FORCES: Tong Dalin and Hu Ping, 'Science and Technology', Yu (ed.), *China's Socialist Modernization*, p. 625. Saich, China's Science Policy, pp. 12, 147.

CIVILIAN USE: Saich, China's Science Policy, pp. 12-19.

ACADEMIC EXCELLENCE: Tong and Hu, 'Science and Technology', p. 625.

PAGE 74

SUSPICIONS: Dittmer, 'China's Opening to the Outside World', pp. 7, 10-12.

REDUCED THE STATE'S CAPACITY: Liu Jianming, *Deng Xiaoping xuanchuan sixiang yanjiu*, pp. 230, 233. Stanley Rosen, 'The Impact of Reform Policies on Youth Attitudes', Deborah Davis and Ezra F. Vogel (eds.), *Chinese Society on the Eve of Tiananmen — The Impact of Reform*, p. 290. Richard Baum, 'Epilogue: Communism, Convergence, and China's Political Convulsion', Richard Baum (ed.), *Reform and Reaction in Post-Mao China: The Road through Tiananmen*, p. 193.

CLASS-HATE: Renmin ribao nongcunbu, 'Women dui nongcun shengchan zerenzhide xuanchuan', pp. 146-147; and An Gang, 'Jingji xuanchuan zhide dashu teshude yinian', p. 70.

CONSECUTIVE CAMPAIGNS: Michel Bonnin and Yves Chevrier, 'The Intellectual and the State: Social Dynamics of Intellectual Autonomy During the Post-Mao Era', *The China Quarterly*, No. 127 (September 1991), p. 576. Thomas Fingar, 'Recent Policy Trends in Industrial Science and Technology', Richard Baum (ed.), *China's Four Modernizations: The New Technological Revolution*, p. 71. See also Man Yuanlai, 'Xinwen xuanchuan yu shangpin jingji', p. 70.

PAGE 75

REAL EXAMPLES: Lü et al. (eds.), *Dangde jianshe qishinian jishi 1919-1991*, p. 527. Guangming ribao zongbianshi, 'Gaijin renwu baodao, tuchu zhishi fenzide xuanchuan', p. 151.

PLAIN OLD...: Alan P.L. Liu, 'Problems in Communications in China's Modernization', *Asian Survey*, Vol. xxii, No. 5 (May 1982), p. 482, and 'Political Decay on Mainland China: On Crises of Faith, Confidence and Trust', *Issues & Studies*, August 1982, pp. 24-38. Peter R. Moody Jr., 'Spiritual Crisis in Contemporary China: Some Preliminary Explorations', *Issues & Studies*, June 1987, pp. 34-66, 55, 59. Victor C. Falkenheim, 'Popular Values and Political Reform: The 'Crisis of Faith' in Contemporary China', Sidney L. Greenblatt, Richard W. Wilson and Amy Auerbacher Wilson (eds.), *Social Interaction in Chinese Society*, pp. 237-251.

SIDE-EFFECTS: Li Peilin, 'Problems in China's Social Transformation', *Social Sciences in China*, Vol. 14, No. 3 (Autumn 1993), pp. 23-34.

PAGE 76

RED-EYE DISEASE: Ann Anagnost, 'Prosperity and Counterprosperity: The Moral Discourse on Wealth in Post-Mao China', Arif Dirlik and Maurice Meisner (eds.), *Marxism and the Chinese Experience: Issues in Contemporary Chinese Socialism*, p. 220. An Gang, 'Jingji xuanchuan zhide dashu teshude yinian', p. 70.

PRIVATE ENTREPRENEURS: Thomas B. Gold, 'Urban Private Business and Social Change', Deborah Davis and Ezra F. Vogel (eds.), *Chinese Society on the Eve of Tiananmen — The Impact of Reform*, p. 164.

SUB-CAMPAIGNS: Stanley Rosen, 'The Impact of Reform Policies on Youth Attitudes', Davis and Vogel (eds.), *Chinese Society on the Eve of Tiananmen*, pp. 303-305.

NAIVE ATTEMPTS: Lull, *China Turned On*, pp. 79, 83, 84, 125.

PAGE 78

FOREIGN PRODUCTS: John Gittings, *China Changes Face — The Road from Revolution 1949-1989*, p. 254; Stross, 'The Return of Advertising in China', pp. 485-502.

EDUCATED YOUTH: Frederick C. Teiwes, *Politics & Purges in China — Rectification and the Decline of Party Norms, 1950-1965*, p. 42. Moody, 'Spiritual Crisis', pp. 41, 56. Link, 'The Limits of Cultural Reform', p. 123.

TITLES REINSTATED: Guangming ribao zongbianshi, 'Gaijin renwu baodao, tuchu zhishi fenzide xuanchuan', pp. 152-153; and Xing Fangqun, 'Guanyu xuanchuan xianjin renwu he xianjin dianxingde jidian yijian', p. 128. Saich, *China's Science Policy*, pp. 12-13, 17-18.

PAGE 79

NEW IDEAS: 'Speech Greeting the Fourth Congress of Chinese Writers and Artists', Editorial Committee for Party Literature under the Central Committee of the Communist Party of China (ed.), *Selected Works of Deng Xiaoping*, pp. 200-207. John Fitzgerald, 'A New Cultural Revolution: The Commercialisation of Culture in China', *Australian Journal of Chinese Affairs*, No. 11, January 1984, p. 105; Thomas B. Gold, 'Youth and the State', *The China Quarterly*, No. 127 (September 1991), p. 600; Dittmer, 'China's Opening to the Outside World', p. 3. Liang Heng and Judith Shapiro, *Intellectual Freedom in China After Mao — with a Focus on 1983* (New York: Fund for Free Expression, 1984), pp. 13, 87. Wang He, 'Traditional Culture and Modernization — A Review of the General Situation of Cultural Studies in China in Recent Years', *Social Sciences in China*, Vol. 7, No. 4, Winter 1986, p. 22.

CORRECT THOUGHTS: Liu, *Deng Xiaoping xuanchuan sixiang yanjiu*, pp. 226-228, 236; Hu Yaobang, 'On the Party's Journalism Work', p. 176. For an overview of the theoretical debates on the relationship between politics and arts following Deng's pronouncement, see Yu Shiqian, Li Yuzhen, Chen Jianzhuo, Hu Rongzhi and Lin Qinshu (eds.), *Xin shiqi wenyi xuelunzheng ziliao (1976-1985) shang, xia*. See also Liang and Shapiro, *Intellectual Freedom*, pp. 76, 95.

RECENT CCP-POLICIES: Bennett Lee, 'Introduction', Lu Xinhua et al., *The Wounded; New Stories of the Cultural Revolution, 77-78*, pp. 3-5. Jerome Silbergeld with Gong Jisui, *Contradictions: Artistic Life, the Socialist State and the Chinese Painter Li Huasheng*, pp. 86-87. Perry Link, 'The Limits of Cultural Reform in Deng Xiaoping's China', *Modern China*, Vol. 13, No. 2 (April 1987), pp. 119-121. Hans van Dijk, 'Painting in China after the Cultural Revolution: Style Developments and Theoretical Debates. Part I: 1979-1985', *China Information*, Vol. 6, No. 3, Winter 1991-1992, pp. 30-32. Joan Lebold Cohen, *The New Chinese Painting 1949-1986*, pp. 98, 99, 101.

PAGE 82

ABSTRACT ART: Cohen, *The New Chinese Painting*, pp. 76-7, 106-7; van Dijk, 'Painting in China', pp. 28, 32.

INSTANT MODERNIZATION: Bruce Doar, 'Speculation in a Distorting Mirror: Scientific and Political Fantasy in Contemporary Chinese Writing', *Australian Journal of Chinese Affairs*, No. 8 (1982), pp. 55-56, 57. Rudolf G. Wagner, 'Lobby Literature: The Archaeology and Present Functions of Science Fiction in China', Jeffrey C. Kinkley (ed.), *After Mao: Chinese Literature and Society 1978-1981*, pp. 17-62. Despite Doar's and Wagner's observations, the use of science fiction in literature came under attack during the spiritual pollution campaign; see Liang and Shapiro, *Intellectual Freedom*, pp. 141-143.

SING THE PRAISES...: Zheng Wenguang in his postface to *Feixiang renmazou*, p. 282, as translated by Doar, p. 57. See also Wagner, 'Lobby Literature', pp. 22-23.

PAGE 87

EXPLOSIVE DIVERSIFICATION: Richard Kraus, 'China's Cultural 'Liberalization' and Conflict over the Social Organization of the Arts', *Modern China*, Vol. IX, No. 2 (April 1983), p. 221; Minick and Jiao, *Chinese Graphic Design*, p. 134.

REFORM PROGRAM: Moody, 'Spiritual Crisis', p. 36.

PAGE 88

MORAL MESSAGES: Gittings, *China Changes Face*, p. 254.

ART SUPPLIES: Kraus, 'China's Cultural Liberalization' p. 219; Minick and Jiao, *Chinese Graphic Design*, p. 134; van Dijk, 'Painting in China', p. 36; Michael Sullivan, 'Painting with a New Brush: Art in Post-Mao China', Robert B. Oxnam and Richard C. Bush (eds.), *China Briefing*, 1980, p. 60. Ellen Johnston Laing, 'Contemporary Painting', The Committee on Scholarly Communication with the People's Republic of China (ed.), *Traditional and Contemporary Painting in China; A Report of the Visit of the Chinese Painting Delegation to the People's Republic of China*, pp. 54-55, 67

CHINESE IDENTITY: James L. Watson mentions the following elements of a shared culture: the role of an ideographic, non-phonetic script; the autocratic power of the Chinese state; the elaborate hierarchy of commercial centres and marketing communities; a shared oral tradition, and the central role of ritual. See 'The Renegotiation of Chinese Cultural Identity in the Post-Mao Era', Jeffrey N. Wasserstrom and Elizabeth J. Perry (eds.), *Popular Protest and Political Culture in Modern China: Learning from 1989*, p. 71. Link, 'The Limits of Cultural Reform', p. 137; van Dijk, 'Painting in China', pp. 25, 40.

OFFICIAL PAINTERS: Kraus, 'China's Cultural Liberalization', p. 218, 220. Miklós Haraszti, *The Velvet Prison; Artists under State Socialism* (New York: Basic Books, Inc., 1987). Barmé, 'The Chinese Velvet Prison', p. 70. Van Dijk, 'Painting in China', pp. 40, 41. According to Silbergeld, East coast artists saw their inspiration by foreign styles as a source of renewal for their art. Contradictions, p. 87.

PAGE 89

GALLERIES: McDougall, 'Breaking Through', p. 59; Zhang and Sang, *Chinese Profiles*, pp. 205-206. Gittings, *China Changes Face*, p. 254, also mentions the 'salons' where showings are organized that can be attended by invitation. Deborah Davis notes, for example, the absence of any decorations with explicit political content in the Shanghai homes she visited in 1987. See 'My Mother's House', Perry Link, Richard Madsen and Paul G. Pickowicz (eds.), *Unofficial China — Popular Culture and Thought in the People's Republic*, pp. 91, 95. Ellen Johnston Laing draws attention to the return of traditional auspicious imagery in both urban and rural domestic interiors and New Year prints. See 'The Persistence of Propriety in the 1980s', ibid., pp. 156-171.

COMPETITION: Barmé, 'The Chinese Velvet Prison', pp. 74, 75. Bonnie S. McDougall, 'Breaking Through: Literature and the Arts in China, 1976-1986', *Copenhagen Papers in East and Southeast Asian Studies*, No. 1, 1988, p. 42. Willy Kraus, *Private Unternehmerwirtschaft in der Volksrepublik China; Wiederbelebung zwischen Ideologie und Pragmatismus*, p. 3.

PAGE 90

BOOKS: Hans J. Hendrischke, *Populäre Lesestoffe — Propaganda und Agitation im Buchwesen der Volksrepublik China*, pp. 320-321.

PAGE 94

WHAT IS PROPER...: China News Analysis 1234, 8 October 1982, p. 4. Hu Yaobang, 'Create a New Situation in All Fields of Socialist Modernization', Report to the 12th National Congress of the Communist Party of China, September 1, 1982, *Beijing Review*, Vol. 25, No. 37, 13 September 1982, pp. 21, 22-23. Chang Ching-li, 'Promotion of Socialist Spiritual Civilization on the Chinese Mainland', *Issues & Studies*, August 1983, p. 25. Deng Xiaoping, 'Build a Socialist Society with Both High Material and High Cultural and Ideological Standards', *Fundamental Issues in Present-Day China*, p. 11. Watson, "The Renegotiation", p. 69. Link, 'The Limits of Cultural Reform', p. 134.

CLEAR INSTRUCTIONS: Moody, 'Spiritual Crisis', p. 53. 'Gaijin renwu baodao, tuchu zhishi fenzide xuanchuan', p. 152. 'Ba jianshe jingshen wenming dangzuo xuanchuande zhongyao zhuti', pp. 209-211.

CONTINUAL DEEPENING...: Dittmer, 'China's Opening to the Outside World', p. 15. Stanley Rosen, 'The Rise (and Fall) of Public Opinion in Post-Mao China', Richard Baum (ed.), *Reform and Reaction in Post-Mao China: The Road through Tiananmen*, p. 75. Wang, 'Traditional Culture and Modernization', pp. 11, 12.

PACE OF REFORM: Stanley Rosen, 'Value Change Among Post-Mao Youth — The Evidence from Survey Data', Link, Madsen and Pickowicz (eds.), *Unofficial China*, pp. 202-203. James T. Myers, 'Socialist Spiritual Civilization and Cultural Pollution: The Problem of Meaning', *Issues & Studies*, March 1985, pp. 52, 63, 72-73, 75.

PAGE 100

POLITICAL SUBJECTS: Qian Daxin, 'Xuanchuanhua chuangzuo he chuban zongshu', p. 229.

PAGE 102

DEPARTED LEADERS: Liu Jianming, *Deng Xiaoping xuanchuan sixiang yanjiu*, pp. 60-65.

PAGE 103

MAO KNEW: See Tony Saich, 'The Fourteenth Party Congress: A Programme for Authoritarian Rule', *The China Quarterly*, No. 132 (December 1992), p. 1143.

PAGE 110

NINE MARSHALLS: The individual posters were published by Sichuan renmin chubanshe, 1982, printnos. 8118.1089, 8118.1267, 8118.1234, 8118.1326, 8118.1269, 8118.1285, 8118.1268, 8118.1270, 8118.1271.

PLA AUDIENCE: The excellent reception of this series by the Chinese peasantry is mentioned by Zhang Daoliang in 'Nianhua chuban zongshu', p. 197.

PAGE 111

ENTREPRENEURSHIP: The number of individual enterprises increased from 0.30 million in 1978 to 14.13 million in 1988. See Thomas B. Gold, 'Guerrilla Interviewing Among the Getihu', Perry Link, Richard Madsen and Paul G. Pickowicz (eds.), *Unofficial China — Popular Culture and Thought in the People's Republic*, p. 177.

PAGE 129

MAINSTREAM PEOPLE: Thomas B. Gold, 'Urban Private Business and Social Change', Deborah Davis and Ezra F. Vogel (eds.), *Chinese Society on the Eve of Tiananmen — The Impact of Reform*, p. 176. Chiang Chen-ch'ang, 'The New Lei Fengs of the 1980s', *Issues & Studies*, May 1984, p. 37. Xing Fangqun, 'Guanyu xuanchuan xianjin renwu he xianjin dianxingde jidian yijian', p. 127, advocates the need for models to have shortcomings, and warns of the danger of using 'absolute models'.

PAGE 130

IN LEI FENG...: Alan P.L. Liu, 'Opinions and Attitudes of Youth in the People's Republic of China', *Asian Survey*, Vol. xxiv, No. 9 (September 1984), p. 992.

PAGE 132

DIFFERENTIATED GROUP: Alan P.L. Liu, *How China is Ruled*, p. 331.

RECURRING EXHORTATIONS: James T. Myers, 'Whatever happened to Chairman Mao? Myth and Charisma in the Chinese Revolution', Victor C. Falkenheim and Ilpyong Kim (eds.), *Chinese Politics from Mao to Deng*, p. 33. Stanley Rosen, 'The Effects of Post-4 June Re-Education Campaigns on Chinese Students', *The China Quarterly*, No. 134 (June 1993), pp. 321-323, supplies information on Lei's decline as a model in 1988.

PAGE 144

FACTORY WORK...: Stanley Rosen, 'Value Change Among Post-Mao Youth — The Evidence from Survey Data', Perry Link, Richard Madsen and Paul G. Pickowicz (eds.), *Unofficial China — Popular Culture and Thought in the People's Republic*, pp. 206-207.

PAGE 150

WOMEN'S FEDERATION: See 'Chinese Women Active in World Arena', *Beijing Review*, 4 March 1985, pp. 17-18.

PAGE 156

TRADITION OF THE PLA: See Lü Liang, 'Ba junshi xuanchuan fangdao shidangde weizhishang', p. 68.

PAGE 158

GREENISH COLOUR: 'Green is the colour of the painted board carried before a criminal going to be executed ...' C.A.S. Williams, *Outlines of Chinese Symbolism & Art Motives*, p. 79.

PAGE 169

PAINTINGS ARE MEANT...: Emil Preetorius, *Catalogue of the Preetorius Collection* (Munich: 1958), quoted in Wolfram Eberhard, *A Dictionary of Chinese Symbols — Hidden Symbols in Chinese Life and Thought*, p. 9.

CONFUCIAN INTERPRETATIONS: David L. Holm, 'Art and Ideology in the Yenan Period, 1937-1945', pp. 154, 157, 193-194.

NEW YEAR PICTURES: Holm, 'Art and Ideology'.

PAGE 172

VISUAL LINKS: See 'Peasant Responses to Current Pictures', described by Ellen Johnston Laing, 'The Persistence of Propriety in the 1980s', Perry Link, Richard Madsen and Paul G. Pickowicz (eds.), *Unofficial China — Popular Culture and Thought in the People's Republic*, pp. 163-169. Deborah Davis, 'My Mother's House', p. 95.

PAGE 182

TRADITIONAL NEW YEAR PICTURES: Holm, 'Art and Ideology', p. 165.

PAGE 187

LONG MARCH: John B. Thompson, 'Editor's introduction', Pierre Bourdieu, *Language and Symbolic Power*, p. 14. Lü Cheng, Zhang Zhuwu, Zhong Bihui, Su Xisheng, He Jinqing (eds.), *Dangde jianshe qishinian jishi 1919-1991*, p. 109.
WINDOW CLEANING: See Joan Lebold Cohen, *The New Chinese Painting 1949-1986*, p. 105.

PAGE 190

TRADITIONAL IDEALS: Laing, 'Persistence of Propriety', pp. 159-160.
DOVE: See Williams, *Outlines of Chinese Symbolism*, p. 131.

PAGE 191

DUODUO: Duoduo, 'Het is geld en anders niets', *NRC-Handelsblad*, 18 June 1993.
UPWARD MOBILITY: Holm, 'Art and Ideology', p. 151.
RED: Stephen White, *The Bolshevik Poster* (New Haven CT and London: Yale University Press, 1988), p. 5; Williams, *Outlines of Chinese Symbols*, pp. 76, 78; Eberhard, *Dictionary of Chinese Symbols*, pp. 248-249.

PAGE 194

ELEGANT COLOURS: Zhang Daoliang, 'Nianhua chuban zongshu', p. 197.

PAGE 200

RED SPOT: Eberhard, *Dictionary of Chinese Symbols*, p. 249.
BLUE: Eberhard, *Dictionary of Chinese Symbols*, pp. 42-43.

PAGE 201

LOTUS: Eberhard, *Dictionary of Chinese Symbols*, pp. 168-169.
CRANES: Eberhard, *Dictionary of Chinese Symbols*, p. 75.

PAGE 206

FOREIGN TELEVISION: In this respect, mention should be made of such popular Chinese television favourites as 'Star trek', 'Man from Atlantis' and 'Falcon Crest', purchased from the United States from 1979 on. Lull, *China Turned On*, pp. 147, 149. See also Lowell Dittmer, 'China's Opening to the Outside World', p. 7; Liu, 'Communications and Development in Post-Mao Mainland China', pp. 77-78; Chang, *Mass Media in China*, p. 214.
VOICE OF THE GOVERNMENT: Lull, *China Turned On*, pp. 1, 17, 27, 79, 145.
PRESENT THE MESSAGE: Lü, 'Ba junshi xuanchuan fangdao shidangde weizhishang', p. 69, stresses this point explicitly. See also Womack (ed.), *Media and the Chinese Public*, p. 73.
COMMERCIALS: Lull, *China Turned On*, pp. 136, 169, 170, 180, 209, 214; Womack (ed.), *Media and the Chinese Public*, p. 73.

PAGE 207

EXHORTATIONS: James Lull, *China Turned On: Television, Reform, and Resistance*, p. 18.
CORRECTNESS OF POLICY DIRECTIVES: An Gang, 'We Must Have a Serious Attitude Toward Surveys of the Media Audience', Brantly Womack (ed.), *Media and the Chinese Public: A Survey of the Beijing Media Audience*, pp. 54-59. The volume edited by Womack contains Chinese media surveys, as does David S.K. Chu (ed. and transl.), 'Sociology and Society in Contemporary China 1979-1983', special issue of *Chinese Sociology and Anthropology*, Vol. xvi, No. 1-2 (Fall-Winter 1983-1984).
FACTIONAL CONFLICTS: An-chia Wu, 'The Anti-Bourgeois Liberalization Campaign: Its Background, Tasks and Impact', *Issues & Studies*, June 1987, p. 13; Lucian W. Pye, 'Communication and Political Culture in China', Godwin C. Chu and Francis L.K. Hsu (eds.), *Moving a Mountain; Cultural Change in China*, pp. 154, 174.

PAGE 208

CONSERVATIVE REACTION: James T. Myers, 'Whatever happened to Chairman Mao? Myth and Charisma in the Chinese Revolution', Victor C. Falkenheim, Ilpyong Kim (eds.), *Chinese Politics from Mao to Deng*, p. 32; Pye, 'Communication and Political Culture', p. 166, mentions that the choice of models is at times a matter of intra-elite 'struggles'.
GREAT NUMBERS OF JOURNALS: The most well-known of these was the *Shijie jingji daobao* [World Economic Herald], published in Shanghai. Chang Won Ho, *Mass Media in China: The History and the Future*, pp. 130-150.
CORRUPT BEHAVIOUR: Various personal observations, including in Guilin, *Spring 1984*. See also Stephen K. Ma, 'Reform Corruption: A Discussion on China's Current Development', *Pacific Affairs*, Vol. 62, No. 1 (Spring 1989), pp. 40-52.

PAGE 210

GLASNOST POSTERS: Viktor Litvinov, in Yegorov and Litvinov (eds.), *The Posters of Glasnost and Perestroika*, p. 1.
IMAGINARY WORLD: Pye, 'Communication and Political Culture', pp. 168, 175.

Ayi you song zanba laile [Auntie has also come to bring zanba], Shanghai renmin chubanshe, early 1970s, No. 86.677

Ai kexue, qin tansuo [Love science, explore diligently], Guangzhou branch Kexue puji chubanshe, July 1985, No. 8051.60413

Ai laodong [Love labor], Shanghai renmin meishu chubanshe, February 1983, No. 8081.13386

Ai renmin [Love the people], Shanghai renmin meishu chubanshe, February 1983, No. 8081.13385

Ai shehui zhuyi [Love Socialism], Shanghai renmin meishu chubanshe, February 1983, No. 8081.13388

Ai weisheng, jiang wenming [Love hygiene, stress civilization], Shanghai renmin meishu chubanshe, April 1983, No. 8081.13397

Ai wo Zhonghua, ai wo changcheng [I love my China, I love my Great Wall], Guangzhou branch Kexue puji chubanshe, July 1985, No. 8051.60407

Ai xuexi, ai laodong [Love study, love labor], Shanghai renmin meishu chubanshe, early 1970s, No. 86-829

Aiguo shouxian yao zhiguo — zhi zhi yu shen, ai zhi yu qie [To love the country one must first know its history — the deeper the knowledge, the more eager the love], Zhejiang renmin meishu chubanshe, January 1984, No. 8156.456

Aihu lühua, zhenxi gushu mingmu [Cherish greening, treasure old and famous trees], Shanghai renmin meishu chubanshe, March 1983, No. 8081.13286

Anquan shengchan, wenmin shengchan [Safe production, intelligent production], Shanghai renmin meishu chubanshe, April 1984, No. 8081.14021

Bai die ying chunchun geng yan [A hundred butterflies welcome an even more colourful spring], Renmin meishu chubanshe, early 1970s, No. 86-833

Baiwen buyan, baitiao bufan [Don't be fed up with a hundred questions, don't be irritated by a hundred choices], Shanghai renmin meishu chubanshe, June 1983, No. 8081.13550

Baiyangdianshang lian wumang [Busy practising martial arts on Lake Baiyangdian], Renmin meishu chubanshe, November 1976, No. 8027.6139

Bangzhu xiao tongxue [Helping a little schoolmate], Shandong renmin chubanshe, July 1982, No. 8099.2378

Baobao renzi tu [Baby recognizes characters], Shandong meishu chubanshe, May 1986, No. 8332.646

Baochi huanjing weisheng [Protect environmental hygiene], Liaoning meishu chubanshe, February 1983, No. 8161.02802

Bixu jianchi Ma Lie zhuyi Mao Zedong sixiang [Firmly uphold Marxism-Leninism, Mao Zedong Thought], Zhejiang renmin meishu chubanshe, January 1984, No. 8156.460

Bixu jianchi shehui zhuyi daolu [Firmly uphold the socialist course], Zhejiang renmin meishu chubanshe, January 1984, No. 8156.459

Bixu jianchi wuchan jieji zhuanzheng [Firmly uphold proletarian dictatorship], Zhejiang renmin meishu chubanshe, January 1984, No. 8156.461

Bianjiang tieqi [Border cavalry], Shanghai renmin meishu chubanshe, September 1978, No. 8081.11252

Brigade Chicken Farm, Renmin meishu chubanshe, c. March 1973, No. 86-626

The Brigade's Ducks, Renmin meishu chubanshe, c. March 1973, No. 86-625

Bu kao tian [Not depending on the sky], Shanghai renmin chubanshe, early 1970s, No. 86-663

Caicai kan [Looking to guess], Renmin meishu chubanshe, early 1970s, No. 86-837

Caoyuan lian Beijing [The grasslands are connected with Beijing], Hebei renmin chubanshe, October 1977, No. 8086.695

Chen Yi, Sichuan renmin chubanshe, 1982, No. 8118.1285

Chen Zhen, Tianjin renmin meishu chubanshe, August 1985, No. 8073.20949

Chun chu [Spring hoeing], Shanghai renmin chubanshe, early 1970s, No. 86-617

Chunfeng chuinuan shao nü xin [Spring wind warmly blows on a young girl's heart], Fazhi xuanchuan chuchuang no. 4, three sheets, colour, Falü chubanshe, December 1983, No. 8004.005

Chunyu [Spring rain], Shanghai renmin chubanshe, early 1970s, No. 86-664

Ci liang shou [Two poems (by Mao Zedong)], Renmin meishu chubanshe, early 1970s, No. 86-683

The Commune's Fishpond, Renmin meishu chubanshe, c. March 1973, No. 86-624

Cong xiao jiang weisheng [Practising hygiene from an early age], Gansu renmin chubanshe, September 1982, No. 8096.797

Cong xiao yangcheng haode xiguan, aihao, qingqu [Foster good habits, hobbies and interests from an early age on], Sichuan renmin chubanshe, May 1985, No. 8118.1439

Cong xiaoxue yingmo, zhangda jian qigong [Studying illustrious models when small, performing outstanding service when grown up], Chongqing chubanshe, July 1986, No. 8114.464

Dafenglangli lian hongxin [Tempering red hearts in stormy waves], Renmin meishu chubanshe, early 1970s, No. 86-681

Dadui tushushi [The production brigade's reading room], Shanghai renmin chubanshe, July 1974, No. 8171.824

Dazhai tianshang xiao Yu Gong [Little Yu Gong's on the fields of Dazhai], Shanghai renmin chubanshe, May 1977, No. 8171.1947

Dazhan quyuhe [Great struggle against crooked valleys and rivers], Shanghai renmin chubanshe, May 1975, No. 8171.893

Dangdai Yu Gong hui xintu [Contemporary Yu Gong's draw a new picture], two sheets, Shanghai renmin chubanshe, June 1974, No. 8171.892

Dangxin chudian [Be careful around live wires]; Shanghai renmin chubanshe, February 1981, No. 8081.12423

Dangxin chuojiao [Be careful not to stab your foot], Shanghai renmin meishu chubanshe, April 1984, No. 8081.14027

Dangxin jixie shangren [Be careful around dangerous machinery], Shanghai renmin meishu chubanshe, April 1984, No. 8081.14026

Dong Cunruide gushi [The story of Dong Cunrui], Renmin meishu chubanshe, August 1974, No. 86-639

Dushu he xiezi zishi [Posture for reading and writing], Shanghai jiaoyu chubanshe, January 1981, No. 7150.1388

Duanlian shenti, duanlian yizhi, wei shixian sige xiandaihua gongxian liliang [Build up a good physique, steel the will, to contribute strength to the realization of the Four Modernizations], Renmin tiyu chubanshe, July 1979, No. 8015.1792

Duogan shishi, shao shuo konghua — Deng Xiaoping [We should do more and engage less in empty talk — Deng Xiaoping], Guangxi meishu chubanshe, August 1992, No. 880582.242

Fayang jianku fendoude chuangye jingshen [Develop the spirit for the bitter struggle of doing pioneering work], Tianjin renmin meishu chubanshe, September 1980, No. 8073.10245

Fanhuade Shanghai Nanjing Lu [The bustling Nanjing Lu of Shanghai], Shanghai renmin meishu chubanshe, June 1989, No. 85322.16083

Fanghuo fangbao [Prevention of fires and explosions], Shanghai renmin meishu chubanshe, April 1984, No. 8081.14023

Fangxiang sa renjian [Scattering fragrance among the people], Shanghai renmin meishu chubanshe, June 1987, No. 8081.15157

Fei xiang taikong [Flying towards outer space], Tianjin renmin meishu chubanshe, June 1979, No. 8073.20390

Fengshou changshang pi xinzhuang [Spreading out new clothes on a bumper harvest market], Shanghai renmin chubanshe, early 1970s, No. 86-675

Fengshou mang [Busy with a bumper harvest], Renmin meishu chubanshe, early 1970s, No. 86-584

Gaige kaifang danzi yao da yixie, ganyu shiyan, bu neng xiang xiaojiao nüren yixiang. Kan zhunlede, jiu dadande shi, dadande chuang — Deng Xiaoping [In the process of reform and opening up, we must be a little more courageous, and we must dare to experiment; we cannot be like women with bound feet. If it looks acceptable, we must courageously experiment, courageously charge — Deng Xiaoping], Guangxi meishu chubanshe, August 1992, No. 880582.243

Gaohao jihua shengyu, cujin jingji fazhan [Do a good job in family planning to promote economic development], Xin jiating baoshe (Liaoning), 1986, not numbered

Gaoyuan shengkai Dazhai hua [The flower of Dazhai is in full bloom on the plateau], Shanghai renmin chubanshe, early 1970s, No. 86-673

Gege zhengdang xiao Lei Feng [All strive to become little Lei Fengs], Shanghai renmin meishu chubanshe, August 1978, No. 8081.11274

Gege zunshou zhixu, renren zhuyi shehui gongde [Everybody observes order, everybody pays attention to social morality], Renmin meishu chubanshe, January 1983, No. 8027.8673

Geming you youle zhangduoren [The revolution still has a helmsman], Shanghai renmin chubanshe, 1977, No. 8171.1941

Gongchan zhuyi yiding yao shixian — Jinian Kaer Makesi shishi yibai zhounian [Communism will certainly be realized — commemorate the day that Karl Marx died 100 years ago], Renmin meishu chubanshe, January 1983, No. 8027.8634

Gonghe xinxi [Happy New Year], Shanghai renmin meishu chubanshe, early 1970s, No. 86-821

Gongshang daji [Discussing great plans together], Tianjin Yangliuqing huashe, June 1985, No. 8174.629

Gongshe chun changzai [It's always spring in the commune], Shaanxi renmin chubanshe, early 1970s, No. 86-691

Gongshede jieri [National Day in the Commune], Renmin meishu chubanshe, early 1970s, No. 86-680

Gongshe zhi chun [Commune's Spring], Hebei renmin chubanshe, October 1977, No. 8086.674

Gongtongde xinyuan [Common aspirations], Shanghai renmin chubanshe, July 1977, No. 8171.1940

Gongye qianqiu xingfu wandai [Achievements and happiness throughout the ages], Tianjin Yangliuqing huashe, June 1990, No. 7-80503.2528

Gushou bianfang [Defending the Borders tenaciously], Yunnan renmin chubanshe, August 1989, No. 8222.1776

Guangzhao qianqiu [Glorious through the ages], Shanghai renmin meishu chubanshe, 1985, No. 8081.14007

Guoqi zai women xinzhong shengqi [The national flag is hoisted in our hearts], Zhongguo xiju chubanshe, October 1984, No. 8069.620

Haigang xinmao [New appearance of the harbour], Shanghai renmin chubanshe, January 1977, No. 7171.926

Haohao xuexi, tiantian xiangshang [Study well, improve daily], Tianjin renmin meishu chubanshe, September 1978, No. 8073.20354

He Long, Sichuan renmin chubanshe, 1982, No. 8118.1326

Hua zhuxi, gezu renmin re'ai nin! [Chairman Hua, the people of all minorities warmly love you!], Jiangsu renmin chubanshe, September 1978, No. 8100.2.305

Hua zhuxi shi zan linglu ren [Chairman Hua shows us the way], Tianjin Yangliuqing huashe, September 1978, No. 8174.087

Huandu jiajie [Celebrate a festival with jubilation], Tianjin renmin meishu chubanshe, 1983, No. 8073.20786

Huanghe gudao hua guoxiang [The fragrance of flowers and fruit in the former course of the Yellow River], Jiangsu renmin chubanshe, September 1973 (?), No. 8100.2.064

Huibi shu haoqing [Putting brush to paper to express lofty sentiments], Shanghai renmin meishu chubanshe, July 1980, No. 8081.11885

Huo Yuanjia, Tianjin renmin meishu chubanshe, August 1985, No. 8073.20948

Jicheng geming chuantong, zhili zhenxing Zhonghua [Carry on the revolutionary tradition, work for the vigorous development of China], Renmin meishu chubanshe, April 1984, No. 8027.9202

Jihua shengyu kepu huabao [Posters popularizing the science of family planning], three sheets, Liaoningsheng jihua shengyu xuanchuan jiaoyu fenzhongxin, 1986, not numbered

Jiji canjia laodong, aixi laodong chengguo [Take part in labor enthusiastically, cherish the fruits of labor], Renmin meishu chubanshe, May 1982, No. 8027.8321

Jinian quan shijie wuchan jiejide weida daoshi Makesi shishi yibai zhounian [Commemorate the day that Marx, the greatest proletarian instructor of the world, died 100 years ago], Shanghai renmin meishu chubanshe, February 1983, No. 8081.13424

Jiaqiang laodong baohu, gaohao anquan shengchan [Strengthen labor safety, make a good job of safe production], Shanghai renmin meishu chubanshe, February 1981, No. 8081.12419

Jianjue weihu funü ertongde hefa liyi [Firmly protect the legal rights and interests of women and children], Falü chubanshe, December 1983, No. 8004.002

Jiangjiu weisheng yufang jibing [Pay attention to hygiene, take precautions against disease], Shanghai renmin meishu chubanshe, April 1983, No. 8081.13395

Jiefangjun [People's Liberation Army], Shanghai jiaoyu chubanshe, June 1980, No. 7150.1461

Jiemei liang [Two sisters], Renmin meishu chubanshe, early 1970s, No. 86-642

Jinfang qizhong shanghai [Guard against injuries while hoisting], Shanghai renmin meishu chubanshe, April 1984, No. 8081.14028

Jintian women zhiri [Today we are on duty], by Shanghai jiaoyu chubanshe, No. 7150.1323

Jingxin zhiliao, jingxin huli [Treat and nurse with the best of care], Shanghai renmin meishu chubanshe, June 1983, No. 8081.13551

Junshi da yanxi [Great war exercise], Shanghai renmin meishu chubanshe, April 1983, No. 8081.13199

Junshi da yanxi [Great war exercise], Shanghai renmin meishu chubanshe, June 1986, No. 8081.14828

Kaichuang shehui zhuyi xiandaihua jianshede weida xin jumian [Create a great new situation in socialist modernized construction], Beijing chubanshe, early 1980s, No. 8071.467

Kaichuang wenming xin shidai [Create a new age of civilization], Liaoning renmin chubanshe, February 1983, No. 8161.0282

Kaiguo dadian [Ceremony proclaiming the founding of the State], Tianjin renmin meishu chubanshe, August 1990, No. 7-5305.21807

Kexuede chuntian [Spring of science], Shanghai renmin meishu chubanshe, June 1979, No. 8081.11452

Kongjiang yanxi [Airborne manoeuvres], Shanghai renmin meishu chubanshe, August 1979, No. 8081.11602

Lao shuji [Old party secretary], Shanghai renmin chubanshe, June 1974, No. 8171.890

Lei Feng yu hong lingjin [Lei Feng and the red scarves], Renmin meishu chubanshe, May 1982, No. 8027.8100

Li Shizhen, Shanghai renmin meishu chubanshe, August 1979, No. 8081.11714

Li Xiulan zhi si [The death of Li Xiulan], Fazhi xuanchuan chuchuang no. 7, two sheets, black-and-white, Falü chubanshe, December 1983, No. 8004.008

Li Zicheng, two sheets, Renmin meishu chubanshe, July 1982, No. 8027.8048

Limao daike, reqing zhoudao, wenming jingshang [Treat customers politely, be enthusiastic and attentive, engage in trade in a cultured way], Renmin meishu chubanshe, January 1983, No. 8027.8672

Lianheguo guoji funü shinian — pingdeng, fazhan, heping [Ten years of the U.N. International women — Equality, Development, Peace], Renmin meishu chubanshe, February 1985, No. 8027.9576

Lianheguo guoji funü shinian — pingdeng, fazhan, heping — Chuangzao zuguo meihaode mingtian [Ten years of the U.N. International women — Equality, Development, Peace — Create a beautiful tomorrow for the mother country], Renmin meishu chubanshe, February 1985, No. 8027.9575

Liening ai haizi [Lenin loves children], Shanghai renmin meishu chubanshe, July 1982, No. 8081.12803

Liu Bocheng, Sichuan renmin chubanshe, 1982, No. 8118.1267

Lulu caishen jin jiamen, zhao cai zhao bao zhao ping'an [The gods of wealth enter the home from everywhere, wealth, treasures and peace beckon], Zhongguo huabao chubanshe, 1993, No. 880024.182

Lühua zuguo [Make the mother country green], Sichuan renmin chubanshe, December 1982, No. 8118.1396

Luo Ronghuan, Sichuan renmin chubanshe, 1982, No. 8118.1271

Mama jiao wo xue Lei Feng [Mama tells me to study Lei Feng], Guangdong renmin chubanshe, July 1982, No. 8099.2366

Manyuan chunse [A courtyard full of Spring colours], Shanghai renmin chubanshe, July 1977, No. 8171.1895

Mao Zedong tongzhi, Zhou Enlai tongzhi, Liu Shaoqi tongzhi, Zhu De tongzhi zai yiqi [Comrades Mao Zedong, Zhou Enlai, Liu Shaoqi and Zhu De together], Renmin meishu chubanshe, April 1982, no. 8027.7565

Mao Zedong tongzhi, Zhou Enlai tongzhi, Liu Shaoqi tongzhi, Zhu De, Deng Xiaoping tongzhi, Chen Yun tongzhi zai yiqi [Comrades Mao Zedong, Zhou Enlai, Liu Shaoqi, Zhu De, Deng Xiaoping and Chen Yun together], Renmin meishu chubanshe, December 1982, No. 8027.8292

Mao Zedong zhuxi he tade zhanyou [Chairman Mao Zedong and his comrades-in-arms], Sichuan renmin chubanshe, June 1983, No. 8118.1278

Mao zhuxi wuliang xinren Hua zhuxi, quanguo junmin relie yonghu Hua zhuxi [Chairman Mao had a boundless confidence in Chairman Hua, the people and the army of the whole nation enthusiastically support Chairman Hua], Shanghai renmin chubanshe, December 1976, No. 8171.951

Meili congming, jiankang ke'ai [Clever and pretty, healthy and lovely], Xin jiating baoshe (Liaoning), 1986, not numbered

Nie Rongzhen, Sichuan renmin chubanshe, 1982, No. 8118.1268

Nongcun gaige, xingshi xiren [The countryside is reformed, the situation pleases the people], Renmin meishu chubanshe, February 1987, No. 8027.10430

Nuli wancheng zhengdang renwu, shixian dangfeng genben haozhuan [Energetically complete the task of party rectification, bring about a basic turn for the better in party spirit], Zhejiang renmin meishu chubanshe, January 1984, No. 8156.457

Peng Dehuai, Sichuan renmin chubanshe, 1982, No. 8118.1234

Pinxue jianyou [Good character and scholarship], Chongqing chubanshe, June 1984, No. 8114.209

Qinqiede guanhuai [Showing loving care], Tianjin renmin meishu chubanshe, August 1975, No. 8073.20229

Qinfen xuexi [Study diligently], Chongqing chubanshe, June 1984, No. 8114.208

Qin xuexi shou jilü [Study diligently, observe discipline], Chongqing chubanshe, July 1986, No. 8114.461

Qingchun wubu [Youthful dancesteps], Lingnan meishu chubanshe, April 1986, No. 8260.1875

Qingnian yingxiongpu, Zhongguo qingnian chubanshe, September 1984, setno. 8009-44 (Xiang Xiuli (1933-1959), Lei Feng (1940-1962), Ouyang Hai (1940-1963), Yan Long (1960-1979), Lan Jianye (1959-1980), Cao Zhenxian (1959-1980), Zhang Hua (1958-1982), Ma Junyou (1962-1982), An Ke (1960-1983), Zhang Haidi (1955-))

Qingsong jingzhang shanhe zhuang [Young pines struggle to develop the magnificence of mountains and streams], Shanghai renmin chubanshe, July 1977, No. 8171.1894

Qingzhu liu.yi guoji ertongjie [Celebrate International Children's Day June 1], Shanghai renmin meishu chubanshe, April 1979, No. 8081.11645

Qingzhu Zhongguo gongchandang jiandang 70 zhounian [Celebrate the 70th anniversary of the founding of the Chinese Communist Party], Chongqing chubanshe, May 1991, Nos. J 5366.530-536 (*Guanghuide yeji* [A glorious, outstanding achievement], No. J 5366.532 *Dang ah dang, qin'aide dang* [Party, oh Party, Beloved Party], No. J 5366.534)

Quanguo renmin tuanjie yizhi wei quanmian kaichuang shehui zhuyi xiandaihua jianshede xin jumian er fendou [The people of the whole country unite to struggle for the creation of a completely new situation of socialist modernized construction], Sichuan renmin chubanshe, August 1983, No. 8118.1394

Quanmin zhishu, zhili heshan [The whole people plant trees and put rivers and mountains in order] Shanghai renmin meishu chubanshe, March 1983, No. 8081.13284

Quan xin quan yi [Heart-and-soul], Renmin meishu chubanshe, early 1970s, No. 86-651

Rang lixiang chashang chibang [Let idealism grow wings], Renmin meishu chubanshe, September 1979, No. 8027.7229

Rang qingchun mei zai xingwei zhong shan guang [Let youthful beauty glitter in behaviour], Shanghai renmin meishu chubanshe, March 1982, No. 8081.12978

Rang wode chengshi geng meihao [Make our cities even more beautiful], Changjiang wenyi chubanshe, April 1982, No. 8107.356

Rang womende shenghuo geng you zhixu [Let our lives have more order], Liaoning meishu chubanshe, February 1983, No. 8161.0279

Re'ai zuguo, qinfen xuexi [Love the mother country, study diligently], Shanghai renmin meishu chubanshe, September 1981, No. 8081.12753

Reqing gongping xiwang tiantian jiandao nin [I'm enthusiastic and fair, I hope to see you everyday], Shanghai renmin meishu chubanshe, March 1984, No. 8081.13952

Ren huan yu yue [People and fish jump for joy], Shanghai renmin meishu chubanshe, April 1978, No. 8081.11033

Ren Yexiang, Zhongguo dianying chubanshe, August 1983, No. 8061.2016

Renmin gongchen [People's heroes], Renmin meishu chubanshe, July 1984 (7th imprint), No. 8027.8750

Renmin liyi gao yu yiqie [The people's interest is placed above everything else], Shanghai jiaoyu chubanshe, July 1983, No. 7150.1794

Ruixue fengnian zhubao ping'an [Timely snow, good year, firecrackers, peace], Tianjin renmin meishu chubanshe, August 1982, No. 8073.20586

Saman Shenzhou chuchu chun — xian geiwei sihua zuo gongxiande renmen [Spread Spring all over the Divine Land (i.e., China) — dedicated to those people who contributed to the 'Four Modernizations'], Shanghai renmin meishu chubanshe, July 1983, No. 8081.13623

San ying zhan Lü Bu [The three heroes battle Lü Bu], Renmin meishu chubanshe, July 1982, No. 8027.8113

Sange 'shizong' de shaonü [Three 'missing' young girls], Fazhi xuanchuan chuchuang no. 5, two sheets, black-and-white, Falü chubanshe, December 1983, No. 8004.006

Shanshou fengshou guo [Selling the fruits of a bumper harvest in a friendly manner], Shanghai renmin meishu chubanshe, April 1978, No. 8081.11120

Shancun xinhu [New household in the mountain village], Shanghai renmin chubanshe, early 1970s, No. 86-668

Shancun yiliaozhan [Mountain village medical station], Shanghai renmin chubanshe, May 1974, No. 8171.896

Shang dangke [Attending Party class], Shanghai renmin chubanshe, May 1974, No. 8171.889

Shangdian xinfeng [Fresh breeze in the shop], Shanghai renmin chubanshe, May 1975, No. 8171.897

Shanghai tan [Shanghai beach], published by Tianjin renmin meishu chubanshe, August 1986, No. 8073.21163

Shao nü [Young girl], Zhongguo sheying chubanshe, no date, No. 8226.020

Shehuizhuyi hao [Socialism is Fine], Shanghai renmin chubanshe, n. d., No. 86-715

Shehui zhuyi song [Ode to Socialism], Renmin jiaoyu chubanshe, December 1989, No. 107-03 (*Zhi you shehui zhuyi cai neng qiu Zhongguo, zhi you shehui zhuyi cai neng fazhan Zhongguo* [Only socialism can save China, only socialism can develop China], *Gongye fazhan rixin yueyi* [Industry develops and changes with each passing day], *Zhongguo nongye mianmao yixin* [Chinese agriculture takes on a new look], *Guofang, keji chengjiu huihuang* [The achievements in national defense and science and technology are glorious])

Shenshengde shiming [Sacred mission], Renmin meishu chubanshe, February 1987, No. 8027.10438

Shengshi longnian yu pang wa [In the heyday of the year of the dragon plump babies are born], Tianjin Yangliuqing huashe, June 1987, No. 8174.1499

Shi shei haisile ta? [Who has murdered her?], Fazhi xuanchuan chuchuang no. 9, two sheets, black-and-white, Falü chubanshe, December 1983, No. 8004.010

Shixing jihua shengyu, guanche jiben guoce [Carry out family planning, implement the basic national policy], Xin jiating baoshe (Liaoning), 1986, not numbered

Shoudu jieri shengkuang [A grand occasion during National Day in the Capital], Shanghai renmin meishu chubanshe, June 1986, No. 8081.14797

Shu jiu lian jingbing [Training crack troops in the coldest time of the year], Jiangsu renmin chubanshe, early 1970s, No. 8100.2.134(2)(75.4)

Shuben shi zhishide yuanquan [Books are a source of knowledge], Guangzhou branch Kexue puji chubanshe, July 1985, No. 8051.60408

Shuji shi zhishide chuanghu — Qingnian pengyoumen, re'ai shuji ba [Books are a window on knowledge — Young friends, enthusiastically love books!], Shanghai renmin meishu chubanshe, March 1984, No. 8081.13950

Sihua jianshe yingxiongbu [Register of heroes of 'Four Modernizations' construction], Sichuan renmin chubanshe, 1983, printnos. 8118.1554-5

Song Qingling tongzhi he haizi [Comrade Song Qingling and children], Shanghai renmin meishu chubanshe, June 1982, No. 8081.12936

Tengfeide shidai [A soaring era], Renmin meishu chubanshe, February 1987, No. 8027.10431

Tiantian duanlian shenti hao [Daily exercise is healthy], Guangzhou branch Kexue puji chubanshe, July 1985, No. 8051.60411

Tiexin ren [Intimate friend], Shanghai renmin meishu chubanshe, 1983, No. 8081.13126

Tuanjie fendou wei zhenxing Zhonghua zuo gongxian [Struggle in unity to contribute to the vigorous development of China], Liaoning meishu chubanshe, June 1984, No. 8161.0521

Tuanjie you'ai yijia qin [Fraternal love as in one family], Shanghai renmin meishu chubanshe, September 1980, No. 8081.12209

Wanhun, wanyu [Marry late, conceive late], 1988 calendar, Liaoningsheng lianhe zhizuo jihua shengyu xuanchuanpin bianji weiyuanhui

Wanwu shengzhang kao taiyang [The growth of all things depends on the sun], Shanghai renmin chubanshe, early 1970s, No. 86-704

Wanzhong yixin xiangqianjin [The myriad masses move forward with one heart], Guangxi renmin chubanshe, July 1984, No. 8113.952.

Wei zuguo xuexi [Studying for the mother country], Lingnan meishu chubanshe, April 1986, No. 8260.1906

Weihu funü ertong hefa quanyi [Protect the legal rights and interests of women and children], Shanghai renmin meishu chubanshe, February 1984, No. 8081.13951

Weihu jiti liyi, zhenxi jiti rongyu [Safeguard the collective interest, cherish the collective honour], Guangzhou branch of Kexue puji chubanshe, July 1985, No. 8051.60410

Weixian — dangxin chudian [Danger— Be careful about live wires], Shanghai renmin meishu chubanshe, April 1984, No. 8081.14022

Wenming limao lühua meihua [Culture, courtesy, greening, beautification], Chongqing chubanshe, May 1982, no. 8114.11

Wenming limao reqing wei guke fuwu [Serve customers in a cultured, civilized and enthusiastic manner], Shanghai renmin meishu chubanshe, March 1982, No. 8081.12975

Wo ai Beijing Tian'anmen [We love Beijing's Tian'anmen], Shaanxi renmin chubanshe, early 1970s, No. 86-690

Wo ai shehui zhuyi shiye [I love the socialist cause], Chongqing chubanshe, July 1986, No. 8114.466

Wo ai wode zuguo [I love my mother country], Chongqing chubanshe, July 1986, No. 8114.465

Wo daishangle hong lingjin [I have put on the red scarf], Shanghai renmin meishu chubanshe, January 1983, No. 8081.13113

Wo shi haiyan [I am a petrel], Renmin meishu chubanshe, February 1973, No. 8027.5595

Wo shi xiaoxiao yishujia [I'm a little artist], Guangzhou branch Kexue puji chubanshe, July 1985, No. 8051.60412

Wo wei zuguo xian baozang [I contribute precious deposits to the mother country], Shanghai renmin meishu chubanshe, February 1979, No. 8081.11425

Wo wei zuguo zheng guangrong [I strive to bring glory to the mother country], Shanghai renmin meishu chubanshe, June 1986, No. 8081.14717

Wo yao zuo sanhao xuesheng [I want to be a three-good student], Heilongjiang meishu chubanshe, September 1985, No. 8358.255

Women ai zuguo [We love the nation], Zhejiang renmin meishu chubanshe, August 1985, No. 8156.892

Women dou shi hao pengyou [We are all good friends], Shanghai renmin meishu chubanshe, June 1983, No. 8081.13326

Women shi zugoude xiwang [We are the hope of the mother country], Shanghai renmin meishu chubanshe, June 1985, No. 8081.14192

Womende jianglai [Our future], Renmin meishu chubanshe, February 1987, No. 8027.10432

Womende zongshe jishi [Our Master Planner], Zhongyang wenxian chubanshe, 1992, No. 175073.12

'Wujiang' 'Simei' [Five do's, four beauties], two sheets, Shanghai jiaoyu chubanshe, January 1983, No. 7150.1713

Xikan bayang bu wanyao [Happy to see that pulling up seedlings no longer needs bending the waist], Shanghai renmin chubanshe, early 1970s, No. 86-674

Xilin men [A blessing descends upon the house], Renmin meishu chubanshe, early 1970s, No. 86-831

Xiqing tongle [Joyous and happy together], Shanghai renmin meishu chubanshe, early 1970s, No. 86-822

Xishua fengshou tao [Playing with a bumper crop of peaches], Shanghai renmin meishu chubanshe, early 1970s, No. 86-828

Xianhua song yingxiong [Presenting fresh flowers to the hero], Xileng yinshe, June 1986, No. 8191.457

Xiang Jiang Zhuying neiyang wei Sihua duozuo gongxian [Make many contributions to the Four Modernizations in the same manner as Jiang Zhuying], Jilin renmin chubanshe, February 1983, No. 8091.1411

Xiang Lei Feng shushu xuexi, zhengdang honghua shaonian [Learn from Uncle Lei Feng, strive to become a red-flowered youth], Sichuan renmin chubanshe, May 1983, No. 8118.1425

Xiang Lei Feng tongzhi xuexi [Study comrade Lei Feng], Sichuan renmin chubanshe, August 1983, No. 8118.1279.

Xiang Lei Feng tongzhi xuexi [Study comrade Lei Feng], Sichuan shaonian ertong chubanshe, March 1990, ISBN no. 7-5365-0567-1

Xiang Lei Feng tongzhi xuexi [Study comrade Lei Feng], Renmin meishu chubanshe, April 1990, No. 8102.11028, with Mao's inscription

Xiang Lei Feng tongzhi xuexi, hongyang Lei Feng jingshen [Study comrade Lei Feng, let Lei Feng's spirit expand], Renmin meishu chubanshe, April 1990,Nno. 8102.11029, with Jiang Zemin's calligraphy

Xiang Lei Feng tongzhi xuexi, peiyang gongchan zhuyi pinde [Study from comrade Lei Feng, foster a Communist moral character], Sichuan renmin chubanshe, May 1983, No. 8118.1426

Xiang Mao zhuxi huibao [Reporting to Chairman Mao], Shanghai renmin chubanshe, early 1970s, No. 86-706

Xiang Zhang Haidi tongzhi xuexi [Learn from comrade Zhang Haidi], Shanghai renmin meishu chubanshe, May 1983, No. 8081.13526.

Xiao yan fei [Little swallows fly], Guangxi renmin chubanshe, June 1976, No. 8113.275

Xiao yongshi [Little warriors], Shanghai renmin meishu chubanshe, April 1986, No. 8081.14701

'Xiaoxuesheng xingwei guifan' xuanchuanhua [Propaganda posters on 'Primary school pupils' behavioral standard'], Shanghai renmin meishu chubanshe, June 1987, setno. 8081.15558 (*Zunshou jiaotong guize, weihu gonggong zhixu* [Observe traffic regulations, safeguard public order], *Zunjing laoshi, zunjing zhangbei* [Honour teachers, honour elders], *Zhuyi qingjie weisheng meihua xiaoyuan huanjing* [Pay attention to sanitation and hygiene, beautify the environment of schoolyards])

Xinde zhandou cong zheli kaishi [The new struggle starts from here], Shanghai renmin chubanshe, early 1970s, No. 86-669

Xin shou [New hand], Renmin meishu chubanshe, early 1970s, No. 86-644

Xiongdi minzu daibiao canguan fangjichang [Representatives of brother nationalities visit a textile machinery plant], Shanghai renmin chubanshe, early 1970s, No. 86.620

Xiu jin bian [Embroidering a silk banner with words of gold], Jiangsu renmin chubanshe, August 1978, No. 8100.2.315(2)

Xu Xiangqian, Sichuan renmin chubanshe, 1982, No. 8118.1270

Xuan duizhang [Electing a team leader], Shanghai renmin chubanshe, early 1970s, No. 86-662

Xue Lei Feng, shu xin feng [Study Lei Feng, establish a new practice], Shandong renmin chubanshe, April 1981, No. 8099.2214

Xue Lei Feng, shu xin feng [Study Lei Feng, establish a new practice], Shanghai jiaoyu chubanshe, February 1982, No. 7150.1647

Xue Lei Feng, shuli gongchan zhuyi lixiang [Study Lei Feng, establish Communist ideals], Shanghai jiaoyu chubanshe, January 1983, No. 7150.1712

Xue yingxiong jingshen, zuo yingxiong daolu [Study a brave spirit, follow a brave example], Renmin meishu chubanshe, early 1970s, No. 86-656

Xuexi Lei Feng hao bangyang [Study Lei Feng's fine example], Jiangxi meishu chubanshe, no date, printnos. 880580.1-5 (*Xiang Lei Feng tongzhi xuexi* [Study comrade Lei Feng], *Re'ai dang re'ai shehui zhuyi re'ai renmin* [Warmly love the Party, socialism and the people], *Nuli xuexi Ma Lie zhuyi Mao Zedong sixiang* [diligently study Marxism-Leninism, Mao Zedong Thought], *Quanxin quanyi wei renmin fuwu* [Serve the people wholeheartedly], *Fayang jianku fendoude jingshen* [Develop the spirit for bitter struggle])

Xuexi Lu Xunde geming jingshen [Study Lu Xun's revolutionary spirit], Renmin meishu chubanshe, October 1978, No. 8027.6932

Yancheng '11.25' an fanzui fenzi, baohu funü ertong hefa quanyi [Severely punish the offenders of the '25 November' case, protect the legal rights and interests of women and children], Fazhi xuanchuan chuchuang no. 3, three sheets, colour, Falü chubanshe, December 1983, No. 8004.004

Yanfang chehuo [Take strict precautions against traffic accidents], Shanghai renmin meishu chubanshe, April 1984, No. 8081.14025

Yange xunlian, zuohao fan qinlüe zhanzhengde zhunbei [Train rigorously, do good in preparing to counter a war of aggression], Shanghai renmin meishu chubanshe, July 1978, No. 8081.11294

Yanli daji xingshi fanzui huodong [Sternly attack criminal activities], Falü chubanshe, December 1983, No. 8004.003

Yanshan chuying [Young eagles on Mount Swallow], Renmin tiyu chubanshe, June 1976, No. 8015.1567

Yanzhe you Zhongguo tesede shehui zhuyi daolu fenyong qianjin [Advance bravely along the road of socialism with Chinese characteristics], Shanghai renmin chubanshe, September 1989, No. 8074.11

Yanzi feihuilaile [The swallows are flying back], two sheets, Shanghai jiaoyu chubanshe, November 1978, No. 7150.1278

Yangzijiangpan Daqing hua [On the banks of the Yangzi river, Daqing blooms], Jiangsu renmin chubanshe, early 1970s, No. 8100.2.154(2)

Yao ba wuchan jieji wenhua dageming jinxing daodi [The great proletarian cultural revolution must be waged to the end], Renmin meishu chubanshe, August 1973, No. 8027.5618

Yao zunzhong shehui gongde [Respect social morality], Shanghai renmin meishu chubanshe, February 1984, No. 8081.13949

Ye Jianying, Sichuan renmin chubanshe, 1982, No. 8118.1269

Yijiusanliunian Zhu De huijian Geda Huofo [The 1936 meeting of Zhu De and Living Buddha Geda], Sichuan minzu chubanshe, October 1982, No. M8140.63

Yi shan zao tian [Moving mountains to create fields], Shanghai renmin chubanshe, June 1977, No. 8171.1908

Yi youzhi chanpin xiangei renmin [Offer high-quality goods to the people], Shanghai renmin meishu chubanshe, August 1981, No. 8081.12706

Yingzi sashuang [Bright and brave], Shanghai renmin meishu chubanshe, May 1982, No. 8081.12927

Yonghu zanmen laobaixing zijide jundui [Supporting an Army of the People and for the People], no date, not numbered

Yongjun youshu [Support the army and give preferential treatment to families of revolutionary armymen and martyrs], Chongqing chubanshe, February 1983, No. 8114.38

Yongyuan genzhe gongchandang, yongyuan genzhe Mao zhuxi [Follow the Communist Party forever, follow Chairman Mao forever], Renmin meishu chubanshe, early 1970s, No. 86.716

You lixiang — you daode — you wenhua — you jilü [Have ideals — Have morality — Have culture — Have discipline], Sichuan meishu chubanshe, February 1986, four sheets, setno. 8373.661.

Yousheng youyu, zhuozhuang chengzhang [Better birth and upbringing, sturdily growing], Xin jiating baoshe (Liaoning), 1986, not numbered

Youyi — weile heping, weile haizi, weile xingfu [Friendship — for peace, children and happiness], Shanghai renmin meishu chubanshe, August 1985, No. 8081.14734

Yu er fei you da [The fish is fat and big], Renmin meishu chubanshe, early 1970s, No. 86-834

Yuanman xingfu [Satisfied and happy], Shanghai renmin meishu chubanshe, August 1980, No. 8081.12008

Yuegong xiao keren [Little guests in the Moon Palace], Renmin meishu chubanshe, early 1970s, No. 86-835

Zai qing zhan [Ask for a new battle assignment], Renmin meishu chubanshe, August 1975, No. 8027.6159

Zhandoude haozhao, guangyaode bangyang [A call to struggle, glorious example], Shanghai renmin meishu chubanshe, March 1978, No. 8081.11113

Zhanyou [Comrades-in-arms], Renmin meishu chubanshe, December 1977, No. 8027.6645

Zhaosheng [Enrolling new students], Hebei renmin chubanshe, October 1977, No. 8086-676

Zhengzheng rikang [Becoming more prosperous every day], Jiangsu renmin chubanshe, early 1970s, No. 8100.2.035(2)(72.11)

Zhigong shouze [Regulations for staff and workers], Renmin meishu chubanshe, January 1983, printnos. 8027.8500-07 (*Re'ai zuguo, re'ai gongchandang, re'ai shehuizhuyi* [Warmly love the country, the communist party and socialism], *Re'ai jiti, qinjian jieyue, aihu gongwu, jiji canjia guanli* [Warmly love the collective, work hard at economizing, take loving care of public property, participate actively in management], *Re'ai benzhi, xue ganxianjin, tigao zhiliang, jiangjiu xiaolü* [Warmly love one's job, study to catch up with the advanced, raise quality, practice efficiency], *Nuli xuexi, tigao zhengzhi, wenhua, keji, yewu shuiping* [Exert oneself in study, raise the level of politics, culture, science and technology, and professional work], *Zunji shoufa, lianjie fenggong, yan'ge zhixing guizhang zhidu* [Observe discipline and be law abiding, be honest in performing one's official duties, rigorously implement rules and regulations], *Guanxin tongzhi, zunshi aitu, hemu jiating, tuanjie linli* [Care for comrades, respect the teacher and love the student, strive for domestic peace, unite with the neighbourhood], *Wenming limao, zhengjie weisheng, jiangjiu shehui gongde* [Cultured and civilized, tidy and hygienic, practice social morality],

Fuzhi zhengqi, dizhi waiqi, ju fushi, yong buzhan [Foster a correct spirit, resist the evil spirit, resist corruption, never get involved with it].)

Zhishu lühua, weihu shengtai pingheng [Plant trees and make green, protect the ecological balance], Shanghai renmin meishu chubanshe, March 1983, No. 8081.13285

Zhixin hua [Heart-to-heart talk], Renmin meishu chubanshe, early 1970s, No. 86-679

Zhongguo gongye . xuri dongsheng [Chinese industry . the sun rises in the Eastern sky], Renmin meishu chubanshe, February 1987, No. 8027.10429

Zhongguo jian'er tengfei wu liu zhou [China's healthy sons soar over the five regions and six continents], Renmin meishu chubanshe, February 1987, No. 8027.10434

Zhongguo yixue shishangde you yici feiyue [Another leap in the history of Chinese medical science], Renmin meishu chubanshe, February 1987, No. 8027.10436

Zhonghua hao ernü [Excellent sons and daughters of China], Sichuan meishu chubanshe, November 1990, printnos. 8541.2251-2258 (Zhongguo nüpai, Mao Erdong zhanshi, Qian Xuesen, Jiao Yulu, Lei Feng, Wang Jinxi, Hao ba lian, Zhou Enlai)

Zhonghua renmin gongheguo wansui [Long live the People's Republic of China], two sheets, Renmin meishu chubanshe, June 1979, No. 8027.7133

Zhonghua yongshi shou piao Changjiang [Chinese braves for the first time trail the Changjiang], Renmin meishu chubanshe, February 1987, No. 8027.10433

Zhonghua zhishu meihua huanjing — Fayang shehui zhuyi xin fengshang [Plant flowers and trees, beautify the environment — Develop new socialist habits], Shanghai renmin meishu chubanshe, April 1982, No. 8081.12974

Zhonghua zhongcao, meihua chengxiang huanjing [Plant flowers and grasses, beautify the environment of cities and villages], Shanghai renmin meishu chubanshe, March 1983, No. 8081.13287

Zhou Enlai he Deng Yingchao tongzhi [Comrades Zhou Enlai and Deng Yingchao], Sichuan renmin chubanshe, 1983, No. 8118-1346

Zhou yeye guanhuai womende chengchang [Grandpa Zhou shows solicitude for our growth], Liaoning meishu chubanshe, 1983, No. 8161.0148

Zhou zongli laidaole xunlianchang [Premier Zhou has come to the training field], Renmin tiyu chubanshe, June 1978, No. 8015.1666

Zhu De, Sichuan renmin chubanshe, 1982, No. 8118.1089

Zi zhu 'jinluandian', mu qi 'muyangjuan' [Son lives in the 'Golden Bell Hall', mother dwells in the 'sheepfold'], Fazhi xuanchuan chuchuang no. 8, two sheets, black-and-white, Falü chubanshe, December 1983, No. 8004.009

Zuguo chuchu shi wo jia — zai zui xuyaode difang shenggen.kaifang [Everywhere in the Mother country is my home — strike root and flower in those places that need it most], Shanghai renmin meishu chubanshe, March 1984, No. 8081.13954

Zuguo wansui [Long live the mother country], Shanghai renmin meishu chubanshe, early 1970s, No. 86-830

Zunshou shehui zhixiu — jiangjiu wenming chengche [Observe social order — pay attention to boarding trains in a civilized way], Shanghai renmin meishu chubanshe, April 1981, No. 8081.12535

BIBLIOGRAPHY

CHINESE LANGUAGE SOURCES

Dianshizhai Huabao [Dianshizhai Pictorial] (Shanghai, 1884 or later)

Huxian nongminhua [Peasant Paintings from Huxian] (Tianjin: Tianjin renmin meishu chubanshe, 1975)

Qingzhu Zhonghua renmin gongheguo chengli ershiwu zhounian quanguo meishu zuopin zhanlan zuopin xuanji [Selection of Works from the National Exhibition of Fine Arts to Celebrate the Twenty-fifth Anniversary of the Founding of the People's Republic of China] (n.p., no publisher, n.d. [1974?])

Shandong minjian nianhua [Popular New Year Prints from Shandong] (Shanghai: Shanghai renmin meishu chubanshe, 1979)

Tianjin meishu zuopinxuan [Selection of Fine Arts Works from Tianjin] (Tianjin: Tianjin renmin meishu chubanshe, 1979)

Yangliuqing nianhuaxuan [Selection of New Year Prints from Yangliuqing] (Tianjin: Tianjin renmin meishu chubanshe, 1979)

Zhonggong dangshi zhuyao shijian jianjie [Short introduction to important events in the history of the CCP] (Chengdu: Sichuan renmin chubanshe, 1982)

Zhonghua renmin gongheguo fazhan guomin jingjide di'yige wunian jihua (1953-1957) tujie [Graphs of the First Five Year Plan (1953-1957) For the Development of the National Economy of the People's Republic of China] (Beijing: Renmin chubanshe, 1955)

Zhonghua renmin gongheguo xingfa tujie [Illustrated Penal Code of the PRC] (Shanghai: Shanghai renmin meishu chubanshe, 1982)

A Ying, *Zhongguo nianhua fazhan shilüe* [A Short History of the Development of Chinese New Year Prints] (Beijing: Zhaohua meishu chubanshe, 1954)

An Gang, 'Jingji xuanchuan zhide dashu teshude yinian' [A Year in Which Economic Propaganda Merited Big and Special Publications], Zhongguo shehui kexueyuan xinwen yanjiusuo (ed.), *Zhongguo xinwen nianjian 1984* [Yearbook of Chinese News 1984] (Beijing: Renmin ribao chubanshe, 1984), pp. 69-72

Guangming ribao zongbianshi, 'Gaijin renwu baodao, tuchu zhishi fenzide xuanchuan' [Improve the Coverage of Personages, Highlight Propaganda towards Intellectuals], *Zhongguo xinwen nianjian 1983* [Yearbook of Chinese News 1983] (Beijing: Zhongguo shehui kexue chubanshe, 1983), pp. 151-153

Guowuyuan wenhuazu meishu zuopin zhengji xiaozu (eds.), *Jinian Mao zhuxi 'Zai Yan'an wenyi zuotanhuishangde jianghua' fabiao sanshi zhounian meishu zuopinxuan* [Selection of Fine Arts Works to commemorate the Thirtieth Anniversary of the Publication of Chairman Mao's 'Talks at the Yan'an Conference on Literature and Art'] (Beijing: Renmin meishu chubanshe, 1973)

Guowuyuan wenhuazu meishu zuopin zhengji xiaozu (eds.), *Shanghai, Yangquan, Lüda gongrenhua zhanlan zuopin xuanji* [Selection of Works from the Exhibition of Workers' Art from Shanghai, Yangquan and Lüda] (Beijing: Renmin meishu chubanshe, 1975)

Jiao Yongfu, 'Jianchi liangtiao zhanxiande sixiang douzheng, Wei jianshe shehui zhuyi jingshen wenming zuochu gongxian — Xuexi Deng Xiaoping tongzhi guanyu lishi zhuanzhe shiqi wenyi wentide lunshu' [Persevere in the ideological struggle on two fronts, Contribute to the creation of a socialist spiritual civilization — On studying comrade Deng Xiaoping's discussion of questions on literature and art in a period of historical transition], Zhongyang renmin guangbo diantai lilunbu (ed.), *Xuexi 'Deng Xiaoping wenxuan' guangbo jiangzuo* [Radio lessons on studying Deng Xiaoping's Selected Works] (Beijing: Guangbo chubanshe, 1983), pp. 114-127

Jiefang ribao bianjibu, 'Tigao xuanchuan xiaoyi shi xinwen gaigede zhongyao keti' [Improving the Effectiveness of Propaganda is an Important Task in the Reform of News], *Zhongguo xinwen nianjian 1983* [Yearbook of Chinese News 1983] (Beijing: Zhongguo shehui kexue chubanshe, 1983), pp. 164-166

Jin Kaicheng, *Wenyixinlixue lungao* [Theories of Psychology in Literature and the Arts] (Beijing: Beijing daxue chubanshe, 1982)

Li Fanfu, *Erjuan He Laoda da Riben* [He Laoda beats Japan] (Guangzhou: Huangse tushu chubanhui, 1938)

Li Zehou, *Meixue Lunji* [Collected Essays on Aesthetics] (Shanghai: Shanghai wenyi chubanshe, 1980)

Liu Jianming, *Deng Xiaoping xuanchuan sixiang yanjiu* [On Deng Xiaoping's Ideas of Propaganda] (Shenyang: Liaoning renmin chubanshe, 1990)

Liu Zhengyan, Gao Mingkai, Mai Yongqian, Shi Youwei (eds.), *Hanyu wailaici cidian* [Dictionary of Loan Words and Hybrid Words in Chinese] (Shanghai: Shanghai cishu chubanshe, 1984)

Liu Zhide a.o., *Huxuan nongminhua* [Peasant Paintings from Huxian] (Shanghai: Shanghai renmin chubanshe, 1974)

Lü Cheng, Zhang Zhuwu, Zhong Bihui, Su Xisheng, He Jinqing (eds.), *Dangde jianshe qishinian jishi 1919-1991* [Chronicle of 70 years of Party construction] (Beijing: Zhonggong dangshi chubanshe, 1991)

Lü Liang, 'Ba junshi xuanchuan fangdao shidangde weizhishang' [Put Army Propaganda in the Right Position], Zhongguo xinwen xuelun lianhehui, Zhongguo shehui kexue xinwen yanjiusuo (eds.), *Zhongguo xinwen nianjian 1988* [Yearbook of Chinese News 1988] (Beijing: Zhongguo shehui kexue chubanshe, 1988), pp. 68-69

Ma Ke, 'Jianguo shinianlaide zhengzhi xuanchuanhua' [Political Propaganda Prints in the Ten Years Since the Founding of Our Country], *Meishu yanjiu* (1959:1), pp. 1-6

Man Yuanlai, 'Xinwen xuanchuan yu shangpin jingji' [News Propaganda and the Commodity Economy], Zhongguo xinwen xuelun lianhehui, Zhongguo shehui kexue xinwen yanjiusuo (eds.), *Zhongguo xinwen nianjian 1988* [Yearbook of Chinese News 1988] (Beijing: Zhongguo shehui kexue chubanshe, 1988), pp. 69-71

'Meishu xiangdao' bianjibu, *Meishu xiangdao (zixue meishu jifa congshu)* [Guide to Fine Arts (series for self-study of methods and techniques of fine arts)] (N.p.: Zhaohua meishu chubanshe, n.d.)

Ningxia Huizu zizhiqu zhanlanguan (ed.), *Bokai 'Sirenbang' huapi* [Ripping off the Mask of the 'Gang of Four'] (n.p.: Ningxia Huizu zizhiqu zhanlanguan, 1977)

Qian Daxin, 'Xuanchuanhua chuangzuo he chuban zongshu' [Summary of the creation and publication of propaganda posters], *Zhongguo chuban nianjian 1984* [Yearbook of Chinese publishing 1984] (Beijing: Shangwu yinshuguan, 1984), pp. 229-230

Renmin meishu chubanshe (eds.), *Gaoju Mao zhuxide weida qizhi shengli qianjin meishu zuopinxuan* [Selection of Fine Arts Works to Promote the Victory of Holding aloft the Great Banner of Chairman Mao] (Beijing: Renmin meishu chubanshe, 1977)

Renmin meishu chubanshe (eds.), *Renwuhua xizuozuan* [Selected exercises in drawing human beings] (Beijing: Renmin meishu chubanshe, 1978)

Renmin meishu chubanshe (eds.), *Qingzhu Zhongguo renmin jiefangjun jianjun wushi zhounian meishu zuopinxuan* [Selection of Fine Arts Works to Celebrate the Fiftieth Anniversary of the founding of the Chinese People's Liberation Army] (Beijing: Renmin meishu chubanshe, 1978)

Renmin meishu chubanshe bianjishi (eds.), *Ba pi Lin pi Kong de douzheng jinxing daodi meishu zuopinxuan* [Selection of fine arts works to carry forward to the end the struggle to criticize Lin [Piao] and Kong [Confucius]] (Beijing: Renmin meishu chubanshe, 1974)

Renmin ribao nongcunbu, 'Women dui nongcun shengchan zerenzhide xuanchuan' [Our Propaganda Concerning the Rural Responsibility System], *Zhongguo xinwen nianjian 1983* [Yearbook of Chinese News 1983] (Beijing: Zhongguo shehui kexue chubanshe, 1983), pp. 145-147

Renmin ribao she (ed.), *Chu sihai manhua ji (er)* [Collection of Cartoons to Exterminate the Four Pests (Vol. II)] (n.p. (Beijing?): Renmin ribao she, n.d.)

Shanghai renmin chubanshe (eds.), *Renwuhua cankao ziliao* [Reference material-also for drawings of human beings] (Shanghai: Shanghai renmin chubanshe, 1973)

Shanghai renmin chubanshe (eds.), *Banhua* [Woodblock Prints] (Shanghai: Shanghai renmin chubanshe, 1974)

Shanghai renmin meishu chubanshe (eds.), *Beidahuang fengqing banhuaxuan* [Selected Woodprints of Scenes in the Great Northern Wilderness] (Shanghai: Shanghai renmin meishu chubanshe, 1986)

Tianjin renmin meishu chubanshe (eds.), *Gongnongbing xingxiang xuan* [Selection of images of workers, peasants and soldiers], Vols. 2 and 3 (Tianjin: Tianjin renmin meishu chubanshe, 1973 (Vol. 2), 1975 (Vol. 3))

Tongsu duwu chubanshe (ed.), *Zhongguo gongchandang guanyu di'erge wunian jihuade jianyi huace* [Illustrated Proposals of the Chinese Communist Party Concerning the Second Five Year Plan] (Beijing: Tongsu duwu chubanshe, 1956)

Wang Shucun (ed.), *Zhongguo minjian nianhua baitu* [100 Popular Chinese New Year Prints] (Beijing: Renmin meishu chubanshe, 1988), unpaginated

Xinmin wanbao bianjibu, 'Ba jianshe jingshen wenming dangzuo xuanchuande zhongyao zhuti' [The Creation of Spiritual Civilization Must Become An Important Topic of Propaganda], Zhongguo shehui kexueyuan xinwen yanjiusuo (ed.), *Zhongguo xinwen nianjian 1984* [Yearbook of Chinese News 1984] (Beijing: Renmin ribao chubanshe, 1984), pp. 209-211

Xing Fangqun, 'Guanyu xuanchuan xianjin renwu he xianjin dianxingde ji-dian yijian' [Some Viewpoints Concerning the Propagation of Advanced Personages and Models], Zhongguo shehui kexueyuan xinwen yanjiusuo (ed.), *Zhongguo xinwen nianjian 1984* [Yearbook of Chinese News 1984] (Beijing: Renmin ribao chubanshe, 1984), pp. 124-128

Yang Sixun, 'Guanyu xinwen yu xuanchuan guanxide taolun zongshu' [A Summary of Discussions Concerning the Relation between News and Propaganda], Zhongguo shehui kexueyuan xinwen yanjiusuo (ed.), *Zhongguo xinwen nianjian 1986* [Yearbook of Chinese News 1986] (Beijing: Zhongguo shehui kexue chubanshe, 1986), pp. 57-59

Yangquanshi renmin wenhuaguan (eds.), *Yangquan gongren huaxuan* [Selection of Workers' Art from Yangquan] (Beijing: Renmin meishu chubanshe, 1975)

Yu Shiqian, Li Yuzhen, Chen Jianzhuo, Hu Rongzhi, Lin Qinshu (eds.), *Xin shiqi wenyi xuelunzheng ziliao (1976-1985) shang, xia* [Materials on the debates on literature and arts in the new age (1976-1985), 2 Vols.] (Shanghai: Fudan chubanshe, 1988)

Zhang Daoliang, 'Nianhua chuban zongshu' [Summary of New Year print publication], *Zhongguo chuban nianjian 1983* [Yearbook of Chinese publishing 1983] (Beijing: Shangwu yinshuguan, 1983), pp. 197-198

Zhonggong zhongyang wenxian bianji weiyuanhui (ed.), *Deng Xiaoping wenxuan* [Selected Works of Deng Xiaoping] (Beijing: Renmin chubanshe, 1983)

Zhonggong zhongyang xuanchuanbu wenyiju (ed.), *Deng Xiaoping lun wenyi* [Deng Xiaoping on Literature and the Arts] (Beijing: Renmin wenxue chubanshe, 1989)

Zhongguo dianying faxing fangyang gongsi (eds.), *Dianying xuanchuanhua xuanji* [A Selection of Film Posters] (Zhongguo dianying faxing fangyang gongsi: n.p., n.d. (presumably 1982/1983))

Zhongguo meishu quanji bianji weiyuanhui (ed.), *Zhongguo meishu quanji — huihuabian 21 minjian nianhua* [Chinese fine arts collection — painting Vol. 21, popular New Year prints] (Beijing: Renmin meishu chubanshe, 1985); this volume's main editor is Wang Shucun

Zhongguo shaonian ertong chubanshe (ed.), *Laodong renmin de hao erzi Lei Feng* [Lei Feng, the good son of the working people] (Beijing: Zhongguo shaonian ertong chubanshe, 1981 [1963])

Zhongguo shehui kexueyuan xinwen yanjiusuo (ed.), *Zhongguo xinwen nianjian 1984* [Yearbook of Chinese News 1984] (Beijing: Renmin ribao chubanshe, 1984)

Zhongguo xinwen xuelun lianhehui, Zhongguo shehui kexue xinwen yanjiusuo (eds.), *Zhongguo xinwen nianjian 1988* [Yearbook of Chinese News 1988] (Beijing: Zhongguo shehui kexue chubanshe, 1988)

Zhongguo xinxing banhua wushinian xuanji bianji weiyuanhui (ed.), *Zhongguo xinxing banhua wushinian xuanji, shang (1931-1949), xia (1950-1981)* [Selections of Modern Prints of China in the Fifty Years from 1931 to 1981, 2 Vols.] (Shanghai: Shanghai renmin meishu chubanshe, 1981)

Zhongyang renmin guangbo diantai lilunbu (ed.), *Xuexi 'Deng Xiaoping wenxuan' guangbo jiangzuo* [Radio lessons on studying Deng Xiaoping's Selected Works] (Beijing: Guangbo chubanshe, 1983)

Zhu Boxiong, Chen Ruilin, *Zhongguo xihua wushi nian 1898-1949* [Western Painting in China 1898-1949] (Beijing: Renmin meishu chubanshe, 1989)

BIBLIOGRAPHY

WESTERN LANGUAGE SOURCES

Documents of the First Session of the Fifth National People's Congress of the People's Republic of China (Peking: Foreign Languages Press, 1978)

Resolution on CPC History (1949-81) (Beijing: Foreign Languages Press, 1981)

Summary of the Forum on the Work in Literature and Art in the Armed Forces with which Comrade Lin Piao entrusted Comrade Chiang Ch'ing (Peking: Foreign Languages Press, 1968)

Alexander, Jeffrey C., and Steven Seidman (eds.), *Culture and Society: Contemporary Debates* (Cambridge, etc.: Cambridge University Press, 1990)

An Gang, 'We Must Have a Serious Attitude Toward Surveys of the Media Audience', Brantly Womack (ed.), *Media and the Chinese Public: A Survey of the Beijing Media Audience* (Armonk: M.E. Sharpe Inc., 1986), pp. 54-59

Anagnost, Ann, 'Prosperity and Counterprosperity: The Moral Discourse on Wealth in Post-Mao China', Arif Dirlik and Maurice Meisner (eds.), *Marxism and the Chinese Experience: Issues in Contemporary Chinese Socialism* (Armonk: M.E. Sharpe Inc., 1989), pp. 210-234

Anagnost, Ann, 'Socialist Ethics and the Legal System', Jeffrey N. Wasserstrom and Elizabeth J. Perry (eds.), *Popular Protest and Political Culture in Modern China: Learning from 1989* (Boulder: Westview Press, 1992), pp. 177-205

Anikst, M., (ed.) *Sovjetreclame en Propaganda in de jaren twintig* [Soviet Commercial Design in the Twenties] (Veenendaal: Gaade Uitgevers, 1987)

Apter, David E., and Tony Saich, *Discourse and Power: The Revolutionary Process in Mao's China* (Harvard University Press, forthcoming)

Arendrup, Birthe, Carsten Boyer Thogersen, Ann Wedell-Wedellsborg (eds.), *China in the 1980s — And Beyond* (London/Malmö: Curzon Press, 1986)

Baburina, Nina, (ed.), *The Soviet Political Poster, 1917-1980* (Harmondsworth, etc.: Penguin Books, 1985)

Barmé, Geremie, 'The Chinese Velvet Prison: Culture in the "New Age", 1976-89', *Issues & Studies* (August 1989), pp. 54-79

Barnett, A. Doak, 'A Note on Communication and Development in Communist China', *Communication and Change in the Developing Countries* (Honolulu: East-West Center Press, 1967), pp. 231-234

Bauer, H., (ed.), *China und die Fremden* (München: Beck, 1980)

Baum, Richard (ed.), *China's Four Modernizations: The New Technological Revolution* (Boulder: Westview Press Inc., 1980)

Baum, Richard, 'Epilogue: Communism, Convergence, and China's Political Convulsion', Richard Baum (ed.), *Reform and Reaction in Post-Mao China: The Road through Tiananmen* (New York, London: Routledge, 1990), pp. 183-199

Baum, Richard (ed.), *Reform and Reaction in Post-Mao China: The Road through Tiananmen* (New York, London: Routledge, 1990)

Baum, Richard, and Frederick C. Teiwes, *Ssu-Ch'ing: The Socialist Education Movement of 1962-1966* (China Research Monographs No. 2) (Berkeley CAL: University of California 1968)

Beaufort, Simon de, *Yellow Earth, Green Jade: Constants in Chinese Political Mores* (Harvard Studies in International Affairs No. 41) (Cambridge Mass: Center for International Affairs, 1978)

Benewick, Robert, & Paul Wingrove (eds.), *Reforming the Revolution — China in Transition* (Houndmills etc.: Macmillan Education Ltd., 1988)

Bennett, Gordon, 'Traditional, Modern, and Revolutionary Values of New Social Groups in China', Richard W. Wilson, Amy Auerbacher Wilson and Sidney L. Greenblatt (eds.), *Value Change in Chinese Society* (New York, N.Y.: Praeger Publishers, 1979), pp. 207-229

Bewig, Jutta (ed.), *Bauernmalerei aus Huxian* [Peasant Paintings from Huxian] (Frankfurt/M: Gesellschaft für Deutsch-Chinesische Freundschaft, 1979)

Bewig, Jutta, 'Huxian — die Heimat der Bauernmalerei', Jutta Bewig (ed.), *Bauernmalerei aus Huxian* [Peasant Paintings from Huxian] (Frankfurt/M: Gesellschaft für Deutsch-Chinesische Freundschaft, 1979), pp. 13-31

Blecher, Marc, 'The Reorganisation of the Countryside', Robert Benewick and Paul Wingrove (eds.), *Reforming the Revolution — China in Transition* (Houndmills etc.: Macmillan Education Ltd., 1988), pp. 91-107

Boehm, Edward, *Behind Enemy Lines; W.W. II Allied / Axis Propaganda* (Secaucus N.J.: The Wellfleet Press, 1989)

Bond, Michael Harris (ed.), *The Psychology of the Chinese People* (Hong Kong etc.: Oxford University Press, 1987 [1986])

Bond, Michael Harris, and Kwang-kuo Hwang, 'The Social Psychology of Chinese People', Michael Harris Bond (ed.), *The Psychology of the Chinese People* (Hong Kong etc.: Oxford University Press, 1987 [1986]), pp. 213-266

Bonnell, Victoria E., 'The Peasant Woman in Stalinist Political Art of the 1930s', *American Historical Review*, February 1993, pp. 55-82

Bonnin, Michel, and Yves Chevrier, 'The Intellectual and the State: Social Dynamics of Intellectual Autonomy During the Post-Mao Era', *The China Quarterly*, No. 127 (September 1991), pp. 569-593

Boorman, Howard L., 'The Literary World of Mao Tse-tung', *The China Quarterly*, No. 13 (January-March 1963), pp. 15-37

Bourdieu, Pierre, *Language and Symbolic Power* (Cambridge, MA: Harvard University Press, 1991)

Brown, J.A.C., *Techniques of Persuasion — From Propaganda to Brainwashing* (Harmondsworth: Penguin Books, 1972 [1963])

Brugger, Bill, *Contemporary China* (London: Croom Helm, 1977)

Burch, Betty B., 'Models as Agents of Change in China', Richard W. Wilson, Amy Auerbacher Wilson, and Sidney L. Greenblatt (eds.), *Value Change in Chinese Society* (New York N.Y.: Praeger Publishers, 1979), pp. 122-137

Blumenthal, Eileen P., *Models in Chinese Moral Education: Perspectives from Children's Books* (Ann Arbor: UMI, 1979)

Bulletin of Concerned Asian Scholars (ed.), *China From Mao to Deng: The Politics and Economics of Socialist Development* (Armonk: M.E. Sharpe Inc./Zed Press, 1983)

Cai Shaoqing, 'Secret Organizations in Modern China', *Far Eastern Affairs*, No. 4 (1991), pp. 137-141

Cannon, Terry, 'Opening up to the Outside World', Robert Benewick and Paul Wingrove (eds.), *Reforming the Revolution — China in Transition* (Houndmills etc.: Macmillan Education Ltd., 1988), pp. 138-148

Cell, Charles P., *Revolution at Work; Mobilization Campaigns in China* (New York: Academic Press, 1977)

Chai, Winberg, *The New Politics of Communist China; Modernization Process of a Developing Nation* (Pacific Palisades CA: Goodyear Publishing Cy., 1972)

Chan, Anita, *Children of Mao; Personality Development & Political Activism in the Red Guard Generation* (London: Macmillan, 1985)

Chandler, Robert W., *War of Ideas: The U.S. Propaganda Campaign in Vietnam* (Boulder: Westview Press, 1981)

Chang, Arnold, *Painting in the People's Republic of China: The Politics of Style* (Boulder: Westview Press, 1980)

Chang, K.C., *Art, Myth and Ritual; The Path to Political Authority in Ancient China* (Cambridge MA: Harvard University Press, 1983)

Chang, Parris H., 'Children's Literature and Political Socialization', Chu and Hsu (eds.), *Moving a Mountain*, pp. 237-256

Chang Won Ho, *Mass Media in China: The History and the Future* (Ames: Iowa State University Press, 1989)

Cheek, Timothy, 'Redefining Propaganda: Debates on the Role of Journalism in Post-Mao Mainland China', *Issues & Studies*, (February 1989), pp. 47-74

Chen, C.S., (ed.), *Rural People's Communes in Lien-chiang; Documents Concerning Communes in Lien-chiang County, Fukien Province, 1962-1963* (Stanford CA: Hoover Institution Press, 1969)

Chen, Theodore H.E., *Thought Reform of the Chinese Intellectuals* (Westport: Hyperion Press, 1981 [1960])

Cheng, Chu-yüan, 'The Modernization of Chinese Industry', Richard Baum (ed.), *China's Four Modernizations — The New Technological Revolution* (Boulder COL: Westview Press, 1980), pp. 21-48.

Chesneaux, Jean (ed.), *Popular Movements and Secret Societies in China 1840-1950* (Stanford: Stanford University Press, 1972)

Chi P'ing, 'Attach Importance to the Role of Teachers by Negative Example', *Peking Review* (31 March 1972), pp. 5-8

Chiang Chen-ch'ang, 'The New Lei Fengs of the 1980s', *Issues & Studies* (May 1984), pp. 22-42

Chin, Ai-li, 'Value Themes in Short Stories, 1976-1977', Chu and Hsu, *Moving a Mountain*, pp. 280-304

Chin, Robert, and Ai-li S. Chin, *Psychological Research in Communist China: 1949-1966* (Cambridge MA: Massachusetts Institute of Technology, 1969)

Chin, Steve S.K. (ed.), *Modernization in China* (Selected Seminar Papers on Contemporary China, Vol. III) (Hong Kong: University of Hong Kong, 1979)

Chinese Woodcutters' Association, The, *Woodcuts of Wartime China, 1937-1945* (Shanghai: Kaiming Book Company, 1946)

Chow Tse-tung, *The May Fourth Movement — Intellectual Revolution in Modern China* (Cambridge MA: Harvard University Press, 1960)

Chu, David S.K. (ed. and transl.), 'Sociology and Society in Contemporary China 1979-1983', special issue of *Chinese Sociology and Anthropology* (Armonk: M.E. Sharpe Inc.), Vol. xvi, No. 1-2 (Fall-Winter 1983-1984)

Chu, Godwin C., Fred Hung, Wilbur Schramm, Stephen Uhalley Jr, Frederick T.C. Yu, *Communication and Development in China*. Communication Monographs Number 1 (Honolulu: East-West Center Press, 1976)

Chu, Godwin C., *Radical Change through Communication in Mao's China* (Honolulu: East-West Center Press, 1977)

Chu, Godwin C. (ed.), *Popular Media in China; Shaping New Cultural Patterns* (Honolulu: University Press of Hawaii, 1978)

Chu, Godwin C., 'Group Communication and Development in Mainland China — The Function of Social Pressure', Wilbur Schramm and Daniel Lerner (eds.), *Communication and Change; The Last Ten Years — And The Next* (Honolulu: University Press of Hawaii, 1978), pp. 119-133

Chu, Godwin C., and Francis L.K. Hsu (eds.), *Moving a Mountain; Cultural Change in China* (Honolulu: University Press of Hawaii, 1979)

Chu, Godwin C., and Francis L.K. Hsu (eds.), *China's New Social Fabric* (London: Kegan Paul International, 1983)

Chu, Godwin C., 'The Emergence of the New Chinese Culture', Wen-Shing Tseng and David Y.H. Wu, (eds.), *Chinese Culture and Mental Health* (Orlando, etc.: Academic Press Inc., 1985), pp. 15-27

Clarke, Donald C., 'Political Power and Authority in Recent Chinese Literature', *The China Quarterly*, No. 102 (June 1985), pp. 234-252

Cochran, Sherman, *Big Business in China — Sino-Foreign Rivalry in the Cigarette Industry, 1890-1930* (Cambridge MA: Harvard University Press, 1980)

Cohen, Joan Lebold, *The New Chinese Painting 1949-1986* (New York N.Y.: Harry N. Abrams Inc., 1987)

Committee on Scholarly Communication with the People's Republic of China (ed.), *Traditional and Contemporary Painting in China; A Report of the Visit of the Chinese Painting Delegation to the People's Republic of China* (Washington DC: National Academy of Sciences, 1980)

Croizier, Ralph C. (ed.), *China's Cultural Legacy and Communism* (London: Pall Mall Press, 1970)

Croizier, Ralph C., 'Review Article: Chinese Art in the Chiang Ch'ing Era', *Journal of Asian Studies*, Vol. XXXVIII, No. 2 (Feb. 1979), pp. 303-311

Croizier, Ralph C., 'The Thorny Flowers of 1979: Political Cartoons and Liberalization in China', Bulletin of Concerned Asian Scholars (ed.), *China From Mao to Deng; The Politics and Economics of Socialist Development* (Armonk: M.E. Sharpe Inc./Zed Press, 1983), pp. 29-38

Croizier, Ralph C., *Art and Revolution in Modern China; The Lingnan (Cantonese) School of Painting, 1906-1951* (Berkeley CAL etc.: University of California Press, 1988)

Crook, Isabel and David, *Mass Movement in a Chinese Village: Ten Mile Inn* (London: Routledge & Kegan Paul, 1979)

Cwik, Hans-Jürgen, '"Flut des Zorns" — die Bewegung des Neuen Holzschnittes', Jerg Haas et al., *Holz Schnitt im neuen China — Zeitgenössige Graphik aus der Volksrepublik China* [Woodcuts in new China — Contemporary Graphics from the People's Republic of China] (Berlin: Gesellschaft für Verständigung und Freundschaft mit China e.V., 1977 [1976]), pp. 78-84

Davis, Deborah, 'My Mother's House', Perry Link, Richard Madsen and Paul G. Pickowicz (eds.), *Unofficial China — Popular Culture and Thought in the People's Republic* (Boulder, etc.: Westview Press, 1989), pp. 88-100

Davis, Deborah, & Ezra F. Vogel (eds.), *Chinese Society on the Eve of Tiananmen — The Impact of Reform* (Cambridge MA: Harvard University Press, 1990)

Deng Xiaoping, *Fundamental Issues in Present-Day China* (Beijing: Foreign Languages Press, 1987)

Dijk, Hans van, 'Painting in China after the Cultural Revolution: Style Developments and Theoretical Debates. Part I: 1979-1985', *China Information*, Vol. 6, No. 3, Winter 1991-1992, pp. 25-43

Dijk, Hans van, 'Painting in China after the Cultural Revolution: Style Developments and Theoretical Debates. Part II: 1985-1991', *China Information*, Vol. 6, No. 4, Spring 1992, pp. 1-18

Dirlik, Arif, and Maurice Meisner (eds.), *Marxism and the Chinese Experience: Issues in Contemporary Chinese Socialism* (Armonk: M.E. Sharpe Inc., 1989)

Dittmer, Lowell, 'China's "Opening to the Outside World": The Cultural Dimension', *Journal of Northeast Asian Studies*, Vol. 6, No. 2 (Summer 1987), pp. 3-23

Dittmer, Lowell, & Chen Ruoxi, *Ethics and Rethoric of the Chinese Cultural Revolution*. Studies in Chinese Terminology No. 19 (Berkeley CAL: University of California, 1981)

Doar, Bruce, 'Speculation in a Distorting Mirror: Scientific and Political Fantasy in Contemporary Chinese Writing', *Australian Journal of Chinese Affairs*, No. 8 (1982), pp. 51-64

Dreyer, June Teufel, *China's Political System — Modernization and Tradition* (London: Macmillan, 1993)

Duoduo [pseudonym of Li Shizhen], 'Het is geld en anders niets' [It's money and nothing else], *NRC-Handelsblad*, 18 June 1993, translated by Michel Hockx

Eberhard, Wolfram, *A Dictionary of Chinese Symbols — Hidden Symbols in Chinese Life and Thought* (London: Routledge, 1988 [1986/1983])

Fairbank, John K., Edwin O. Reischauer and Albert M. Craig (eds.), *East Asia — Tradition and Transformation* (London: George Allen & Unwin Ltd., 1973)

Falkenheim, Victor C., 'Popular Values and Political Reform: The "Crisis of Faith" in Contemporary China', Sidney L. Greenblatt, Richard W. Wilson, Amy Auerbacher Wilson (eds.), *Social Interaction in Chinese Society* (New York N.Y.: Praeger Publishers, 1982), pp. 237-251

Falkenheim, Victor C., 'Chinese Politics in Transition', Victor C. Falkenheim, Ilpyong Kim (eds.), *Chinese Politics from Mao to Deng* (New York: Paragon House, 1989), pp. 3-14

Falkenheim, Victor C., Ilpyong Kim (eds.), *Chinese Politics from Mao to Deng* (New York: Paragon House, 1989)

Farquhar, Mary, 'Revolutionary Children's Literature', *Australian Journal of Chinese Affairs*, No. 4 (1980), pp. 61-84

Findlay, Ian, 'When art goes to work in the cause of communism', *Far Eastern Economic Review*, 17 November 1983, pp. 106-109

Fine Arts Collection Section of the Cultural Group Under the State Council of the People's Republic of China (eds.), *Peasant Paintings from Hubsien County* (Peking: People's Fine Arts Publishing House, 1976 [1974])

Fingar, Thomas, 'Recent Policy Trends in Industrial Science and Technology', Richard Baum (ed.), *China's Four Modernizations: The New Technological Revolution* (Boulder: Westview Press Inc., 1980), pp. 61-101

Fitzgerald, John, 'A New Cultural Revolution: The Commercialisation of Culture in China', *Australian Journal of Chinese Affairs*, No. 11 (January 1984), pp. 105-120

Fitzpatrick, Sheila, *The Commissariat of Enlightenment — Soviet Organization of Education and the Arts under Lunacharsky, October 1917-1921* (London: Cambridge University Press, 1970)

Foulkes, A.P., *Literature and Propaganda* (London, New York: Methuen, 1983)

Fraser, Stewart E. (ed.), *100 Great Chinese Posters: Recent Examples of 'the People's Art' from the People's Republic of China* (New York: Images Graphiques Inc., 1977)

Friedman, Edward, 'The Politics of Local Models, Social Transformation and State Power Struggles in the People's Republic of China: Tachai and Teng Hsiao-p'ing', *The China Quarterly*, No. 76 (December 1978), pp. 873-890

Gibbs, Donald A., 'Shao Ch'üan-lin and the "Middle Character" Controversy', Kai-yu Hsu (ed.), *Literature of the People's Republic of China* (Bloomington: Indiana University Press, 1980), pp. 642-652

Gittings, John, *China Changes Face — The Road from Revolution 1949-1989* (Oxford: Oxford University Press, 1990)

Goffman, Erving, *Gender Advertisments* (New York: Harper Colophon Books, 1979)

Gold, Thomas B., '"Just in Time!" China Battles Spiritual Pollution on the Eve of 1984', *Asian Survey*, Vol. XXIV, No. 9 (September 1984), pp. 947-974

Gold, Thomas B., 'Guerrilla Interviewing Among the Getihu', Perry Link, Richard Madsen and Paul G. Pickowicz (eds.), *Unofficial China — Popular Culture and Thought in the People's Republic* (Boulder, etc.: Westview Press, 1989), pp. 175-192

Gold, Thomas B., 'Urban Private Business and Social Change', Deborah Davis and Ezra F. Vogel (eds.), *Chinese Society on the Eve of Tiananmen — The Impact of Reform* (Cambridge MASS: Harvard University Press, 1990), pp. 157-178

Gold, Thomas B., 'Youth and the State', *The China Quarterly*, No. 127 (September 1991), pp. 594-612

Goldman, Merle, *Literary Dissent in Communist China* (New York: Atheneum, 1971 [1967])

Goldman, Merle, 'The Unique 'Blooming and Contending' of 1961-62', *The China Quarterly* 37 (January-March 1969), pp. 54-83

Goldman, Merle, Timothy Cheek, Carol Lee Hamrin (eds.), *China's Intellectuals and the State: In Search of a New Relationship* (Cambridge: Harvard University Press, 1987)

Goodman, David S.G., *Beijing Street Voices — The Poetry and Politics of China's Democracy Movement* (London, Boston: Marion Boyers Publishers Ltd., 1981)

Gramsci, Antonio, 'Culture and ideological hegemony', Jeffrey C. Alexander and Steven Seidman (eds.), *Culture and Society: Contemporary Debates* (Cambridge, etc.: Cambridge University Press, 1990), pp. 47-54

Greenblatt, Sidney L., Richard W. Wilson and Amy Auerbacher Wilson (eds.), *Social Interaction in Chinese Society* (New York: Praeger Publishers, 1982)

Guerman, M., *Art of the October Revolution* (Leningrad: Aurora Art Publishers, 1979)

Guillain, Robert, *L'autre Chine — Photographies de Henri Cartier-Bresson* (Paris: Centre National de la Photographie, 1989)

Guttman, Cynthia, 'Mao's Children Fly Avant-Garde Flag — A Mix of Tradition and Subversion', *International Herald Tribune*, 26 October 1991

Haas, Jerg, 'Kontinuität und Bruch — Tradition und Moderne in der chinesischen Kunst', Jerg Haas et al., *Holz Schnitt im neuen China — Zeitgenössige Graphik aus der Volksrepublik China* [Woodcuts in new China — Contemporary Graphics from the People's Republic of China] (Berlin: Gesellschaft für Verständigung und Freundschaft mit China e.V., 1977 [1976]), pp. 52-62

Haas, Jerg, et al., *Holz Schnitt im neuen China — Zeitgenössige Graphik aus der Volksrepublik China* [Woodcuts in new China — Contemporary Graphics from the People's Republic of China] (Berlin: Gesellschaft für Verständigung und Freundschaft mit China e.V., 1977 [1976])

Hamrin, Carol Lee, 'Conclusion: New Trends under Deng Xiaoping and His Successors', Merle Goldman, Timothy Cheek, Carol Lee Hamrin (eds.), *China's Intellectuals and the State: In Search of a New Relationship* (Cambridge: Harvard University Press, 1987), pp. 275-304

Haraszti, Miklós, *The Velvet Prison; Artists under State Socialism* (New York: Basic Books Inc., 1987)

Harding, Harry, *China's Second Revolution: Reform after Mao* (Washington DC: The Brookings Institution, 1987)

Harris, P.B., 'Modernization in China: The Word and The Deed', Steve S.K. Chin (ed.), *Modernization in China* (Selected Seminar Papers on Contemporary China, Vol. III) (Hong Kong: University of Hong Kong, 1979), pp. 243-265

Hayes, James, 'Specialists and Written Materials in the Village World', David Johnson, Andrew J. Nathan, Evelyn S. Rawski (eds.), *Popular Culture in Late Imperial China* (Berkeley: University of California Press, 1985), pp. 75-111

Heller, Mikhail, *Cogs in the Wheel — The Formation of Soviet Man* (New York: Alfred A. Knopf Inc., 1988)

Hendrischke, Hans J., *Populäre Lesestoffe — Propaganda und Agitation im Buchwesen der Volksrepublik China* (Bochum: Studienverlag Brockmeyer, 1988)

Henley, Lonnie D., 'China's Military Modernization: A Ten Year Assessment', Larry M. Wortzel (ed.), *China's Military Modernization — International Implications* (New York etc.: Greenwood Press, 1988), pp. 97-118

Hiniker, Paul J., *Revolutionary Ideology & Chinese Reality — Dissonance under Mao* (Beverly Hills/London: Sage Publications Inc./Ltd., 1977)

Holbrook, Bruce, *Mainland China's External Propaganda Values, 1958-1974: A Content Analysis of 'Peking Review'* (Ann Arbor: UMI, 1976)

Holm, David L., 'Art and Ideology in the Yenan Period, 1937-1945' (unpublished Ph.D. thesis, University of Oxford, 1979)

Holm, David L., *Art and Ideology in Revolutionary China* (Oxford: Clarendon Press, 1991)

Houn, Francis W., *To Change a Nation; Propaganda and Indoctrination in Communist China* (Glencoe: The Free Press/Michigan State University, 1961)

Howkins, John, 'China: This Society is Communications', *InterMedia* (Journal of the International Institute of Communications), Vol. 8, No. 2 (March 1980), pp. 10-17

Howkins, John, *Mass Communication in China* (New York: Longman Inc., 1982)

Hsia, T.A., *Metaphor, Myth, Ritual and the People's Commune, Studies in Chinese Communist Terminology*, No. 7 (Berkeley: University of California, 1961)

Hsiao Kung-chuan, *Rural China; Imperial Control in the Nineteenth Century* (Seattle: University of Washington Press, 1967)

Hsu, Kai-yu (ed.), *Literature of the People's Republic of China* (Bloomington: Indiana University Press, 1980)

Hsu Kuang-t'ai, 'Problems in Sweeping away "Illiteracy of Law" in Mainland China', *Issues & Studies* (August 1986), pp. 44-54

Hu Yaobang, 'Create a New Situation in All Fields of Socialist Modernization', Report to the 12th National Congress of the Communist Party of China, September 1, 1982, *Beijing Review*, Vol. 25, No. 37, 13 September 1982, pp. 11-40

Hu Yaobang, 'On the Party's Journalism Work (1985)', Brantly Womack (ed.), *Media and the Chinese Public: A Survey of the Beijing Media Audience* (Armonk N.Y.: M.E. Sharpe Inc., 1986), pp. 174-198

Hua Junwu, *Chinese Satire and Humor — Selected Cartoons of Hua Junwu (1955-1982)* (Beijing: New World Press, 1984)

Hua Kuo-feng, 'Unite and Strive to Build A Modern, Powerful Socialist Country! — Report on the Work of the Government delivered at the First Session of the Fifth National People's Congress on February 26, 1978', *Documents of the First Session of the Fifth National People's Congress of the People's Republic of China* (Peking: Foreign Languages Press, 1978), pp. 1-118

Huang, Chun-chieh, and Erik Zürcher (eds.), *Norms and the State in China* (Leiden: E.J. Brill, 1993)

Huang, Joe C., *Heroes and Villains in Communist China; The Contemporary Chinese Novel as a Reflection of Life* (New York: Pica Press, 1973)

Huang, Joe C., 'Ideology and Confucian Ehtics in the Characterization of Bad Women in Socialist Literature', Amy Auerbacher Wilson, Sidney L. Greenblatt and Richard W. Wilson (eds.), *Deviance and Social Control in Chinese Society* (New York, N.Y. / London: Preager Publishers, 1977), pp. 37-51

Hung, Fred C., 'Appendix A: Some Observations on Confucian Ideology', Godwin C. Chu and Francis L.K. Hsu (eds.), *Moving a Mountain; Cultural Change in China* (Honolulu: University Press of Hawaii, 1979), pp. 419-423

Hunter, Edward, *Brain Washing in Red China; The Calculated Destruction of Men's Minds* (New York: Vanguard Press, 1951)

Hwang, Kwang-kuo, 'A Psychological Perspective of Chinese Interpersonal Morality', Carl-Albrecht Seyschab, Armin Sievers, Slawoj Szynkiewicz (eds.), *Society, Culture, and Patterns of Behaviour* (Unkel/Rhein: Horlemann Verlag, 1990), pp. 10-24

Johnson, David, 'Communication, Class, and Consciousness in Late Imperial China', David Johnson, Andrew J. Nathan, Evelyn S. Rawski (eds.), *Popular Culture in Late Imperial China* (Berkeley, etc.: University of California Press, 1985), pp. 34-72

Johnson, David, Andrew J. Nathan, Evelyn S. Rawski (eds.), *Popular Culture in Late Imperial China* (Berkeley: University of California Press, 1985)

Jowett, Garth S., and Victoria O'Donnell, *Propaganda and Persuasion* (Newbury Park: Sage Publications, 1988 [1986])

Kaal, Ron, *Oplage 1 Miljoen; Modern Drukwerk in China* [One Million Copies; Modern Prints in China] (Rotterdam: Museum voor Land- en Volkenkunde, 1983)

Kao, Mayching M., *China's Response to the West in Art: 1898-1937* (Ann Arbor: UMI, 1990 [1972])

Kenez, Peter, *The Birth of the Propaganda State; Soviet Methods of Mass Mobilization, 1917-1929* (Cambridge MA: Cambridge University Press, 1985)

King, Ambrose Y.C., and Michael H. Bond, 'The Confucian Paradigm of Man: A Sociological View', Wen-Shing Tseng and David Y.H. Wu (eds.), *Chinese Culture and Mental Health* (Orlando: Academic Press Inc., 1985), pp. 29-45

King, David, and Cathy Porter, *Images of Revolution; Graphic Art from 1905 Russia* (New York: Pantheon, 1983)

Kinkley, Jeffrey C. (ed.), *After Mao: Chinese Literature and Society 1978-1981* (Cambridge MA: Harvard University Press, 1985)

Kraus, Richard, 'China's Cultural "Liberalization" and Conflict over the Social Organization of the Arts', *Modern China*, Vol. IX, No. 2 (April 1983), pp. 212-227

Kraus, Willy, *Private Unternehmerwirtschaft in der Volksrepublik China; Wiederbelebung zwischen Ideologie und Pragmatismus* (Hamburg: Institut für Asienkunde, 1989)

Kulp II, Daniel H., *Country Life in South China — The Sociology of Familism, Vol. I: Phenix Village, Kwangtung, China* (New York: Bureau of Publications, Teachers College, Columbia University, 1925; reprinted Taipei: Ch'eng-wen Publishing Co., 1966)

Kuo Mo-Jo (Guo Moruo), 'Romanticism and Realism', *Peking Review* (15 July 1958), pp. 7-11

Laing, Ellen Johnston, 'Contemporary Painting', The Committee on Scholarly Communication with the People's Republic of China (ed.), *Traditional and Contemporary Painting in China; A Report of the Visit of the Chinese Painting*

Delegation to the People's Republic of China (Washington DC: National Academy of Sciences, 1980), pp. 54-67

Laing, Ellen Johnston, *The Winking Owl: Art in the People's Republic of China* (Berkeley: University of California Press, 1988)

Laing, Ellen Johnston, 'The Persistence of Propriety in the 1980s', Perry Link, Richard Madsen and Paul G. Pickowicz (eds.), *Unofficial China — Popular Culture and Thought in the People's Republic* (Boulder, etc.: Westview Press, 1989), pp. 156-171

Lan Jian'an and Shi Jicai (comp.), *Cartoons from Contemporary China* (Beijing: New World Press, 1989)

Landsberger, Stefan R., *'After the Bumper Harvest': China's Socialist Education Movement as seen through short stories from the Sixties*, ZZOA Working Paper No. 46 (Amsterdam: University of Amsterdam, 1984)

Landsberger, Stefan R., 'Role Modelling in Mainland China During the "Four Modernizations" Era: The Visual Dimension', Chun-chieh Huang and Erik Zürcher (eds.), *Norms and the State in China* (Leiden: E.J. Brill, 1993), pp. 359-376

Landsberger, Stefan R., 'A Chinese Future with Western Characteristics: Chinese Visual Propaganda during the "Four Modernisations" (1978-1988)', Kurt Werner Radtke and Tony Saich (eds.), *China's Modernisation: Westernisation and Acculturation* (Stuttgart: Franz Steiner Verlag, 1993), pp. 177-194

Lee, Leo Ou-fan, & Andrew J. Nathan, 'The Beginnings of Mass Culture: Journalism and Fiction in the Late Ch'ing and Beyond', David Johnson, Andrew J. Nathan, Evelyn S. Rawski (eds.), *Popular Culture in Late Imperial China* (Berkeley: University of California Press, 1985), pp. 360-395

Lerner, Daniel, and Wilbur Schramm (eds.), *Communication and Change in the Developing Countries* (Honolulu: East-West Center Press, 1967)

LeVine, Robert A., and Merry I. White, *Human Conditions: The Cultural Basis of Educational Development* (New York: Routledge & Kegan Paul, 1986)

Leyda, Jay, *Dianying — Electric Shadows; An Account of Films and the Film Audience in China* (Cambridge MA: MIT Press, 1972)

Li Peilin, 'Problems in China's Social Transformation', *Social Sciences in China*, Vol. 14, No. 3 (Autumn 1993), pp. 23-34

Liang Heng & Judith Shapiro, *Intellectual Freedom in China After Mao — with a Focus on 1983* (New York: Fund for Free Expression, 1984)

Lifton, Robert J., *Thought Reform and the Psychology of Totalism* (New York: W.W. Norton, 1961)

Lin Senmu, Zhou Shulian and Qi Mingchen, 'Industry and Transport', Yu Guangyuan (ed.), *China's Socialist Modernization* (Beijing: Foreign Languages Press, 1984), pp. 271-349

Link, Perry, 'The Limits of Cultural Reform in Deng Xiaoping's China', *Modern China*, Vol. 13, No. 2 (April 1987), pp. 115-176

Link, Perry, Richard Madsen and Paul G. Pickowicz, 'Introduction', Perry Link, Richard Madsen and Paul G. Pickowicz (eds.), *Unofficial China — Popular Culture and Thought in the People's Republic* (Boulder: Westview Press, 1989), pp. 1-13

Link, Perry, Richard Madsen and Paul G. Pickowicz (eds.), *Unofficial China — Popular Culture and Thought in the People's Republic* (Boulder: Westview Press, 1989)

Liu, Alan P.L., *Communications and National Integration in Communist China* (Berkeley: University of California Press, 1971)

Liu, Alan P.L., 'Problems in Communications in China's Modernization', *Asian Survey*, Vol. XXII, No. 5 (May 1982), pp. 481-499

Liu, Alan P.L., 'Political Decay on Mainland China: On Crises of Faith, Confidence and Trust', *Issues & Studies* (August 1982), pp. 24-38

Liu, Alan P.L., 'Opinions and Attitudes of Youth in the People's Republic of China', *Asian Survey*, Vol. XXIV, No. 9 (September 1984), pp. 975-996

Liu, Alan P.L. *How China is Ruled* (Englewood Cliffs: Prentice Hall, 1986)

Liu, Alan P.L., 'Communications and Development in Post-Mao Mainland China', *Issues & Studies* (December 1991), pp. 73-99

Liu Bingwen and Xiong Lei (eds.), *Portraits of Ordinary Chinese* (Beijing: Foreign Languages Press, 1990)

Liu Shaoqi, 'How to be a good Communist', Liu Shaoqi, *Three Essays on Party-Building* (Beijing: Foreign Languages Press, 1980), pp. 1-98

Lockett, Martin, 'The Urban Economy', Robert Benewick & Paul Wingrove (eds.), *Reforming the Revolution — China in Transition* (Houndmills: Macmillan Education Ltd., 1988), pp. 108-126

Lu Xinhua et al., *The Wounded; New Stories of the Cultural Revolution, 77-78* (Hong Kong, London: Joint Publishing Co., Guanghwa Company, 1979)

Lull, James, *China Turned On: Television, Reform, and Resistance* (London: Routledge, 1991)

Ma, Stephen K., 'Reform Corruption: A Discussion on China's Current Development', *Pacific Affairs*, Vol. 62, No. 1 (Spring 1989), pp. 40-52

Mair, Victor H., 'Language and Ideology in the Written Popularizations of the Sacred Edict', David Johnson, Andrew J. Nathan, Evelyn S. Rawski (eds.), *Popular Culture in Late Imperial China* (Berkeley: University of California Press, 1985), pp. 325-359

Mann, Susan, 'Widows in the Kinship, Class, and Community Structures of Qing Dynasty China', *Journal of Asian Studies*, Vol. 46, No. 1 (February 1987), pp. 37-56

Mao Zedong, *Selected Works of Mao Tse-tung* (Beijing: Foreign Languages Press, 1967 [1965])

Mao Zedong, *Mao Tse-tung on Literature and Art* (Beijing: Foreign Languages Press, 1967 [Second Revised Translation of 1960])

Martin, Helmut, *Cult & Canon — The Origins and Development of State Maoism* (Armonk: M.E. Sharpe Inc., 1982)

McDougall, Bonnie S., *Mao Zedong's 'Talks at the Yan'an Conference on Literature and Art': A Translation of the 1953 Text with Commentary*. Michigan Papers in Chinese Studies No. 39 (Ann Arbor: University of Michigan, 1980)

McDougall, Bonnie S., 'Breaking Through: Literature and the Arts in China, 1976-1986', *Copenhagen Papers in East & Southeast Asian Studies* (1988:1), pp. 35-65

Menshikov, Lev, (ed.), *Chinese Popular Prints* (Leningrad: Aurora Art Publishers, 1988)

Minick, Scott, and Jiao Ping, *Chinese Graphic Design in the Twentieth Century* (London: Thames and Hudson Ltd., 1990)

Moody, Jr., Peter R., 'Spiritual Crisis in Contemporary China: Some Preliminary Explorations', *Issues & Studies* (June 1987), pp. 34-66

Munro, Donald J., 'The Malleability of Man in Chinese Marxism', *The China Quarterly*, No. 48 (October-December 1971), pp. 609-640

Munro, Donald J., *The Concept of Man in Contemporary China* (Ann Arbor: University of Michigan Press, 1977)

Munro, Donald J., 'Belief Control: the Psychological and Ethical Foundations', Amy Auerbacher Wilson, Sidney L. Greenblatt and Richard W. Wilson (eds.), *Deviance and Social Control in Chinese Society* (New York: Preager Publishers, 1977), pp. 14-36

Munro, Robin (ed. and transl.), 'Syncretic Sects and Secret Societies: Revival in the 1980s', *Chinese Sociology and Anthropology*, (Armonk, N.Y.: M.E. Sharpe Inc.), Vol. xxi, No. 4 (Summer 1989)

Myers, James T., 'Religious Aspects of the Cult of Mao Tse-tung', *Current Scene*, Vol. X, No. 3 (10 March 1972), pp. 1-11

Myers, James T., 'Socialist Spiritual Civilization and Cultural Pollution: The Problem of Meaning', *Issues & Studies* (March 1985), pp. 47-89

Myers, James T., 'Whatever happened to Chairman Mao? Myth and Charisma in the Chinese Revolution', Victor C. Falkenheim, Ilpyong Kim (eds.), *Chinese Politics from Mao to Deng* (New York: Paragon House, 1989), pp. 17-40

Myers, Samuel M., and Albert D. Biderman (eds.), *Mass Behavior in Battle and Captivity; The Communist Soldier in the Korean War* (Chicago: The University of Chicago Press, 1968)

Ng Mau-sang, *The Russian hero in modern Chinese fiction* (Albany/Hong Kong: State University of New York Press/Chinese University Press, 1988)

Novikov, Boris, 'The Anti-Manchu Propaganda of the Triads, ca. 1800-1860', Jean Chesneaux (ed.), *Popular Movements and Secret Societies in China 1840-1950* (Stanford: Stanford University Press, 1972), pp. 49-63

Oshima, Harry T., 'How Workable is Mao's Strategy?', Wilbur Schramm and Daniel Lerner (eds.), *Communication and Change; The Last Ten Years — And The Next* (Honolulu: University Press of Hawaii, 1978), p. 138

Oxnam, Robert B., and Richard C. Bush (eds.), *China Briefing, 1980* (Boulder: Westview Press, 1980)

Palaia, Franc, *Great Walls of China* (Westfield: Eastview Editions Inc., 1984)

Pan Jia-ching, 'Mass Political and Ideological Dissent: Big-Character Posters and Underground Publications in Mainland China', *Issues & Studies* (August 1980), pp. 42-62

Parsons, Talcott, and Edward Shills, 'Values and Social Systems', Jeffrey C. Alexander and Steven Seidman (eds.), *Culture and Society: Contemporary Debates* (Cambridge: Cambridge University Press, 1990), pp. 39-46

People's Publishing House of Shantung (eds.), *New Year Pictures of Weifang, Shantung* (Jinan: People's Publishing House of Shantung, 1978)

Philippe, Robert, *Political Graphics — Art as a Weapon* (Oxford: Phaidon, 1982)

Pickowicz, Paul, *Marxist Literary Thought and China: A Conceptual Framework*. Studies in Chinese Terminology No. 18 (Berkeley: University of California, 1980)

Piltz, Georg, *Russland wird Rot* [Russia turns Red] (Berlin: Eulenspiegel Verlag, 1977)

Possony, Stefan T., *The Revolution of Madness* (Republic of China: Institute of International Relations, 1971)

Price, Don C., *Russia and the Roots of the Chinese Revolution 1896-1911* (Cambridge MA: Harvard University Press, 1974)

Pusey, James R., 'On Liang Qichao's Darwinian "Morality Revolution", Mao Zedong's "Revolutionary Morality", and China's "Moral Development"', Richard W. Wilson, Sidney L. Greenblatt, and Amy Auerbacher Wilson (eds.), *Moral Behavior in Chinese Society* (New York N.Y.: Praeger Publishers, 1981), pp. 73-103

Pye, Lucian W., *The Spirit of Chinese Politics; a Psychocultural Study of the Authority Crisis in Political Development* (Cambridge MA: MIT Press, 1968)

Pye, Lucian W., 'Communication and Political Culture in China', Godwin C. Chu and Francis L.K. Hsu (eds.), *Moving a Mountain; Cultural Change in China* (Honolulu: University Press of Hawaii, 1979), pp. 153-178

Pye, Lucian W., *The Mandarin and the Cadre: China's Political Cultures* (Ann Arbor: Center for Chinese Studies/University of Michigan, 1988)

Raddock, David M., *Political Behavior of Adolescents in China; The Cultural Revolution in Kwangchow* (Tucson: University of Arizona Press, 1977)

Radtke, Kurt Werner, and Tony Saich (eds.), *China's Modernisation: Westernisation and Acculturation* (Stuttgart: Franz Steiner Verlag, 1993)

Ridley, Charles P., Paul H.B. Godwin and Dennis J. Doolin, *The Making of a Model Citizen in Communist China* (Stanford: Hoover Institution Press, 1971)

Rose, Margaret A., *Marx's Lost Aesthetic; Karl Marx and the Visual Arts* (Cambridge MA: Cambridge University Press, 1989 [1984])

Rosen, Stanley, 'Value Change Among Post-Mao Youth — The Evidence from Survey Data', in Perry Link, Richard Madsen and Paul G. Pickowicz (eds.), *Unofficial China — Popular Culture and Thought in the People's Republic* (Boulder: Westview Press, 1989), pp. 193-216

Rosen, Stanley, 'The Impact of Reform Policies on Youth Attitudes', Deborah Davies and Ezra F. Vogel (eds.), *Chinese Society on the Eve of Tiananmen — The Impact of Reform* (Cambridge MA: Harvard University Press, 1990), pp. 283-305

Rosen, Stanley, 'The Rise (and Fall) of Public Opinion in Post-Mao China', Richard Baum (ed.), *Reform and Reaction in Post-Mao China: The Road through Tiananmen* (New York, London: Routledge, 1990), pp. 60-83

Rosen, Stanley, 'The Effect of Post-4 June Re-education Campaigns on Chinese Students', *The China Quarterly*, No. 134 (June 1993), pp. 310-334

Saich, Tony, 'Political and Ideological Reform in the People's Republic of China: An Interview with Professor Su Shaozhi', *China Information*, Vol. 1, No. 2 (Autumn 1986), pp. 19-25

Saich, Tony, *China's Science Policy in the 80s* (Manchester: Manchester University Press, 1989)

Saich, Tony, 'The Fourteenth Party Congress: A Programme for Authoritarian Rule', *The China Quarterly*, No. 132 (December 1992), pp. 1136-1160

Scheck, Frank Rainer, *Chinesische Malerei seit der Kulturrevolution: Eine Dokumentation* [Chinese Paintings since the Cultural Revolution: A Documentary] (Köln: Verlag M. DuMont Schauberg, 1975)

Schein, Edgar H., with Inge Schneier and Curtis H. Barker, *Coercive Persuasion: A Socio-Psychological Analysis of the 'Brainwashing' of American Civilian Prisoners by the Chinese Communists* (New York: W.W. Norton, 1971 [1961])

Schell, Orville, *To Get Rich is Glorious — China in the 80s* (New York: NAL Books, 1986)

Schell, Orville, *Discos and Democracy — China in the Throes of Reform* (New York: Pantheon Books, 1988)

Schramm, Wilbur, and Daniel Lerner (eds.), *Communication and Change; The Last Ten Years — And The Next* (Honolulu: University Press of Hawaii, 1978)

Schramm, Wilbur, Godwin C. Chu, and Frederick T.C. Yu, 'China's Experience with Development Communication — How Transferable is it?', Wilbur Schramm and Daniel Lerner (eds.), *Communication and Change; The Last Ten Years — And The Next* (Honolulu: University Press of Hawaii, 1978), pp. 139-148

Schurmann, Franz, *Ideology and Organization in Communist China* (Berkeley: University of California Press, 1968 [1966])

Semsel, George S., (ed.), *Chinese Film; The State of the Art in the People's Republic* (New York: Praeger Publishers, 1987)

Seyschab, Carl-Albrecht, Armin Sievers, Slawoj Szynkiewicz (eds.), *Society, Culture, and Patterns of Behaviour* (Unkel/Rhein: Horlemann Verlag, 1990)

Sheridan, Mary, 'The Emulation of Heroes', *The China Quarterly*, No. 33 (January-March 1968), pp. 47-72

Shryock, John K., *The Origin and Development of the State Cult of Confucius* (New York: The Century Co., 1932)

Shue, Vivienne, 'China: on the wire', *InterMedia* (Journal of the International Institute of Communications), Vol. 8, No. 2 (March 1980), pp. 18-21

Silbergeld, Jerome, with Gong Jisui, *Contradictions: Artistic Life, the Socialist State and the Chinese Painter Li Huasheng* (Seattle: University of Washington Press, 1993)

Stross, Randall, 'The Return of Advertising in China: A Survey of the Ideological Reversal', *The China Quarterly*, No. 123 (September 1990), pp. 485-502

Sullivan, Michael, 'Painting with a New Brush: Art in Post-Mao China', Robert B. Oxnam and Richard C. Bush (eds.), *China Briefing, 1980* (Boulder, COL.: Westview Press, 1980), pp. 53-63

Taylor, Rodney L., *The Way of Heaven — An Introduction to the Confucian Religious Life* (Leiden: E.J. Brill, 1986)

Teiwes, Frederick C., *Politics & Purges in China — Rectification and the Decline of Party Norms 1950-1965* (White Plains, Folkestone: M.E. Sharpe Inc., Dawson, 1979)

Thompson, John B., 'Editor's Introduction', Pierre Bourdieu, *Language and Symbolic Power* (Cambridge, MA: Harvard University Press, 1991), pp. 1-31

Tillman Durdin, F., 'How Durable is Mao's Policy?', Wilbur Schramm and Daniel Lerner (eds.), *Communication and Change; The Last Ten Years — And The Next* (Honolulu: University Press of Hawaii, 1978), pp. 134-137

Tong Dalin and Hu Ping, 'Science and Technology', Yu Guangyuan (ed.), *China's Socialist Modernization* (Beijing: Foreign Languages Press, 1984), pp. 619-672

Townsend, James R., *Politics in China (2nd Edition)* (Boston: Little, Brown and Co., 1980 [1974])

Tschichold, J., *Der Holzschneider und Bilddrucker Hu Cheng-yen* (Basel: Holbein Verlag, 1943)

Tseng, Wen-Shing, and David Y.H. Wu (eds.), *Chinese Culture and Mental Health* (Orlando: Academic Press Inc., 1985)

Tseng, Wen-Shing, and David Y.H. Wu, 'Directions for Future Study', Wen-Shing Tseng and David Y.H. Wu (eds.), *Chinese Culture and Mental Health* (Orlando, etc.: Academic Press Inc., 1985), pp. 395-406

Tu Wei-ming, 'Confucianism: Symbol and Substance in Recent Times', Richard W. Wilson, Amy Auerbacher Wilson, and Sidney L. Greenblatt (eds.), *Value Change in Chinese Society* (New York: Praeger Publishers, 1979), pp. 21-51

Tun Li-ch'en, *Annual Customs and Festivals in Peking*, Derk Bodde trans. and annot. (Peiping: Henri Vetch, 1936)

Tung, Ricky, 'Communist China's Economic Reforms in the Wake of the CCP's Thirteenth National Congress', *Issues & Studies* (December 1987), pp. 40-65

Valkenier, Elizabeth K., *Russian Realist Art: The State and Society: The Peredvizhniki and their Tradition* (New York/Guildford, Surrey: Columbia University Press, 1989 [1977])

Wagner, Rudolf G., 'Lobby Literature: The Archeology and Present Functions of Science Fiction in China', Jeffrey C. Kinkley (ed.), *After Mao: Chinese Literature and Society 1978-1981* (Cambridge MA: Harvard University Press, 1985), pp. 17-62

Wang He, 'Traditional Culture and Modernization — A Review of the General Situation of Cultural Studies in China in Recent Years', *Social Sciences in China*, Vol. 7, No. 4 (Winter 1986), pp. 9-30

Wang Shucun (ed.), *Ancient Chinese Woodblock New Year Prints* (Beijing: Foreign Languages Press, 1985)

Wasserstrom, Jeffrey N., & Elizabeth J. Perry (eds.), *Popular Protest and Political Culture in Modern China: Learning from 1989* (Boulder: Westview Press, 1992)

Watson, James L., 'The Renegotiation of Chinese Cultural Identity in the Post-Mao Era', Jeffrey N. Wasserstrom & Elizabeth J. Perry (eds.), *Popular Protest and Political Culture in Modern China: Learning from 1989* (Boulder: Westview Press, 1992), pp. 67-84

Wedgwood Benn, David, *Persuasion & Soviet Politics* (Oxford: Basil Blackwell, 1989)

Weill, Alain, *Plakatkunst International* (Berlin: Frölich & Kaufmann, 1985[1984])

White III, Lynn T., 'Local Newspapers and Community Change, 1949-1969', Godwin C. Chu and Francis L.K. Hsu (eds.), *Moving a Mountain; Cultural Change in China* (Honolulu: University Press of Hawaii, 1979), pp. 76-112

White, Stephen, *The Bolshevik Poster* (New Haven: Yale University Press, 1988)

Whyte, Martin K., *Small Groups and Political Rituals in China* (Berkeley: University of California Press, 1974)

Whyte, Martin K., 'Small Groups and Communication in China: Ideal Forms and Imperfect Realities', Godwin C. Chu and Francis L.K. Hsu (eds.), *Moving a Mountain; Cultural Change in China* (Honolulu: University Press of Hawaii, 1979), pp. 113-124

Williams, C.A.S., *Outlines of Chinese Symbolism & Art Motives* (New York: Dover Publications Inc., 1976 [1941])

Wilson, Amy Auerbacher, 'Deviance and Social Control in Chinese Society: An Introductory Essay', Amy Auerbacher Wilson, Sidney L. Greenblatt and Richard W. Wilson (eds.), *Deviance and Social Control in Chinese Society* (New York: Preager Publishers, 1977), pp. 1-13

Wilson, Amy Auerbacher, Sidney L. Greenblatt and Richard W. Wilson (eds.), *Deviance and Social Control in Chinese Society* (New York: Preager Publishers, 1977)

Wilson, Richard W., Amy Auerbacher Wilson and Sidney L. Greenblatt (eds.), *Value Change in Chinese Society* (New York: Praeger Publishers, 1979)

Wilson, Richard W., Sidney L. Greenblatt, and Amy Auerbacher Wilson (eds.), *Moral Behavior in Chinese Society* (New York: Praeger Publishers, 1981)

Womack, Brantly (ed.), *Media and the Chinese Public: A Survey of the Beijing Media Audience* (Armonk: M.E. Sharpe Inc., 1986)

Worth, Robert M., 'Strategy of Change in the People's Republic of China — The Rural Health Center', Daniel Lerner and Wilbur Schramm (eds.), *Communication and Change in the Developing Countries* (Honolulu: East-West Center Press, 1967), pp. 216-230

Wortzel, Larry M. (ed.), *China's Military Modernization — International Implications* (New York: Greenwood Press, 1988)

Wu, An-chia, 'The Anti-Bourgeois Liberalization Campaign: Its Background, Tasks and Impact', *Issues & Studies* (June 1987), pp. 11-33

Wu, An-chia, The Theory of the "Initial Stage of Socialism": Background, Tasks and Impact', *Issues & Studies* (July 1988), pp. 12-32

Wu, David Y.H., and Wen-Shing Tseng, 'Introduction: The Characteristics of Chinese Culture', Wen-Shing Tseng and David Y.H. Wu (eds.), *Chinese Culture and Mental Health* (Orlando: Academic Press Inc., 1985), pp. 3-13

Yegorov, Alexander, and Viktor Litvinov (eds.), *The Posters of Glasnost and Perestroika* (London: Penguin Books, 1989)

Ying Wenzu (comp.), *Satire and Humour — Selected Chinese Cartoons* (Hong Kong: Joint Publishing Co., 1981)

Yoon, Chong K., 'Problems of Modernizing the PLA: Domestic Constraints', Larry M. Wortzel (ed.), *China's Military Modernization — International Implications* (New York: Greenwood Press, 1988), pp. 1-25

Yu, Frederick T.C., *Mass Persuasion in Communist China* (New York: Praeger, 1964)

Yu, Frederick T.C., 'Campaigns, Communications, and Development in Communist China', Daniel Lerner and Wilbur Schramm (eds.), *Communication and Change in the Developing Countries* (Honolulu: East-West Center Press, 1967), pp. 195-215

Yu Guangyuan (ed.), *China's Socialist Modernization* (Beijing: Foreign Languages Press, 1984)

Zeman, Zbynek, *Selling the War; Art and Propaganda in World War II* (New York: Exeter Books, 1982 [1978])

Zhan Wu and Liu Wenpu, 'Agriculture', Yu Guangyuan (ed.), *China's Socialist Modernization* (Beijing: Foreign Languages Press, 1984), pp. 209-270

Zhang Xiaodong, 'Interchange and Conflict Between Pluralistic and Monistic Concepts: A Thesis on the Pattern of Contemporary Chinese Artistic Culture', *Social Sciences in China*, Vol. X, No. 3 (September 1989), pp. 53-69

Zhang Xinxin and Sang Ye, *Chinese Profiles* (Beijing: Panda Books, 1987 [1986])